AN OUTPOURING OF PRAISE FOR
INTERVIEW WITH AN ANGEL

"Hardly ever do . . . channeler and researcher interact in the same volume as they do in *Interview with an Angel*. Thayer and Nathanson provide much food for both sides of the brain."
—Rhea A. White, editor of *Journal of the American Society for Psychical Research*

"The truth contained within these words penetrates beyond the limited parameters of the intellect, bringing me to tears more than once. Few books speak directly to the heart, but the love that resonates from every page of *Interview with an Angel* is undeniably real. This is the wisdom that nourished and sustains—it is food for the soul."
—Paula Sirois, holistic nutritional consultant

"*Interview with an Angel* is an exceptionally well-researched and well-written book, packed with inspiring and insightful messages from the realm beyond. I concur with all of the metaphysical information presented in the book. It checks out 100% against all of my research and my personal mystical experiences. In fact, I can't wait to ask my own questions."
—Donna McGrath, author of *Corporate Mentality to Spiritual Reality*

"I was completely overwhelmed and awestruck by the messages in *Interview with an Angel*. Through my tears of joy and wonder, my heart rejoiced in the truth of Ariel's words. I felt each page was written only for me, each message directed solely to me."
—Barbara Apostolou Torres, holistic practitioner, director, The Reiki Room, Point Pleasant Beach, NJ

"Read it! And know angels are around you."
—Rabbi Joseph H. Gelberman, Ph.D., president, The New Seminary, NYC

QUANTITY SALES

Most Dell books are available at special quantity discounts when purchased in bulk by corporations, organizations, or groups. Special imprints, messages, and excerpts can be produced to meet your needs. For more information, write to: Dell Publishing, 1540 Broadway, New York, NY 10036. Attention: Special Markets.

INDIVIDUAL SALES

Are there any Dell books you want but cannot find in your local stores? If so, you can order them directly from us. You can get any Dell book currently in print. For a complete up-to-date listing of our books and information on how to order, write to: Dell Readers Service, Box DR, 1540 Broadway, New York, NY 10036.

Interview
with an
Angel

BY
STEVAN J. THAYER
AND
LINDA SUE NATHANSON, Ph.D.

INTRODUCTION
ALFRED S. ALSCHULER, Ph.D.

A Dell Book

Published by
Dell Publishing
a division of
Random House, Inc.
1540 Broadway
New York, New York 10036

Integrated Energy Therapy is a registered service mark of The Center of Being, Inc.

Special thanks to The Parapsychology Foundation in New York City for their invaluable research assistance.

Editors: Allan Varian, Paula Sirois

Tape transcription: Christine Kessler

The trademark Dell® is registered in the U.S. Patent and Trademark Office.

ISBN: 0-440-23507-3

Reprinted by arrangement with Edin Books, Inc.

Printed in the United States of America

Published simultaneously in Canada

May 1999

10   9   8   7   6   5   4   3   2   1

OPM

We wish to dedicate this work to
all of those souls
who have dared to look,
who have risked finding
and who have faced tremendous fear
in what they have found.

Those souls who have followed their hearts
and have discovered
what their journey has led them to find.
And having found, have shared.
And having shared,
have continued.

Ariel

Contents

Introduction

Inner Voices and Inspired Lives Through the Ages
  Alfred S. Alschuler   2

Preface

In Search of Guidance
  Stevan J. Thayer   78
In Search of Alternatives
  Linda Sue Nathanson   88

The Interview

Invitation   101
Angelic Life   115
Life Passages   155
Life on Earth   179
Extraterrestrial Life   223
Our Selves   243
Unseen Universe   279
Biblical Life   319
Return to Eden   335

Index   351
From the Authors   369

Interview
with an
Angel

Introduction

Inner Voices and Inspired Lives
Through the Ages

Alfred S. Alschuler, Ph.D.

Reverend Stevan J. Thayer, an ordained Interfaith Minister and co-author of this book, began receiving inner messages in 1994 from a voice identifying itself as an angel named *Ariel*. Dr. Linda Sue Nathanson, a research psychologist and co-author of this book, listened to Ariel through Reverend Thayer. It had dramatic effects on her health, work and direction in life. Now they want to share Ariel's wisdom with others.

Should you listen?

Most of my university colleagues dismiss such claims as harmless delusions, or worse, as a sign of psychosis. That is the prevailing view of scientists, psychiatrists, clinical psychologists and counselors. After nearly 20 years of study, however, I am convinced they are wrong. In this introduction, I present my case for listening to inner voices in general and to Ariel in particular.

Some of you may see this as trying to prove what needs no proof. Even if you are a believer in inner voices, you may be surprised by the number of famous people in history who make this claim, the number of people today who are guided by inner voices, and that there can be dangers in listening. The world of inner voices is as rich, complex and diverse as our outer world.

Inner voices have been reported for more than 3000 years. Even today, the experience is far more common than most people realize. Four national surveys in the United States and Great Britain have consistently shown that one-third to one-half of all adults have had an ecstatic, life-changing experience of visions, sudden total knowing or an ineffable eternal moment of unity.[1] Twenty percent of those experiences include a voice, usually attributed to a religious figure or higher power. These surveys also report that virtually no one tells others—not spouses, friends, clergy or counselors. As valuable as these graces may be in giving meaning and purpose to life, they are hidden and appreciated in complete privacy. Why? Why this conspiracy of silence?

---

*One-third to one-half of all adults
have had an ecstatic,
life-changing experience of visions. . . .*

Seventeen years ago I began to hear an inner voice, daily. As a clinical psychologist, I thought I was going crazy. Although I was fascinated by these psychic fireworks, I knew that the road to psychological hell can be paved with good intentions and optimistic assumptions. I needed to know if it was safe, or at least how to recognize dangers so that I could avoid them. I hoped, like so many others, that this "crack in the cosmic egg" might help me rise above the dulling details of daily life and do something truly good and lasting.

As a first step, I looked for other people who had heard inner voices, whose lives were so spectacular that I could take refuge among the super sane, whose accomplishments would be strong inducements to unlock this weightless power. Surely there must be others in history.

I searched libraries, bookstores and encyclopedias of psychic sciences for autobiographies and biographies and discovered that the tradition is ancient.[2] Prophets from Abraham and Moses to Ezekiel and Jeremiah, and later Mohammed, all resisted, then proclaimed, "Thus saith the Lord." There is a medieval tradition of Catholic women who heard a voice from heaven telling them to write down the marvels they heard. After the Spanish Inquisition in 1492, a number of Jewish scholar-lawyer-mystics settled in the northern Palestinian town of Safed. All heard *maggidem* (inner voices) and transcribed the lessons they learned about the Torah, the Kabbalah and the hidden things of God.

I uncovered a number of more recent "inspired" writers who earned a well-deserved obscurity. There are the undigested outpourings of Washington Danskin's 1858 *How and Why I Became a Spiritualist* [3] and several dozen other gushing confessions since 1900. There are better known books by modern authors who present the words of their inner voices: Alice Bailey's *Tibetan*, Benjamin Creme's *Master*, Ruth Montgomery's *Guides*, Mary-Margaret Moore's *Bartholomew*, Pat Rodegast's *Emmanuel*, Helen Schucman's *Voice*, David Spangler's *John*, Meredith Young's *Mentor*, J. Z. Knight's *Ramtha*, and in this book, Stevan Thayer's *Ariel*.

There are remarkable similarities in the lives of well-known men and women from a dozen cultures over a 3000-year period. Their changed outlooks and sudden vitality made it seem as if they had been living half asleep. Their claims could not be discounted easily. They are the majority, but I also discovered exceptions. One chilling set of case histories described inner voices in people who were "possessed," an earlier version of multiple personality disorders. Listening to "God" is not sufficiently safe to be marketed like soap, nor always so satanic that exorcists and psychiatrists should be called.

The tradition is ancient . . .
from a dozen cultures
over a 3000-year period.

When Dr. Nathanson contacted me about the possibility of writing an introductory historical overview to *Interview with an Angel*, I was delighted. She was particularly interested in having readers understand that Ariel is not the first, that she (Dr. Nathanson) and Reverend Thayer are among many in a long history. Rather than diminishing the value of their collaboration, this highlights similarities with other extraordinary inner teaching.

With this goal in mind, I have tried to answer the central questions that cover the topic of inner voices using illustrations from the lives and words of famous historical figures: What is it like to hear an inner voice? Who are they and what do they say? What do the good voices do? What is the best and the worst that can happen? How do you stay safe, sane and healthy? What are inner voices, really? And, where do they come from?

What Is It Like to Hear an Inner Voice?

Try this quick experiment. Think of a number between one and ten. Do you have it clearly in mind? Write it down, or say it out loud. Please do that before reading further.

Hearing an inner voice is almost like that. Some people describe it as *thought forms*, but clear and distinct enough to report out loud or write down. The major difference is the listeners' passivity. The words come to them, instead of being actively chosen by them as you chose the number.

Inner Listening

It would be so convenient if these voices could be heard by others. The controversy and loneliness would disappear. Unfortunately, with a few exceptions, hearers report that the voices only are heard inwardly.

Teresa's description is typical and eloquent. In 1531, at the age of 16, Teresa entered the Augustinian convent of St. Mary of Grace as a boarder and took her vows as a Carmelite nun six years later. She was a sickly woman until she was 34. At 40, she began to hear inner voices, have visions and revelations. Seven years later, after overcoming the resistance of her confessor and superiors, the Pope authorized her to start a stricter order of Carmelites, a task her inner teacher had requested. By age 50, she had completed her autobiography, a spiritual classic. Over the next 15 years, she started 18 additional convents and monasteries and wrote *The Way of Perfection, Exclamations from the Soul of God, Foundations* and her most famous book, *The Interior Castle*—all books she claimed were dictated by an inner voice. Forty years after she died, Pope Gregory XV canonized her. Her accomplishments and the imprimatur of the Pope demand that we take seriously her claims about the nature of her inner voices.

> Though perfectly formed, the words are not heard by the bodily ear; yet they are understood much more clearly than if they were so heard. [The difference] is like that between speaking and listening. While I am speaking, my understanding is composing what I am saying, whereas if I am being spoken to, I do nothing but listen and it requires no effort. . . . Divine speech we listen [to] as we would to a person of holiness, learning and authority, who we know will not lie to us. Sometimes the words are of such majesty that we tremble if they are words of reproof, and if they are words of love, fill us with a love that is all-consuming. Human speech produces no effect on the soul, whereas when the Lord speaks, the words are accompanied by effects.[4]

Four centuries after Saint Teresa's description, reports show the experience has not changed. Beginning in 1963, Helen Schucman, a Jewish atheist with a Ph.D. in psychology, began transcribing the words of her inner voice into what became the three-volume *Course in Miracles*, currently being studied by several hundred groups in the United States.[5] She explains, "It can't be an hallucination, really, because the voice does not come from outside. It's all internal. There is no actual sound and the words come mentally, but very clearly. It's a kind of inner dictation, you might say."

Hearing this inner dictation sometimes takes the form of lectures. "For a year my occult preceptor educated me by means of mental talks," admitted Frederick Oliver, a lazy, dreamy, 16-year-old high school dropout who transcribed a 400-page book, *A Dweller on Two Planets,* dictated by Phylos the Tibetan, his inner voice.[6]

Hearing occurs in a state of alert passivity. "Thoughts were given to my mind." "He put [musical] notes in my head." "I felt the words, real words, crowding into my mind." For Madam Guyon, a martyred 17th-century French Christian mystic, it was not even mental: "What surprised me most was the [words] flowed from my central depth and did not pass through my head."[7]

Hearing occurs
in a state of alert passivity.

A few—very few—report that the voice sometimes seems to come from outside, though not heard by others. Richard Bach, author of nine books, recently told me that he was walking on the beach one evening when he heard a distinct voice outside and behind his head say to him, "Jonathan Livingston Seagull." Bach had no idea what it meant, but knew it was important. He went home and sat for an hour with pen and paper in hand before the first part of his most famous book played out before him as if it were a movie.

Several biblical figures may have heard voices in the same way. Peter, James and John simultaneously heard a voice during

Jesus' transfiguration, according to Matthew and Mark, as did Saul and his companions on the road to Damascus. Reports by St. Thomas, St. Joan and Freud about the location of their voices are ambiguous.[8]

These are the few possible exceptions. As a rule, anyone who claims verifiable voices are coming out of trees, animals or the air has lost sane contact with reality and is hallucinating. This is a disruption of normal, healthy interactions with the physical world and is cause for serious concern.

Hearing an inner voice, however, is not. The good work of too many saints and the ecstatic experiences of too many ordinary people contradict this fashionable belief. Hearing an inner voice, by itself, is not sufficient reason to prescribe medication, electric shocks or hospitalization.

Hearing an inner voice,
by itself,
is not sufficient reason
to prescribe medication. . . .

It's Not Me

Although these voices are inner, hearers claim that they are not their own, that they are dramatically different from their normal inner chatter. Again, Saint Teresa speaks for others before and after her.

If all locutions came from [us], we could hear them whenever we liked. But with Divine locutions, I may listen for days, and although I may have a desire to hear them, I am unable to do so. And then, at other times, when I have no desire to hear them, I am compelled to. And sometimes it happens that the soul and the understanding are so perturbed that they could not put together a single sentence, and yet the soul hears long set speeches which it could not have composed even if completely recollected [calm and relaxed]. They are things of which the memory has no recollection.[9]

Helen Schucman experienced the "otherness" of her inner voice through her resistance and its persistence. She did not like hearing the voice, felt anxious and feared insanity.[10] Early in her relationship with "The Voice" she telephoned her colleague, Bill Thetford.

"You know that inner voice? It won't leave me alone."

"What's it saying?"

"It keeps saying, 'This is a course in miracles. Please take notes.' What am I going to do?"

Calmly and supportively, Bill said, "Why don't you take notes? Take them down in that shorthand you use."

"But Bill, what if it's gibberish? Then I'll know I'm crazy. I'm not a mystical poet. I'm a psychologist and I don't know that I believe in this."

"Well, since you can't make it go away, why don't you take it down?"

"And if it's gibberish?"

"We'll tear it up and no one will know."

The first night she recorded two paragraphs before she panicked and stopped, in spite of The Voice's desire to continue.

Other hearers recognize a separate, distinct personality, much as we know by the style who has written a letter, long before we see the signature at the end.

Some find themselves emotionally transformed while the voice is heard. Dorothy Maclean, founder of the Scottish Findhorn community, admitted that "the personal side of me resisted and did not want to listen, yet in the presence of my resplendent God-self [her name for her inner voice], I was softened, awed, enlarged and beautified."[11] Even Nietzsche, who announced the death of God, described in a letter to a friend how his masterpiece, *Thus Spake Zarathustra,* was received.

> It invaded me. One takes; one does not ask who gives. A thought flashes out like lightning, inevitably without hesitation. I never had a choice about it. One can hardly reject completely the idea that one is the mere incarnation, or mouthpiece or medium of some almighty power.[12]

Alice Bailey, secretary for 19 arcane books dictated in as many years, said she took psychic dictation from a living Tibetan sage thousands of miles away.[13] Bailey was amused by Carl Jung's attempt to trap it in the complex web of his own theory. "I have been told that Jung takes the position that the Tibetan is my personified higher self and that Alice Bailey is my lower self. One of these days I will ask him how my higher self can send me packages all the way from India, for that is what he has done."

Denial of personal responsibility for the voice is neither false modesty nor an attempt to mystify, but a simple statement of what the hearer experiences. "There are two me's," says Ray Bradbury, author of *Fahrenheit 451*, "the one that writes and the one that watches. So he has his life and I have mine, and I take credit for what he does." Robert Louis Stevenson claimed that "the whole of my published fiction [is] the single-handed product of some unseen collaborator." He believed he was in communication with "my brownies, the little people."

Richard Strauss reported "while the ideas were flowing in upon me, measure by measure, it seemed to me that I was dictated to by two wholly different Omnipotent Entities." No doubts were expressed by Giacomo Puccini regarding his *Madam Butterfly*. It "was dictated to me by God; I was merely instrumental in putting it on paper."[14]

On and on it goes, like a religious litany. Rudolf Friml, operetta composer in the early 20th century, said, "I sit down at the piano, and put my hands on the piano. And I let the spirit guide me! No, I never do the music. I never compose it; oh no, no! I am a tool. I am nothing. I am being used. It comes from someone, a spirit perhaps, using me." Even Harlan Howard, composer of hundreds of country and western songs, reported in some amazement how "The Blizzard" was written: "The pencil kept on moving and I didn't know when it would end. Did some great songwriter in the sky use me as a medium?"[15]

Sometimes the voice appears in a vision, as it did for Shirley MacLaine.

I saw the form of a very tall, almost androgynous human being. A graceful, folded cream-colored garment flowed over a figure seven feet tall, with long arms resting calmly at his sides. . . . And I had the intuitive feeling that it was extremely protective, full of patience, yet capable of great wrath. It was simple, yet so powerful that it seemed to "know" all there was to know. . . .

"Who are you?" I asked.

"I am your higher unlimited self," it said. . . .

"Oh, my goodness," I heard myself saying stupidly to it. "Are you really there?"

"Yes," it said, "I have always been here. I have been here with you since the beginning of time. I am never away from you. I am you. I am your unlimited soul. I am the unlimited you that guides you and teaches you through each incarnation."[16]

Pat Rodegast presented her conversations in *Emmanuel's Book* (I, II, III).[17] Corresponding to the "otherness" of inner voices, the hearer is addressed as *you*, as in Shirley MacLaine's vision. Emmanuel's language in the Preface to "his" book is typical.

> The gifts I wish to give you
> Are my deepest love,
> The safety of truth,
> The wisdom of the universe,
> And the reality of God.
> With these four things,
> Nothing will deter you,
> You will follow your heart
> Swiftly to your destination,
> Which is home."

Rodegast ends her introduction with, "So, I give you my dearest, wisest, sweetest, funniest, absolute friend, Emmanuel."

The single most common pressure to treat the voice as *not me* is its announcement of a name. Like many others, when I asked my own inner voice if it had a name, I heard:

"A name is not necessary. It would distract you from our message."

"Well, what are you called?" I pressed disrespectfully.

"We are called 'The Great White Brotherhood.' "

The "we" surprised me, and I felt discouraged. It was just my luck to get a racist, sexist spiritual organization!

I felt its amusement.

" 'Great' means cosmic, 'White' refers to light and 'Brotherhood' indicates the bonds of love among us."

Still, I asked inwardly, "Well, what should I call you? GWB?"

"If you must have a single name, use Victor," it said patiently.

Immediately I got the sense that *Victor* meant success in life's struggles and was chosen to appeal to my hopes more than being an encompassing title for them. Stevan Thayer's Ariel expressed a similar point of view (page 84).

Who Are They? What Do They Say?

If they are inside the person, but *not me*, who and what are they? I wondered if there might be clues in the several hundred names I had collected, so I compiled a list to see if they fell into any obvious groups. A few of the names illustrating each category are given below.

Personalities

Dead People Unknown to the Listener

Abdul Latif, Bethelda, Belle, Chom, Deturno, Dew Drop, Familiars (generic name for spirits), Feda, Harmony, Kabilla, Loas (Voodoo generic name), Nellie, Dr. Ono Yono, Patience Worth, Roophal, Snow Drop, Tren-Sen-Tie, Wonta, Yolande, X.

Friends and Relatives

(Too many of too little general interest.)

Famous Dead People

Achillini, Aknahton, Al Ghazali, Alexander, Appolonius of Tyana, Appolus Munn, Aristotle, Athandorus, Brahms, Beethoven, Byron, Arthur Ford, Benjamin Franklin, Galalius, Hyppolytos, William James, Jefferson, Liszt, Sir Henry Owen Morgan, Nefertiti, Newton, Plato, Plotinus, Schubert, Schumann, Seneca, Shelley, Solon, Swedenborg, Washington.

Guides

Native Americans

Azruth, Big Bear, Blackhawk, Grey Wolf, Kokum, Red Cloud, Segaske, Tecumseh, White Eagle.

Biblical Figures and Saints

Angels Daniel and Gabriel, God, Haggai, Jehovah, Mary, Miriam, Saints Catherine, Germaine, John, Michael, Paul.

Ascended Masters

Agam Parusha, Aman, Ariel, Bodhisattvas (generic name for Buddhist teachers), Cuzco, Djwal Kuhl, Elohim, Emmanuel, Fubic Quanty, Great Divine Director, Hoot Kumi, Isis, K-17, Lao Tzu, Lazaris, Mentor, Mohada, Qootubis, Rami Nuri, Ra Mu, Ramtha, Seth, Sohang, Tobia, Urani, Yaubi, Yavata.

Spiritual Groups

Association of Beneficents, Galactic Man, Galaxy Medallion, Hierarchy, Inyokern Brothers, New Light Era, Pre-Adamic Man, Race Guardians, Ukana of Mercury.

The Rest

Difficult to classify: Ass of Balaam, Brownies, Lion of Androcles, Nature Devas, Old Man of the Hills, Shadow of the Tomb.

The names of dead people refer to personalities, as if death were simply the loss of one's body-tool that did physical work while on earth. These voices usually have a personal agenda and seek assistance from those who still have a body—asking forgiveness; reassuring loved ones; completing unfinished poetry, novels or music; setting the record straight or getting help in growing up.

Some people who hear these voices are convinced by the unique phraseology or references to long-forgotten events that the voice belongs to a dead person whose consciousness, therefore, survives. Many of the "gosh-wow" books containing this spirit chit-chat, usually published at the authors' expense, consist of dialogues one might overhear on a long-distance phone call.

It is easy to be distracted by the claim of "communication from life beyond death." A certain caution here is just as important as caution in conversations with strangers who have bodies. For instance, the novelist Henry James, reacting to a rash of these books at the turn of the century, called these voices "ghostly busybodies" and "vermin." They are not "very saintly or sweet persons whose acquaintance it were deifying or even comfortable to make."[18]

In my experience and reading, "vermin" is too harsh. The voices rarely are malicious. Their typical tone is light and optimistic: "Mommy, please believe that I am alive, never have felt better or been busier. I am closer to you now than I ever was on earth." Such reassurance may be vastly comforting to those who have lost loved ones, but does not constitute evidence to dissuade critics like James.

---

*The voices rarely
are malicious.*

Personally, I have heard stunningly accurate predictions as well as silliness and sinister threats from inner voices claiming to be the disembodied remains of a former person. Once the voice of Azruth came to me. He said he was a North American Indian cave painter "of little importance" from the 10th century B.C. I declined his offer to teach me "the wisdom of my race." At best, a soul who still identifies with his body after 3000 years has a serious problem of arrested development. Another time, I heard the voice of a dead Nazi spouting Aryan tripe. I yelled at him, inwardly, to get out of my head. It was *my* head, and I did not want him there. That voice never returned.

In general, the voices of dead people are the most numerous and least interesting to casual readers. Just because they are dead does not make them smarter. Discernment is necessary.

Guides wear names like loose-fitting clothes. Their former personalities, if revealed at all, are completely secondary to the role of loving teacher. The best, like Victor and Ariel, are selfless in their patience, gentleness, love and desire to help, as if the only thing they wanted was the opportunity to serve. They provide lofty guidance for mundane problems faced by hearers, rarely giving direct advice about what to do but defining the challenges to love and forgive. They are superior models for worldly counselors and psychotherapists. Some of my professional colleagues have told me in confidence that they consult their inner voices for help when they reach a difficult point with a client.

Guides wear names
like loose-fitting clothes. . . .
The best . . . are selfless
in their patience, gentleness, love
and desire to help. . . .

The worst guides are destructive and evil. Sometimes hearers are seduced by initial compliments and promises of personal power, wealth and fame. Then their gullibility is exploited. These inner relationships can become as unhealthy, dysfunctional and abusive as relationships between two people. Conversations with spiritual con artists usually are recorded in psychiatric case notes or police records. We have read too often of murderers who said they were directed by an inner voice. Again, discernment is necessary.

Statements purporting to come from group spirits claim that work without bodies occurs in groups in other realities throughout eternity. From their perspective, this physical world is a remote outstation, a brief home away from home. If true, we would have to reverse our egocentric, geocentric assumptions. It would be a new Copernican revolution. That is the frequent message from the best of group spirits. Most of their statements, however, seem cryptic and impenetrable to me. Sometimes I am less charitable and wonder whether the flecks of gold in these piles of sludge are worth the effort to extract.

In compiling these lists, I assumed that those who heard inner voices felt honored and humbled by the famous people giving them personal attention. Some of the names, however, made me smile and wonder. Do Race Guardians make us safer? Where do they pin the Galaxy Medallion? Just where is the Ass of Balaam located, and what does its voice sound like? Dr. Ono Yono sounds like a cosmic panic reaction. Would Aristotle mind being quoted out of context? Does Snow Drop become Dew Drop in celestial summers?

My ambivalence typifies the range of reactions by others who, confronted with the profound and the inane, the uplifting and the degrading, must make sense of it all. The worlds of inner voices and visions are as diverse, complex and contradictory as this outer world of form and action. There are thorns among the berries, and some of the berries are poisonous. Being able to recognize the difference is essential. At their best, inner voices are aspects of ineffable, ecstatic, life-enhancing experiences. At worst, they should be ignored, laughed at or exiled.

What Do the Good Voices Do?

At a workshop, I once asked "Emmanuel" through Pat Rodegast why I should believe him just because he did not have a body. Pat reported that Emmanuel laughed. "That is reverse prejudice," he said. "Actually, I'm not smarter. I just have access to the smarts." This purported access often results in *information* far beyond the most precise predictions of the world's best futurists, in *inspiration* that transforms lives and in *authorization* for a mission, including authoring books, poems and music. These effects convince the hearers that the voices are superior.

Provide Superior Information

The word *prophet* comes from the Greek word *prophetes*—people who speak for an inner, divine voice. The biblical prophets prefaced or concluded their own statements with, "Thus saith the Lord." They accurately predicted earthquakes, volcanoes, plagues and the outcomes of battles, offered military advice (Haggai) and even located where the enemy had made its camp (Elisha).

These prophets often were improbable, having neither wealth nor status nor worldly power. Amos was a herdsman and fruit gatherer; David was a shepherd. The superiority of their inner voice was clear by contrast, as it has been for many modern prophets—janitors, cafeteria aides and auto mechanics—with limited education.

The superiority of inner voices also can be seen in contrast with the limits of worldly knowledge. Emanuel Swedenborg probably was the last person to know "everything in the world."[19] Born in 1688, he worked as an assessor of mines in Sweden until a small income from his books allowed him to concentrate entirely on scholarship. He wrote 155 books in 17 sciences. His pattern was to learn what was known in a particular field, then summarize, integrate and extend it in a definitive book. He mastered the fields of astronomy, economics, magnetism, physics, hydrostatics, engineering, chemistry, mathematics, geology, paleontology, anatomy, physiology, optics, metallurgy, cosmogony, cosmology and psychology. He founded the science of crystallography. His anatomical discoveries were ignored for 200 years before independent medical confirmation. He was fluent in nine languages and competent in seven crafts, from bookbinding and watchmaking to engraving and lens grinding. His inventions included crude but viable designs for a submarine, flying machine and rapid-firing gun. He created plans for the world's largest dry dock, a tank for ships, stoves, an ear trumpet, pumping methods, fire extinguishers, a music-making machine and a steel rolling mill. And, he was a respected member of the Swedish parliament. None of this, however, prepared him for the new worlds that opened to him, which he considered superior to all this worldly knowledge.

At the age of 54, while Swedenborg was working on the last of his 155 scientific books, he began exploring his inner world. A voice in a vision said "that he [the inner voice] was the Lord God, the creator of the world, and the redeemer, and that he had chosen me to explain the spiritual sense of the scripture, and that he, himself, would explain to me what I should write on the subject." The Lord did enough explaining to fill an additional 282 books in the remaining 32 years of Swedenborg's life. A number of these books were substantial tomes of more than 1,000 pages. They were "dictated by an angel," Swedenborg told a friend who asked him how he wrote so much.

There are numerous verified instances of superior information available to Swedenborg through his inner voices. After Count de Marteville died, his wife asked Swedenborg at a dinner party for assistance in finding the receipt for a valuable silver piece her husband had given her. The silversmith was demanding payment, even though she was sure he had been paid. She could not afford the money and could not find the receipt. Swedenborg said he would try to contact her dead husband. Three days later, in the presence of 11 witnesses, Swedenborg reported that her husband said the receipt was in a bureau upstairs. The countess said the bureau had already been searched. Swedenborg related her husband's instructions to pull out a specific drawer that had a false back with a concealed compartment. The countess and her company went upstairs, found the compartment, the receipt and other lost papers.

Once Swedenborg "saw" and reported to a group of friends the progress and precise details of a devastating fire in Stockholm while it was occurring some 300 miles away. A week later, every detail, down to the fire's near miss of a friend's home, was confirmed in news reports and by messengers.

Swedenborg quoted back to Christopher Springer, Sweden's negotiator, his verbatim conversation in secret talks with Prussia. On another occasion, he described the strangulation of Emperor Peter III of Russia in Kopscha prison several days before the event occurred. Later it was reported in the newspaper.

One evening after his favorite social pastime—dining out with friends—Swedenborg was asked to prove his reputed ability to communicate with spirits. He was asked to say which of them would die first. After a period of silent meditation, he said, "Olaf Olafsohn will die tomorrow morning at 45 minutes past four o'clock." A friend of Olafsohn's went to his home the following morning. On the way, he met the man's servant who said a fit of apoplexy had killed Olafsohn. The clock by his bed had stopped at 4:45.

In February 1772, Swedenborg wrote a letter to the great religious reformer, John Wesley:

Sir, I have been informed in the world of spirits that you have a strong desire to converse with me; I shall be happy to see you if you will favor me with a visit.

I am, Sir, your humble servant,
Emanuel Swedenborg

Wesley told those present that he did want to see Swedenborg, but had not told anyone. Wesley wrote Swedenborg that the meeting would have to take place in six months, after his speaking tour. Swedenborg responded that a meeting then would not be possible because he (Swedenborg) was to die on the 29th of the coming month. Following a stroke the next month, Swedenborg was cared for by a maid who innocently commented afterward that Swedenborg predicted the day of his death. She said he seemed pleased, "as if he was going to have a holiday, to go to some merrymaking."

Frequently, voices of farewell come in ghostly visions at the precise moment of a person's death. Voices of warning are common. Nearly 2500 years ago, Socrates was warned of dangerous situations in his life.[20] "Since childhood," Socrates said, "I have been attended by a semi-divine being whose voice, from time to time, dissuades me from some undertaking, but never directs me what I am to do." Socrates called this voice "The Sign."

---

*Frequently, voices of farewell
come in ghostly visions. . . .
Voices of warning are common.*

Once, Socrates attended a dinner party where a politician named Timarchus was also a guest. When Timarchus was about to leave to participate in an assassination plot known only to the conspirators, The Sign came to Socrates. "By no means rise from the table," warned Socrates. After a time, Timarchus again got up to go. "And The Sign came to me again; and again I made him stay." A third time Timarchus sneaked out while Socrates' attention was diverted to others. "Thus he went forth, and was gone, and did that which was to be his doom."

Plutarch, in his essay "The Genius of Socrates," describes a conversation with Euthyphron while they were walking. Suddenly Socrates stopped and warned his friends to use another route. Most followed him, but some continued and met a herd of pigs who knocked them down. Charillus, who had not followed Socrates' advice, "returned home with legs and clothes full of mire, so that we all remembered Socrates' familiar voice, with roars of laughter, marveling how the divinity took care of him continually."

After a lifetime of accurate warnings, Socrates trusted the voice so much that he was able to face death in prison with absolute confidence. The Sign warned him not to speak in his own defense against charges of impiety. In his address to the court, after he was sentenced to die, Socrates said:

> In other speeches of mine The Sign has often stopped me in the midst. But now it has not hindered me in any deed or word of mine connected with this present business. What then do I suppose to be the reason? I will tell you. I think what has happened to me is a good thing; and we must have been mistaken when we supposed that death was an evil. That accustomed Sign would assuredly have checked me, had I been about to do anything that was evil.[21]

Complete Unfinished Work

Sometimes, as with Swedenborg, psychic information can be verified, and like Socrates, can affect the lives of others. In 1977,

Victoria Mariccio, a practicing psychic in Virginia Beach, was awakened in the middle of the night by "an immensely huge Indian [who] jumped into view, out of nowhere, with a tomahawk. We were in a field, a prairie, with beating drums, a dark blue sky and stars above. He said to me, 'Do not be afraid. I'm your spiritual Indian. My name is Blackfoot. I'm a Crow Indian.' "[22] Mariccio said she verified his claim by finding a picture of Blackfoot in an obscure book in the local library.

Chief Blackfoot was known as a tall, strikingly handsome, wise and eloquent spokesman for the Crow. He developed the Crow's democratic governance system, still in use today, and conducted negotiations with the United States government that obtained 38 million acres in Montana. In 1868, after the chief died, the government unilaterally reduced the Crow land to 8 million acres. The white European foreigners continued to take Crow land.

Over time, Crow Indians lost track of his burial place. By the early 1900s, Chief Blackfoot had disappeared from books about the Crow. Then the Crow Nation, like the chief, nearly disappeared. The reservation was further reduced in size. The buffalo were almost exterminated by greedy white traders.

Economic exploitation was followed by cultural domination. The Federal government outlawed most of their religious practices, making them punishable crimes. By 1900, the Crows went to white schools, learned methods of mass production and earned a reputation as one of the most economically and politically progressive Indian Nations.

Based on Victoria Mariccio's inner conversation with Chief Blackfoot, she reported:

> There were a lot of things he was worried about—the way they were cutting the reservation down from 8 million to 2.5 million acres, about the desecration of graves out there and about the four corners, which made no sense to me at the

time, until I went out to the reservation, and found that they were the four foundation stones he laid for the size of the reservation. He was worried about the alcoholism that is in his people, about the minerals in the ground that should not be stolen from his people. One night, Chief Blackfoot told me to go to the reservation, that now was the time to see his people. I was able to make contact and arrangements. I arrived there on Tuesday in July of 1978. I was there four days when he came to me on a Saturday morning, and said, "I'm buried in White man's land, and I want to be brought back to my people. They will find me through you."

A group of Crow Indians, curious about what Victoria Mariccio had said, decided to search for Chief Blackfoot's grave. David Stewart, a member of the search party, described their efforts. "We went to the approximate location of the burial site and spent all day looking. The chief had described the general area in one of his visitations to Victoria. The information was that there were three prominent boulders marking the grave."

Two trips were unsuccessful. Then Victoria had to return to Virginia Beach. On the third trip, taking directions from Chief Blackfoot through Victoria by telephone from Virginia Beach, they arrived at a sandstone butte with three large rocks in front of a cave. Inside were the bones of a very tall man, buried with beads that the chief would have had at the time of his death.

Chief Blackfoot was reburied in a park beside the office of the Bureau of Indian Affairs where he said, through Victoria Mariccio, it would be conspicuous and bring many visitors. He wanted people to know he had returned.

The story of Chief Blackfoot's rediscovery and reburial illustrates the superior information that inner voices can provide. Inner voices also have other special powers.

Inspire at Times of Doubt and Fatigue

While superior information may persuade doubters, and completing earthly tasks may satisfy the spirits, inspiration changes lives. One-third to one-half of adult Americans have had an ecstatic experience. The effects are positive for some 85 percent: it "strengthened my belief in God," "gave me strength," "made me a better person, more happy, understanding, and appreciative."

Actually, calling it *positive* is too weak. It is uplifting, healing, transformational. It comes at moments of indecision, resolves conflicts, converts unbelievers, floods the personality with new light, creates a sense of certainty, calm and quiet. The superiority of these moments over one's best normal states is marked in time and space as an unforgettable memory of ecstasy.

[An ecstatic experience] is
uplifting, healing, transformational.

For nearly twenty years prior to Saint Teresa's founding of the new order of Carmelites, she had tried unsuccessfully to give up special friendships, as required by the Carmelites.[23] They were not causing her to offend God, she reasoned, and abandoning her friends seemed like ingratitude. Finally she placed the problem before God, praying that she learn how to be "most pleasing in all things." As she was reciting the Veni Creator, "the rapture almost carried me away." Then she heard an inner voice: "I will have thee converse now, not with human beings, but with angels." This unequivocal answer with no wasted words carried with it the force of conviction and the courage to act. "The Lord set me free and gave me strength to carry my resolution into action."

Annie Besant, a modern occult version of Saint Teresa, was a tireless advocate of women's rights at the turn of this century. During a moment of particularly deep discouragement about her attempts to bring human beings together, she heard an inner voice.

> Sitting alone in deep thought as I had accustomed to do after the sun had set, filled with an intense, but nearly hopeless longing to solve the riddle of life and mind, I heard a Voice that was later to become to me the holiest sound on earth, bidding me to take courage for the light was near.[24]

Soon she discovered Theosophy, the mystic philosophy of a charismatic Russian, Madam Blavatsky. With Charles Leadbeater, Besant became one of the two primary spokespersons for the Theosophical Movement that brought forth such luminaries as Krishnamurti, Rudolf Steiner, Alice Bailey and Robert Assagioli.

As an Augustinian monk in the 16th century, Martin Luther wanted assurance that God forgave him for his sins.[25] After extensive penance, Luther finally felt he had done enough. Then he heard a challenging inner voice: "Well done, Brother Martin! Soon you will not need God at all." Luther realized that God's favors are not earned, but given.

Martin Luther's namesake heard an equally effective, but opposite message from an inner voice in the 20th century.[26] Instead of deflating a puffed-up ego, Martin Luther King, Jr. needed support. During a critical moment in the bus boycott in Birmingham, Alabama, he had become frightened. Every day he received between 30 and 40 calls and letters threatening him and his family. King began to doubt, thought about giving up and taking his family to some safe place to live. Then he heard the voice of the "inner Christ" say to him, "Martin Luther, stand up for righteousness. Stand up for justice. Stand up for truth. And lo, I will be with you, even unto the end of the world." This transformed "the fatigue of despair into the buoyancy of hope," and gave him the strength to continue the struggle.

Christopher Columbus also needed support when returning

from his fourth voyage to America, tired, sick and depressed by a difficult crew and other adversities.[27] According to a letter written to a friend, Columbus then heard an inner voice that reassured him about the external conditions, raised his spirits and gave him courage to complete his trip.

Convert Unbelievers

For most people, the inner voice is so inspiring that hearing it once is enough to cause a change in heart or mind. John Bunyan is an exception. Born in 1628, he described his wayward, sinful youth in *Grace Abounding*, his autobiography.[28] One day while playing "cat" [apparently an early version of croquet], he struck the ball once.

> Just as I was about to strike it a second time, a voice from heaven suddenly did dart into my soul, which said, "Wilt thou leave thy sins and go to heaven, or have thy sins and go to hell? . . ." Suddenly this conclusion was fastened on my spirit . . . that I had been a great and grievous sinner, and that now it was too late to look after heaven, for Christ would not forgive me nor pardon my transgressions . . . and therefore resolved in my mind to go on in sin. I [might as well] be damned for many sins as be damned for few.

The inner voice is so inspiring
that hearing it once
is enough to cause a change
in heart or mind.

Though the best voices get to the point with the speed and accuracy of a surgeon's knife, their efforts sometimes go unrewarded.

Having rejected the offer of heaven, Bunyan later felt doubly damned. He could find no biblical examples of sinners who were given a third chance.

For more than a decade Bunyan despaired that he deserved saving. Occasionally he heard inner voices that succeeded in comforting him, but only briefly. During this period Bunyan gave up the sweetness of ringing bells, then of dancing, swearing and friends who were sinful. He read the Bible, then read it many more times looking for clues to his salvation. This righteous but melancholy man believed he was the worst sinner in history, the only person beyond hope, and condemned to eternal hell no matter what he did. It was a delusion of grandeur in reverse.

> One day as I was passing into the field . . . suddenly this sentence fell upon my soul: Thy righteousness is in heaven. I saw with the eyes of my soul Jesus Christ at God's right hand. There was my righteousness. It was not my good frame of heart that made my righteousness better, nor my bad frame that made my righteousness worse, for my righteousness was Jesus Christ.[29]

Like Luther, Bunyan concluded that God's grace was not given because he had earned it. God's love for Jesus was so strong that it overflowed to others, and Bunyan experienced it as *grace abounding*. This time Bunyan's transformation was permanent, undoubtedly a great relief to his patient wife as well. He became a minister and fearlessly preached the word of God, for which he was imprisoned. There he wrote *Pilgrim's Progress*, an allegorical account of his exploration of every wrong turn "delivered under the similitude of a dream."

Whatever real or imagined sins had polluted Bunyan's life, they were mild in comparison with the physical vengeance world heavyweight boxing champion George Foreman inflicted on his opponents. He took pride in destroying their bodies and their will. In 47 fights he knocked out 42 men. In 1973, he took the heavyweight championship by nearly killing Joe Frazier. In 1974, Mohammed Ali took it from him. To show that he still had plenty of fight left in him, Foreman went to Toronto where he crushed five fighters in one evening. In 1976, he destroyed Joe Frazier again and announced to the world, "I am bad." He kept a lion and a tiger as pets because they were "bad." Then he lost a 12-round decision to Jimmy Young in Puerto Rico.

> I was walking to the dressing room, trying to cool down. I was telling myself, "You don't have to box. You can retire to your ranch and die." Die? Where did that come from? I didn't put that word in there. But the word kept sneaking into my head. Then a voice said, "You believe in God. Why you scared to die?" I said, "I can still give money to charities and cancer," and the voice in my head said, "I don't want your money. I want you." I was nothing. I was dead. And a dirty smell came with it. I was dead, and I said, "I don't care if I am dead, I still believe in God." Whap! I was back.[30]

Foreman started yelling hallelujahs. The people in the dressing room "looked at me like I was crazy. All I know is, since that day I wasn't a believer, I was a knower. In all my wildest imagination, I never thought up nothin' like that."

From that night, Foreman "wore out more Bibles than I can count." He preached the word on the street corners of Houston, his hometown, and in 1981 erected his own Church of the Lord Jesus Christ where he preached Sunday mornings and Wednesday nights. "This is the only thing I've ever done that I really did with all my heart and stuck with it." From this transformative event we have today a lovable heavyweight champion who advertises a "seafood diet: I eat any food I see."

According to Mahatma Gandhi, an inspiring inner voice is available to everyone.

For me the Voice of God, of Conscience, of Truth, or the Inner Voice or "the Still Small Voice" mean one and the same thing. It was as unmistakable as some human voice definitely speaking to me, and irresistible. . . . The hearing of the voice was preceded by a terrific struggle within me. Suddenly the Voice came upon me. I listened, made certain it was the Voice, and the struggle ceased. . . . For me the Voice was more real than my own existence. It has never failed me, or for that matter, anyone else. And everyone who wills can hear the Voice. It is within everyone.[31]

Dr. Nathanson, co-author of this book, was inspired by Ariel to start a publishing company to produce and distribute this and other books. Inner voices often provide this type of guidance.

Authorize Missions

In one of my graduate classes, I asked students to write down the five most important questions in their lives. Most people, even the cynics, wanted to know, "What is my mission in life?" The question is revealing. Most of us believe that we have a special reason for being alive, but don't know what it is. Inspiration may bring joy to our hearts, but conversion is incomplete without a clear mission.

Often inner voices define a mission and authorize action. A voice in a vision of a burning bush authorized Moses to liberate the Israelites. His inner voice predicted disasters, suggested military strategy, advised Moses for forty years in the desert and dictated the Ten Commandments. Isaiah said: "The Lord has appointed me to preach good tidings to the meek; he has sent me to bind up the heartbroken, to proclaim liberty to the captives and . . . to comfort all who mourn."[32]

---

*Inner voices
define a mission
and authorize action.*

Authorizations often are sudden, surprising and ask for outcomes that defy the odds. Saint Joan was authorized to throw the English out of France by raising the siege at Orleans and to bring her Dauphin to his throne by having him crowned at Rheims.[33] Saint Joan had six prohibitive handicaps: she was a peasant, a girl, seventeen, with no knowledge of military strategy or politics and had to rejuvenate a dispirited army that considered the cause already lost. When an inner voice calls for action, however, the mission is more important than the means. There is faith that God will provide, somehow. Frequently the improbable is achieved and called a miracle.

Swedenborg was authorized to explain the spiritual sense of the Bible. Saint Teresa was authorized by her inner voice to begin her mission: "After communion, the Lord gave me the most explicit commands to work [for the creation of a stricter convent] with all my might and made me wonderful promises that the convent would not fail to be established."[34] In this century, Mother Teresa was authorized by an inner voice to leave her cloistered convent, to go out and minister to the poorest of the poor. Similar stories, albeit with less worldwide impact, are told by many others who say their life work was authorized by an inner voice.

Inspire Writing

Authorizations for missions have echoes in the claims of modern men and women who say they received epigrams, poems, plays, novels, epics, philosophy, even small libraries of books and musical scores. They were literally "author"-ized. Their inspired writing differs from ordinary writing in five ways: ease, speed, precision, coherence and transcendence.

---

*Inspired writing differs
from ordinary writing. . . .*

EASE

Biographer Stephen Oates once described his usual experience of writing: "I sit with pencil and paper and wait until the blood forms on my brow."[35] After a period of avoidance, blocking and wandering in a mental desert, when a few stray ideas are found, there is an agonized search for good sentences, then painful self-criticism of what is written and continual revisions to make it clear, interesting and stylish. Such are the normal tortures of writing.

By contrast, inspired writing is easy, in the sense that it requires little mental effort. A meditative calm exists while the words of the inner voice are written down like a student taking verbatim notes at a lecture. "It costs me no labor," said Saint Teresa. Geraldine Cummins described how she produced the purported afterlife conversations of several recently dead people. "I am a stenographer taking down words from dictation and employing as it were, an inner hearing."[36] In her autobiography, Alice Bailey explained how she was given 19 arcane books in as many years by a master while he was living thousands of miles away in a Tibetan Monastery: "I simply listen and take down the words that I hear, and register the thoughts which are dropped one by one into my brain."[37]

For Ray Bradbury, author of *Fahrenheit 451*, allowing characters to make contact requires passivity. He recommends that you "lie in bed early in the morning when you are waking up and your mind is relaxed, it's floating, and the voices begin to talk, whoever or whatever they are, for whatever reasons, and you never question that, and you listen to them, and at a certain point, or when you get a certain metaphor, you jump out of bed, and run to get it down before it's gone."[38]

Judith Rossner, author of *Looking for Mr. Goodbar*, reports a similar relaxed receptivity.

> I just give her time to sit down in my head. All I have to do is to go to a place, sit down and have the patience to wait and not give up on her and not accept all the possible distractions. Often it seems as though the process bypasses my brain, or at least my conscious brain, entirely. . . . It's certainly true that at times when I have had difficulty with my work, it's because I'm not just letting those voices speak to me and taking dictation from them.[39]

SPEED

After Jacob Boehme, a famous Catholic mystic, transcribed his first inspired book, *Aurora,* in 1610, it was condemned by a local tribunal and he was forbidden to write any more. After seven years of compliance, "a new motion from on high" commanded him to write.

> All was ordered according to the direction of the spirit, which often went in haste. . . . I could have written in a more accurate and plain manner, yet the reason was this, that the burning fire often forced me forward with speed and the hand and the pen must hasten directly after it; for it comes and goes as a sudden shower.[40]

It took Madam Guyon—a tragic 18th-century Christian mystic—only one-and-a-half days to write the book on prayer that was the cause of her 14-year imprisonment for heresy: "The copyist could not, however diligent, copy in five days what I wrote in a single night." Saint Teresa was so busy providing direction for her nuns and doing her own daily devotions that writing five long books seems miraculous. She lamented, "Oh that I could write with many hands so that none of it were forgotten." Three secretaries working in shifts were needed to transcribe Saint Catherine's *Divine Dialogues* as they were given to her by "Sweet Truth": five books in as many days. Aurobindo acted as the willing scribe for the wisdom his inner teacher wanted to impart: some 5,000 printed pages in a brief six years, the majority of his most substantive literary work. Aurobindo said, "I have made no endeavor in writing. I have simply left the Higher Power to work. . . . I never think or seek for expressions or try to write in good style; it is out of a silent mind that I write whatever comes ready-shaped from above."[41]

In contrast with the normally slow, labored production of prose, poetry or music, this quantum leap in ease and speed leaves little doubt in the authors' minds that it is a gift from beyond themselves.

This quantum leap in ease and speed
leaves little doubt in the authors' minds that
it is a gift from beyond themselves.

From Robert Blake's introduction to *Jerusalem*, we know that he had heard inner voices:

Reader! Lover of Books! Lover of heaven
And of that God from whom all things are given,
Who in mysterious Sinai's awful cave
To Man the wondrous art of writing gave;

Again he speaks in thunder and in fire!
Thunder of Thought and flames of fierce desire:
Even from the depths of Hell his voice I hear
Within the unfathomed caverns of my Ear.[42]

If this poetic description is not sufficiently clear, we have Blake's assertion in a letter to his friend, Thomas Butts, on April 25, 1803:

> I have written [Jerusalem] from immediate dictation, twelve, or sometimes twenty or thirty lines at a time without premeditation, and even against my will. The time it has taken in writing was thus rendered nonexistent, and an immense poem exists which seems to be the labor of a long life, all produced without labor or study.

In another letter to Butts, Blake states that "I may praise it, since I dare not pretend to be any other than the secretary. The authors are in eternity."

PRECISION AND HIDDEN COHERENCE

Since inspired writing usually is not considered one's own, the stenographers usually are meticulous in respecting the higher source, as if to change a word would profane the work. "Much that I wrote did not come out of my own head," confessed Saint Teresa. "I have been told it by this heavenly Master of mine and I am extremely scrupulous about not adding or subtracting so much as a single syllable."[43] In testimony given during St. Teresa's beatification, several of her nuns said she wrote quickly without any erasures, corrections or subsequent editing. Her first draft was her final copy.

Alice Bailey echoes Saint Teresa: "I have never changed anything the Tibetan has given me. If I once did so, he would never dictate to me again. I do not always understand what is given. I do not always agree. But I record it all honestly and then discover that it does make sense."[44] Even that supreme intellect and prolific writer of his own books, Emanuel Swedenborg, expressed his admiration for the inner author who chooses words "much better and more readily than the man himself."

Inner dictation is frequently so clear, sequential and complete that it can be published without revisions, although the plan is not known to the secretary in advance. Often not even the end of each sentence is foreseen. Charles Linton, a 22-year-old blacksmith of good intelligence but limited education, was told by his inner voice to get ready for the transcription of a great work. During a brief four months in 1854, Linton took down *The Healing of Nations*, a 340-page religious rhapsody consisting of epigrams in the style of the King James Bible.[45] The writing was witnessed by a Mr. Tallmadge who said it was done rapidly without erasures or alterations, even though Linton had no idea beforehand of the plan of the book, and frequently did not even know the next word he would write.

Helen Schucman, who heard *The Course in Miracles* dictated by her Voice, never knew how a sentence would end when she started.[46] Once she took a break for three days. When she returned, The Voice began exactly where it had left off, as if it had been waiting patiently for 72 hours to finish the sentence. After three years and 944 typed pages, the first of three volumes was complete. It was published exactly as dictated, the only changes being divisions into subsections for readability, with the permission and assistance of The Voice.

Frederick Oliver, a nearly illiterate 16-year-old dropout, took daily dictation from Phylos the Tibetan who described two incarnations of a soul.[47] In the preface, Oliver observed, "the whole thing was as if [Phylos] had the manuscript already prepared when he first began dictation."

The belief that a whole book or composition has been completed by the voice prior to its dictation is shared by Madam

Guyon. A considerable portion of Guyon's manuscript on Judges was lost. From inner dictation she completed it a second time. "Long afterward these [lost pages] were found in a place no one could have imagined they would be; and the old and the new versions were exactly alike, a circumstance which greatly astonished those persons of learning and merit who undertook its verification."[48]

These inspired compositions seem to be constructed in advance outside the awareness of the worldly author or composer. Some, like George Gershwin, simply report the phenomenon. While riding on a train to Boston, under pressure to finish *A Rhapsody in Blue*, he was astonished and relieved when he "suddenly heard, even saw on paper, the complete construction of the rhapsody from beginning to end."[49]

Steve Halpern, a northern California New Age composer, reminisced:

> Amongst the redwoods, I very clearly heard this music— what sounded like the Spectrum Suite—and I heard instruments that had not been invented then and I was basically told this is what you are supposed to work with. It was not a voice, but it was knowing. I started recording what I received in trance or altered states. I had known that there should be music that would help and heal. I ended up being guided.[50]

For others who receive inspired messages, the attribution is clear, consistent and without need for further explanation. Johannes Brahms believed that at least on occasion, he was "in touch with the Infinite...."

> When I feel the urge I begin by appealing directly to my Maker. I immediately feel vibrations which thrill my whole being. Is this a semi-trance to get results, a condition when the conscious mind is in temporary abeyance? Measure by

measure, the finished product is revealed to me when I am in those rare, inspired moods. Straight away the ideas flow in upon me, directly from God.[51]

TRANSCENDENCE

These testimonies state that a power transcending time, space, causality and the puny boundaries of our bodies is responsible. For those who experience it, the source of their inspired writing is an article of faith. Yet belief, in itself, proves nothing. The capacity for self-deception is powerful and well documented. There are, however, a few instances that support this belief more strongly than mere assertions.

The most extreme examples of inspired writing, the most rare and difficult to explain in terms of latent natural abilities, are written in a language not known to the hearer. These events, if true, give weight to the simple idea that separate intelligence can communicate with us. The hypothesis is radical. It drives rationalists to frenzies of debunking and frantic efforts to find alternative explanations.

The most extreme examples
of inspired writing. . . .
are written in a language
not known to the hearer.

Alice Bailey commented on the Sutras of Patanjali.[52] She says she relied on the Tibetan who dictated translations of the Sutras because she did not know Sanskrit. While this is impressive if true, it is not a strong example. Bailey did not actually write in a foreign language unknown to her, and it would have been easy to get an English translation of the Sutras from the local library.

Gopi Krishna was a low-level Indian bureaucrat and the

founder of modern Kundalini Yoga. Twelve years after the "kundalini rose up his chakras," bringing a permanent alteration in his consciousness, he became interested in writing poetry. His own efforts were sterile and painfully slow.

> The standard of the compositions did not improve in the least, and I had often to labor for hours to complete a line and then longer to find a line to match it. [Then, one day] near me, in a blaze of brilliant light I suddenly felt what seemed to be a mighty conscious presence encompassing me and overshadowing all the objects around, from which two lines of a beautiful verse in Kashmiri poured out to float before my vision, like luminous writing in the air.[53]

Several days later the next lines came to him.

> Couplets, like falling snow flakes . . . came fully formed complete with language, rhyme and meter, finished products originating, as it seemed, from the surrounding intelligence.

Over the next few weeks he wrote a few stanzas in Kashmiri delivered in this way. Usually they dealt with aspects of the unknown, or an approaching apocalypse. Then poems in English arrived, followed by poems in Urdu, succeeded by poems in Punjabi. But Gopi Krishna had at least a passing knowledge of these languages. "My surprise knew no bounds," he says, "when a few days later the direction came that I should prepare to receive verses in Persian. I had never read the language nor could I in the least understand or speak it." Poems in Persian were followed by poems in German, French, Italian, Sanskrit and Arabic, all of which he claims were unintelligible to him because he was completely ignorant of these languages. He simply transcribed the inner voice phonetically as precisely as he could.

The results are unremarkable on their literary merits, most

closely resembling nursery rhymes or folk songs. For instance, here is the English translation of a poem in German:

> A beautiful bird always sings
> In my heart with a gentle voice.
> And when the night wind sheds
> Its tears on the green grass,
> Then the bird is watching.

A simple, plausible, though uncharitable explanation for Krishna's poems is that he wrote them in a normal state of consciousness and lied about their origins. This is possible because it never happened again, it was not witnessed, the literary quality bordered on the infantile, it came at a time when he admitted feeling disappointed that for twelve years (sufficient time to write a few simple poems) no special powers had accompanied his kundalini experience. Did his disappointment make him cheat? We'll never really know.

Rosemary Brown was an Englishwoman with an eighth-grade education and two years of piano instruction as a youth. After her husband died, she took a job as an elementary school cafeteria assistant to support her children. She rarely played the piano after adolescence until an inner voice identifying itself as Franz Liszt began dictating music to her note by note. "Before he [Liszt] put the notes in my mind or at my fingertips, he would tell me the name of the piece we were going to play together." [54]

The musical equivalents of dialects and foreign languages are a composer's style and type of composition. Brown claims to have transcribed more than 400 pieces of music for 13 dead composers: Chopin, Schubert, Beethoven, Bach, Brahms, Schumann, Debussy, Grieg, Berlioz, Rachmaninoff, Monteverdi, Mozart and Schweitzer.

During a six-year period, she transcribed songs, string quartets, the beginning of an opera, partially completed concertos and symphonies. For several years, she kept the scores in her home and played them for no one. Then "Liszt" insisted that they be given to others. A seemingly fortuitous sequence of events led to publication of several scores, then recitals, radio and television interviews and commercial recordings. Most of it does not match the composers' finest works, but then, neither did most of the pieces they composed during their own lifetimes.

Brown said that Sir Donald Tovey, a distinguished musician who died in 1940, dictated to her on January 1, 1970, the words of explanation to appear on the record jacket of "their" new music:

> In communicating through music and conversation, an organized group of musicians who have departed from your world, are attempting to establish a precept for humanity, i.e., that physical death is a transition from one state of consciousness to another wherein one retains one's individuality. The realization of this fact should assist man [sic] to a greater insight into his own nature and potential superterrestrial activities.[55]

All of her public appearances were opportunities to spread the word about the nature of higher realities, life after death and the need for more enlightened policies.

Did Brown tell the truth? Or did she practice and compose in secret for many years? Even if she lied, we must acknowledge that she transcended her previous limits in most remarkable ways.

Lying is a less likely explanation for Pearl Curran. One day in 1912, this St. Louis housewife with an eighth-grade education said a voice calling itself Patience Worth began dictating through her and spoke in an archaic, little known dialect not used for over three centuries. Patience said she had lived in Dorsetshire, England in the 17th century. Some of her descriptions of the countryside have been verified. Over a period of more than 20 years, Patience Worth gave Pearl Curran more than one-and-a-half million words in poems and historical novels, mostly set in the time of Jesus or having religious themes.[56]

Much of it was critically acclaimed. Dr. Usher, Professor of History at Washington University, considered *The Sorry Tale*, a composition of 350,000 words, "the greatest story penned of the life and times of Christ since the Gospels were finished."

This enthusiasm was generated not simply by the sudden literary work of an undereducated woman, but also by the language employed. Professor C.H.S. Schiller of London University analyzed *Telka*, a 70,000-word poem. The book does not contain a single word originated after 1600. "When we consider that the authorized version of the Bible has only 70% Anglo Saxon, and it is necessary to go back to Lyomen in 1205 to equal Patience' percentage (over 90%) of Anglo Saxon words, we realize we are facing a philological miracle." Even if we assume it was not a miracle and was not dictated by a discarnate personality, it is a spectacular demonstration of how much human potential each of us may be able to realize.

We are facing a philological miracle . . .
a spectacular demonstration
of how much human potential
each of us may be able to realize.

What Is the Best That Can Happen?

Inner voices can "do" many things—provide superior information, predict, warn, inspire conversions, authorize a mission, dictate music, poems and novels. What happens, we may ask, if a person listens for a long time and develops a stable relationship with the inner voice? What is the best that can happen with the tutelage of an inner voice? [57]

Hearers' responses are as different as Sunday strollers and world-class sprinters. Most people hide their inner guidance and pretend they never heard it. A few—very few—respond with the full weight of their special genius at ripe historical moments and leave an indelible trace. They provide examples of the best that can happen.

Mohammed was thoroughly embedded in a materialistic existence before he began to hear an inner voice. Mirza Husayn Ali [Baha'u'llah], founder of the Bahai Faith, illustrates how the relationship develops. The lives of Saint Catherine of Siena; Emanuel Swedenborg; George Fox, founder of the Quakers; and Sri Aurobindo, father of the Indian Independence movement, Integral Yoga and the utopian village of Auroville, show what happens after the inner development is complete.

Contact and Enrollment

Most hearers resist the initial contact. They fear becoming whatever their culture has condemned about it—a witch, possessed, psychotic or just intolerably different. There is a point, however, when some hearers choose to learn from the inner voice. They choose to "enroll."

There is a point . . .
when some hearers choose
to learn from the inner voice.

Consider Mohammed, for example. One night during a retreat on Mount Hira, Mohammed had a lucid dream. Gabriel came carrying a piece of brocade with writing on it.

"Recite!" Gabriel ordered.

"What shall I recite?"

Gabriel pressed the brocade against Mohammed's chest so hard that he could not breathe, then released the pressure.

"Recite!"

"What shall I recite?"

Again Gabriel almost crushed Mohammed before letting him go. "Recite!"

"But what shall I read?"

"Recite:

> In the name of your God who created,
> Created man from blood clotted.
> Recite! Your Lord is the most beneficent, who taught by
>   the Pen,
> Taught that which they knew not unto men."

Mohammed complied and Gabriel left. Mohammed reported later that, "It was as though these words were written on my heart." Probably *written* is a diluted translation. Engraved, carved or gouged would be more accurate.

Mohammed reacted as if he had been violated by the dream. He was ashamed and angry to the point of fanatic intolerance. "None of God's creatures was more hateful to me than an ecstatic poet, or a man possessed. I could not even bear to look at them. I thought, 'Woe is me—poet or possessed. Never shall the

Quraysh [Mohammed's tribe in Mecca] say that of me! I will go up the mountain, jump off, kill myself, and find peace.'" It was better to stop consciousness altogether than to remember this violation, risk another invasion or endure others' disgust with him.

Fear is the common reaction when people first hear an inner voice: fear of the unknown; fear of being obligated to change; fear of having to give up hard won comforts and live an ascetic life; fear of others' ridicule; fear of being asked to do something unethical, immoral, illegal or dangerous; fear of losing control; fear of going crazy; fear that the inner voices are satanic. It takes great courage to open one's consciousness just a crack and listen again.

Fear is the common reaction
when people first hear
an inner voice. . . .

Because the intensity of Mohammed's resistance was extreme, his conversion is particularly instructive. He reported the morning after his dream:

> When I was halfway up the mountain, I heard a voice from heaven saying, "O Mohammed! You are the Apostle of God, and I am Gabriel." I raised my head towards heaven to see, and lo Gabriel in the form of a man, stood with feet astride the horizon. . . . I stood gazing at him, moving neither forward or backward. Then I began to turn my face from him, but toward whatever region of the sky I looked, I saw him.

Mohammed was pulled in opposite directions by Gabriel's call to be "The Messenger" and his own decision to commit suicide.

Since he did not know what to do, he did nothing and did not move for what must have been an exceedingly long time. "Then Gabriel departed from me, and I from him, returning to my family."

Gabriel was subjectively real—real enough to provoke and then prevent a suicide, mobile enough to make contact in dreams and visions—too real to be explained away. Perhaps only voices in visions of such surpassing power could have dislodged Mohammed's treasured sense of who he was and driven him to become so much more—more than husband, father, merchant and righteous man; more than an ecstatic poet; not a man possessed by demons, but God's apostle.

For most people, the process of conversion starts with a miraculous event, something that seems to defy the laws of nature, something so unusual that attention is fixed, at least for a moment. The experience cannot be denied even if it is not understood, like Mohammed's lucid dream.

A single miracle seldom is enough, however. Often a second miraculous contact is needed to show that the first was not an accident, to fulfill an earlier promise or to reassure, like Mohammed's seeing Gabriel astride the horizon in every direction. Sometimes these contacts are years apart but so perfectly coordinated and unforgettable that the hearer can no longer doubt their reality and the power of this paranormal force.

------

*A single miracle
seldom is enough. . . .*

Moses' conversion followed the same sequence. The psychology of his response is valid, even if it is legend rather than fact. A miraculous voice in a vision of a burning bush got Moses' attention. He hid his face "for he was afraid to look at God." He felt like an impostor: "Who am I that I should go to Pharaoh?" He argued that others "will not believe me, or listen to my voice, for they will say, 'The Lord did not appear to you.' "

Moses pestered God for more miracles and was given a rod that turned into a snake, an arm that became diseased then healthy again and water that turned into blood. They convinced him he was encountering some mysterious power great enough for the task. Even then, Moses begged not to be the one. "Oh, my Lord, I am not eloquent. I am slow of speech and tongue. Send, I pray some other person." Moses was reassured that the Lord would be with him and with his brother, Aaron, who would say to Pharaoh what the Lord told to Moses.

Self-Transcendence

Contact is complete when the person is willing to continue listening. This does not require absolute trust and obedience, only an openness to hearing more. Then an intensive period of instruction begins in the form of lectures, dialogues or commentary on life experiences. A coherent philosophy is taught about the primacy of love, discerning good from evil, the survival of consciousness beyond bodily death, the eternal path of return to God and the importance of manifesting these truths in one's life in a body on earth. Usually this occurs during a period of solitude from 40 days to three years: Moses' days in the Sinai, Buddha's isolation in the wilds of India, Jesus' time in the wilderness of Judea, Mohammed's walks in the sun-baked hills of Arabia, Baha'u'llah's two years in the Kurdistan caves, St. Catherine's three years of isolation in her room and Aurobindo's year in the Alipore jail.

The pull to lead a normal life with family, friends and worldly comforts tempts the person to stop this inner relationship.

Other inner voices argue for different truths and test the person's ability to choose the highest course. Each time this path is chosen, it increases commitment to the larger purpose. There is a gradual shift in allegiance from this world to that one, and a new sense of identity: "I am not my body, my belongings or the groups I belong to. Nor am I my personality, my history or the roles I play. I have these things like a carpenter has tools or adults have their childhoods." The old self is transcended. A new Self is "real"-ized, literally made real in a relationship with the inner voice.

The pull to lead a normal life . . .
tempts the person to stop
this inner relationship.

The process of self-transcendence usually culminates with three types of mystic unitive experiences that bond the new Self to that world. For Saint Catherine, a mystic marriage *united* her transcendent Self with the personality belonging to the inner voice, Jesus, in an unforgettable ceremony dedicating her life to a new role—the bride of Jesus, servant of God and God's messenger. Second, after being joined in this way, consciousness visits its spiritual *community* in a tour of heavens and hells, the "many mansions in my Father's house." After experiencing those spiritual communities, life in a body in this heavy material world is a prison, an exile from one's true home and family, a brief adventure as a naturalized citizen on earth. Third, there is an ineffable state, a complete loss of individuality as it merges simultaneously with all time, space and being, a *union* with God. Those who have experienced it don't talk about it, and those who do probably haven't experienced it.

---

*Those who have experienced it
don't talk about it. . . .*

Not surprisingly, after unitive experiences, these elevated souls feel passionately committed to that world and are ready to leave this one at any moment. This is evident in their total absence of fear about bodily death. It is liberation and a blessed return Home. For example, faced with an assassin, George Fox calmly said, "Put away your sword. It means no more to me than a piece of straw." Saint Catherine, hearing that two men had come to kill her, ran to them saying, "Here I am, I'm Catherine." They fled. Baha'u'llah, when a group of men were coming to kill him, dismissed his loyal followers guarding his home, went out to meet the mob and invited them in for tea.

Unification

Inspiring unitive experiences, like commencement exercises, complete the curriculum and start an apostolic stage. A mission is authorized. After experiencing union with one's teacher, heavenly communities and All, the new Self tries to make this world more like that one. The mission reflects needs of the historical moment and their personal history. Always they heal conflicts and disunities.

Mohammed unified the warring tribes of the southern Arabian peninsula and gave them one religion, a feat as remarkable eight centuries ago as a similar feat would be in today's Middle East. Saint Catherine devoted her adult life to healing the schisms among the Italian city-states and the rival factions within the Catholic church. Fox preached a way for all to turn inward and find a direct-person route to union with God. Baha'u'llah gave the world a new faith based on the unity of religions, languages and nationalities. For Aurobindo, the utopian community of Auroville and Integral Yoga were outward and inward ways to the unity of God.

In their lives, we can see how inner-voice experiences are woven together into a transcending sequence; how inner, other, superior voices inform, inspire and authorize a mission of unification and "divinely inspired" books like the Koran, Baha'u'llah's 100 Tablets, Aurobindo's 5000 pages of spiritual commentary and Swedenborg's 282 books during the last 32 years of his life. While this complete development is rare, their lives show the possible course for those who listen and serve as beacons for our own spiritual growth. With guidance from inner voices and judicious choices, we can follow their path. That is the best that can happen.

There are dangers, however.

What Is the Worst That Can Happen?

Edison harnessed electricity and invented both the light bulb and the first electric chair. Experiencing inner voices, like any power, can be used to guide self-transcendence or to explore the depths of evil, illness and degradation.

Without risk of hyperbole, I can say confidently that one particular inner-voice experience had the most disastrous consequences for humanity. Adolf Hitler reported during the First World War:

> I was eating my dinner with several comrades. Suddenly a voice seemed to be saying to me, "Get up and go over there." It was so clear and so insistent that I obeyed automatically, as if it had been a military order. I rose at once to my feet and walked twenty yards along the trench carrying my dinner in

its tin can with me. Then I sat down to go on eating, my mind being once more at rest. Hardly had I done so when a flash and deafening report came from the part of the trench I had just left. A stray shell had burst over the group in which I had been sitting, and every member of it was killed.[58]

Hitler came to believe in the superiority of his inner voice. Providence (the name of his inner voice) was supreme, not the Nazi Party.

I carry out the commands that Providence has laid upon me. . . . Unless I have the incorruptible conviction "this is the solution," I do nothing, not even if the whole Party tried to drive me to action. I will not act. I will wait, no matter what happens. But if the voice speaks, then I know the time has come to act.

Hitler was fanatically obedient to his inner voice and demanded the same unthinking loyalty to him. Few people understood Hitler in 1936 when he said "I follow my course with the precision and security of a sleep walker." Instead of gathering information, exploring options and consequences with his generals before choosing a strategy, Hitler occupied himself with diversions until his voice spoke. Hitler would leave Berlin suddenly, without telling anyone, and go to Berchtesgaden where he could walk alone in silence for hours to better hear his inner voice. As a result, critical decisions did not proceed logically or in a timely manner. This procrastination often drove his generals to despair. Yet Allied generals considered Hitler a tactical military "genius." The timing of his decisions was "uncanny," his intelligence "astonishing," his political intuition "miraculous," his moral sense "void."

Fortunately, strict servitude to an evil inner voice seldom reaches the apex of political power or mindless murdering. Usually only the "servant" suffers. However, the development of rigid obedience and the failure to exercise discernment and choose what's good appear to be similar.

In one typical case from the 1960s, a 24-year-old mother of two began to receive messages from various entities who identified themselves as dead friends or relatives.[59] The messages concerned neighbors who were amazed at the accuracy of the information. Like Mohammed and Moses, these several miraculous contacts eased her concerns and she enrolled.

There the similarities end. She heard a soft whisper outside and behind her left ear. The more she followed the instructions blindly, the louder and clearer the voices became. She was warned of accidents and told where to find missing objects, until her obedience was complete. She no longer thought for herself, double-checked the advice or maintained herself as a free partner in the relationship. This submissive posture seemed to invite exploitation and abuse by the entity, who said he was in love with her. She was told she did not belong to her husband, and that she would be killed in order to bring her to the entity's "plane." She would find all food sickening, be unable to eat and eventually die from starvation. The voice kept insisting that she would soon be able to see and feel his presence.

She tried fighting the voice, with occasional success. At those times she was able to eat small quantities of food. At first, she and her husband were afraid to see a psychiatrist for fear of her being committed.

When her husband was put on a different shift at work, she was alone at night. One night she became aware of the entity in her bed, and despite her fear and abhorrence, she was unable to prevent being sexually stimulated and reaching orgasm. She made an emergency call to her husband, and they decided to seek the assistance of a sympathetic psychiatrist. With his help, prayer, and the support of a local psychic, she and her husband eventually were able to return to a normal life.

Inner voices, then, can stimulate self-transcendence or self-abandonment, spiritual ecstasies or sexual excitement, selfless service or self-abasement, union with God or with "the devil." Inner voices cannot be banned, disarmed or licensed. They need to be understood and managed for good.

Inner voices . . . can stimulate . . .
union with God
or with "the devil."

How Do You Stay Safe, Sane and Healthy?

There are yellow lights and red lights on the road to enlightenment. You must be able to recognize them if the journey is to be safe, sane and healthy. The most important rule is to keep thinking, evaluating, assessing and judging for yourself, no matter how superior the inner voice seems to be. Not all inner voices are angelic. The invitations of ancient cave painters probably should be refused. The inner voices of Nazis should be expelled. Silly names and foolish information should cause laughter. Safe, sane and healthy responses to inner voices are the same as safe, sane and healthy responses to people with bodies.

Keep thinking, evaluating,
assessing and judging for yourself,
no matter how superior
the inner voice seems to be.

Reject Temptation

The path of self-transcendence is narrow. On one side there is a deep chasm of self-abandonment. Both Hitler and the 24-year-old wife and mother fell into absolute obedience. They abandoned their responsibility to double-check, to maintain a healthy skepticism, to question authority. It is as if they left their homes, and thus allowed others to occupy and possess them. This is neither psychologically healthy nor spiritually sound. It is said that God does not want us to return in bondage or as robots, but because we have chosen to return freely, every step of the way.

On the other side of the path of self-transcendence is self-inflation. Beware of inner voices that flatter with assertions that "you have been chosen," "you are my messenger," "you are one of the select few whose goodness qualifies you to receive the secrets." In medieval Catholicism, both self-inflation and self-abandonment were called temptations of the devil.

In her *Divine Dialogues*, Sweet Truth recalled for Catherine how she had rejected these temptations.

Once when the devil wished to conquer you, wishing to prove that your life had been deluded, you rose, humbly trusting My mercy and said, "I confess to my Creator that my life has been passed in darkness, but I will hide myself in the wounds of Christ crucified . . . and so shall my iniquities be consumed." You remember that the devil fled, and, turning around to the opposite side, he tried to inflate you with pride, saying, "You are perfect and pleasing to God, and there is no more need for you to afflict yourself, or to lament your sins." And once more I gave you the light to see your true path, namely humiliation of your self, and you answered the devil with these words: "I have committed so many sins, and have hardly begun to know them with grief and true contrition."

Then the devil said, "I can find no way to take you. If I put you down through confusion, you rise to heaven on the wings of mercy, and if I raise you on high, you humble yourself to hell."[60]

This dual challenge has its modern equivalent in the struggles of authors who successfully court the muse and hear the inner voices of characters demanding to be put in their novels. Authors often must fight to control or silence their inner characters. Their struggles illustrate the challenge in staying free, in charge of their lives, while avoiding self-inflation and self-abandonment.

Maintain Final Authority

Authors talk about their relationship to these inner characters as if they were directing an improvisational theater group composed of talented but temperamental actors. They control their actors, barely, by accepting their foibles and whims, letting them speak but reserving final authority for editing the work.

When Dickens was writing *Martin Chuzzlewit*:

Mrs. Gamp kept him in such paroxysms of laughter by whispering to him in the most inopportune places—sometimes even in church—that he was compelled to fight her off by main force, as it were, when he did not want her company, and to threaten to have nothing more to do with her unless she behaved better and came only when she was called.[61]

Herbert Gold, author of the best seller *Fathers*, said ruefully:

Sometimes I have to cut a voice if a voice goes too far and wants to dominate a scene and he or she shouldn't. Then I'll have to cut her short and say, "shut up now. . . ." I remember one book of mine. There was a scene I did not want to write and there was a character I did not want to have. I did not like her. I didn't want her in the book and yet the logic of what was happening to the main character required it. That's the only time in my life I can remember being seriously blocked. Finally I said to myself, I'm going to let her play but then I'm going to just cut her out. . . . And I let her speak, and she just exploded. It was like someone who had been in solitary. I hadn't been letting her speak.[62]

Mozart describes a similar but less contentious editorial process:

When I feel well and in a good humor, or when I am taking a drive or walking after a good meal, or in the night when I cannot sleep, [musical] thoughts crowd into my mind as easily as you could wish. Whence and how do they come? I do not know and have nothing to do with it. [Melodies] which please me, I keep in my head and hum them. Once I have my theme, another melody comes, linking itself to the first, in accordance with the needs of the composition as a whole: the counterpoint, the part of each instrument and all these melodic fragments at last produce the entire work. Then my mind seizes it. It is in its entirety that my imagination lets me hear it.[63]

Modern songwriters have described similar experiences. In *The Beatles Anthology*, Paul McCartney said:

I just woke up one morning with this tune in my head and I thought, I don't know this tune or do I. . . . Maybe I just remembered it . . . so I went to the piano, found the chords to it. . . . I made sure I remembered it and then I just hawked it 'round to all my friends and stuff and said "What's this? It's got to be something. It's like a good little tune, you know, and

I couldn'ta written it 'cause I just dreamed it, ya know. You don't get that lucky."[64]

Leading and following this interview, the film ran clips of Paul singing the Beatles' classic "Yesterday."

These examples suggest that one aspect of creative genius may be the simple act of listening inwardly, recognizing which voices or sounds are superior, then choosing to give them birth. In this type of authorization, the worldly author is neither a passive secretary simply taking dictation from an inner voice (which is, therefore, a dictator), nor some puffed up egotist who claims special access and powers. The author is in charge, finally, challenged but triumphant, taking full responsibility for the quality of what is done. It is a model for anyone hearing an inner voice who wants to stay on the path to self-transcendence.

Avoiding temptations and maintaining final authority are so important that two more examples are warranted.

In 1857, John Murray Spear published recommendations from his inner voice that claimed to be a group of spirits. "The Association of Beneficents" said through Spear that they had chosen him to deliver certain revelations on the structure of society, the responsibilities of human beings, the process of creation, the laws of health and even a plan for a utopian colony to realize heaven on earth.[65] Noble aims, certainly, and consistent with the human impulse to reunite with a higher power and share that knowledge with those on the path. If only the wisdom of all who claimed special knowledge lived up to the advertisements!

From Spear's Association of Beneficents, readers learned that the sun is the eye of God and is made up of vitalized energy. Its rays consist of fine, angular, diamond-shaped particles, the same substance as the diamond itself, and penetrate the interior of the earth where they "copulate, cohere, multiply, expand, grow and take the form of gold." Water can be magnetized to acquire medicinal powers. Tuberculosis is caused by minute, floating, barbed particles which also cause the mold on stones and vegetables. Human hairs are tubular and are organs of perception; eyebrows and eyelashes see the future while hairs at the back of the head contain certain memories. Thus, Spear generously warns those "who intertwine or twist the posterior conductors [hair at the back of the head], thereby ignorantly rendering themselves less able to recall or recollect."

Undoubtedly, Spear was well-intended. Acceptance of good intentions, however, does not require suspension of critical appraisal. Neither unexamined faith nor knee-jerk skepticism is appropriate. The values of messages from inner voices are as diverse as television programming.

Stay Away from Cults

Consider the spiritual progress report for 1975 from "Pallas Athena, Goddess of Truth," announced by an inner voice delivered to and through Elizabeth Clare Prophet.

> I Am come in the fullness of the light of truth. I Am come in the light of Freedom. I come bearing scroll to deliver to you the deliberations of the Lord of Karma concerning the flow of light, of freedom and of truth to mankind. Great inroads have been made of light penetration in the souls of mankind by dispensations invoked from the heart of the light bearer. Side by side, those who have been elected to remain part of the veil of Maya have also been made victims of inroads made by those who move across the margent [sic] of the world sowing yet the seeds of the enemy among the good wheat.[66]

Elizabeth Clare Prophet claims to translate the words of The Great White Brotherhood, a surprising coincidence. Her utterances sound flatulent compared to what I hear. Could our inner voices possibly be from the same source, I wondered? To me, her words seem like a collection of pious abstractions strung together randomly like so many beads on a string. They seem to roll off her tongue without passing through her cortex. Single words and phrases have a certain majesty and suggest mild cosmic emotions, but they do not nourish. Elizabeth Clare's wisdom is the frozen yogurt of esoteric thought.

That initial assessment seemed both accurate and harsh to me. Then I read the "Tenets" in the back of her book, *The Great White Brotherhood,* which I bought several years after my inner voice announced its name to me. Apparently her followers had to sign certain articles of faith. The Tenets include these requirements:

> We accept the message of salvation and the statement of cosmic law contained in all of the sacred scriptures of the world according to the interpretation of the Holy Spirit given to the Messengers Mark L. Prophet and Elizabeth Clare Prophet.

Lest her followers miss the point, it is restated two more times:

> We accept the progressive revelations of God as dictated through his [sic] emissaries, the ascended masters, to their Messengers Mark L. Prophet and Elizabeth Clare Prophet and their appointed successors.

and

> We accept the way of the Christ and the Buddha as the path of initiation defined by the Messengers Mark L. Prophet and Elizabeth Clare Prophet.

These Tenets required followers to submit to the Prophets' final authority, just as Hitler demanded absolute obedience from all

Nazis and the 24-year-old woman blindly followed the dictates of the entity she heard within her.

Tenet XI called for "Selflessness, Sacrifice and Surrender," and the Prophets' final Tenet, number XII, was the Law of the Tithe, a promise by their followers to translate selflessness, sacrifice and surrender into precisely one-tenth of their income. It had to be given to the Church Universal and Triumphant.

It would be convenient if evil came in unambiguous forms with clear labels. Usually, though, it comes after a resounding political success or amazingly accurate predictions, or is mixed in with the loving climate of others who share the faith.

Imagine Elizabeth Clare in a white dress, with her head turned up, eyes closed, arms outstretched, against a background of the full moon above a snow-capped Mt. Shasta. A large, hushed audience listens to the eerie monotone of the spirits speaking through her. It is tempting to confuse the glittery wrapping with the worth of the contents (a human tendency that has allowed hoaxes in séance rooms, the Stanford Research Institute and even at a dinner given by President Carter). Were her words high revelation beyond mere human comprehension? Or simple nonsense uttered with a fine actor's guile. At minimum, there was room for deep suspicion.

When Elizabeth Clare prophesied an apocalypse on a particular day, faithful followers retreated with her to the Montana mountains, a triumph of theater over good sense and more than 2000 years of perfectly incorrect doomsday predictions. While Elizabeth Clare focused inward and upward on heavenly matters, she neglected certain downward and outward bodily matters. Her apocalyptic community eventually was shut down by the federal government for lack of Porta Potties and for illegally stockpiling arms. Apparently Elizabeth Clare had "crossed the margent [sic] of the world."

Admiration for the great mystics who took what they heard to heart, to body, to life and to others should not blind us to inferior forms of inspiration. There is a deep wisdom in acknowledging this mix. It forces us to be cautious, neither to reject it automatically and run away, nor to accept uncritically and head to the hills with a self-proclaimed prophet.

Admiration for the great mystics . . .
should not blind us
to inferior forms of inspiration.

Staying safe, sane and healthy calls for restraint and courage. We should listen, discern, make a choice and take the consequences— a forward step on the path, stumbling and picking ourselves up or acknowledging that we took a wrong turn and retracing our steps.

Where Do They Come From? What Are They?

Famous listeners, like shooting stars, have been recognized briefly, then largely forgotten. Each generation rediscovers the phenomenon of inner voices and assumes it is an exotic event reserved for the chosen few—or the damned. It is neither.

The Debate

Hearers experience their inner voice as coming from a separate, superior personality. Social scientists discount these claims, so convinced are they of the profound human capacity for self-deception. It would be encouraging, after more than 2000 years of debate, if there were some agreement among theoreticians. Instead, theories have increased with each new intellectual fad.

Hearers experience their inner voice
as coming from
a separate, superior personality.

More than 60 years have passed since George Bernard Shaw wrote the preface to *Saint Joan*, but unfortunately, little has changed.

> Joan's voices and visions have been held to prove that she was mad, that she was a liar and impostor, that she was a sorceress (she was burned for this), and finally, that she was a saint. They do not prove any of these things. The variety of conclusions reached shows how little our matter-of-fact historians know about other people's minds, or even their own.[67]

Roughly, there are two theoretical camps: those who argue that inner voices come from some deep well inside the consciousness of each person, and those who claim that the source of inner voices exists outside.

In Jaynes' classic book, *The Origin of Consciousness in the Breakdown of the Bicameral Mind*, he traces the evolution of inner voices over several thousand years.[68] He argues, incorrectly, that in modern times they are nearly extinct, being confined to moments of poetic inspiration or psychosis. Jaynes says that voices come from one side of the brain, a claim about as helpful as explaining political events in the old Soviet Union by pointing to an area on the map, or assuming that the origin of music has been discovered by locating speaker systems.

Psychiatrists assert that inner voices reflect the *unconscious* at work, giving a different name to the place on the map. Jungians say that place should be called *archetypes* in our collective unconscious, nurtured into awareness by active imagination. Some have tried to capture it within traditional psychology by reducing it to a *sub-personality*, or dialogue between two autonomous I's within a polyphonic self. At best, these theories describe the phenomenon, the first canon of a scientific theory, but fail to provide useful insights into prediction and control, essential elements of any adequate theory.

Other theorists believe inner voices originate outside the person. Philo, the Alexandrian Jewish philosopher who lived during the life of Jesus, wrote that:

Sometimes, when I have come to my work empty, I have suddenly become full, ideas being in an invisible manner showered upon me, and implanted in me from on high, so that through the influence of divine inspiration, I have become greatly excited, and have known neither the place in which I was, nor those who were present, nor myself, nor what I was saying, nor what I was writing; for then I have been conscious of a richness of interpretation, an enjoyment of light, a most penetrating insight, a most manifest energy in all that was to be done.[69]

Reviewing more than 2000 years of this experience, Evelyn Underhill, in her famous book *Mysticism*, grants the uniform experience of *otherness* without admitting it may be true:

The great religion, invention, work of art, always owes its inception to some sudden uprush of intuitions or ideas for which the superficial self cannot account, its execution to powers so far beyond the control of the self that they seem, as their owner sometimes says, to "come from beyond." This is inspiration; the opening of the sluices, so that those waters of truth in which all life is bathed may rise to the level of consciousness.[70]

Do inner voices rise to the level of consciousness from depths within the person? Or descend into it from outside?

Religious theorists have a bias equal and opposite to that of social scientists. Inner voices come from a cosmic, ultra- or super-consciousness and herald the next evolutionary step as isolated human beings tap into a shared transpersonal source. Some Christians welcome the Holy Spirit, but also warn of evil spirits and possession. New Age groups describe spirit guides and ascended masters channeling their wisdom through a chosen few. Spiritualists say they are voices of the dead. Some psychics tell us they are entities from other planets and receive broadcasts from extraterrestrials. Tabloids simply assert the facts: "Famed psychic's head explodes." (That one really worried me until the reason emerged: a crosstown rival shot him in the head.)

All of these theorists agree that the phenomenon exists, but they resemble physicists arguing about the nature of electrons—are they waves or particles?—while engineers are busy making computers.

In this area, however, there are no engineers. Obvious practical questions have not been answered: How does it get started? What is it like to hear an inner voice? How do you decide if the relationship is safe and healthy? What happens if you listen for a long time? Do you sail off the edge of the sane world, or discover a new land? How do you climb the peaks and avoid the chasms? Does anything of lasting value come from this half-hidden human inheritance? The route to these practical answers starts with reports from explorers of this inner space, the approach I have taken in this introduction.

The experience is not random and incoherent. Inner voices, sometimes with visions, are understood as the mysterious contact points between the human personality and another wiser, more powerful personality that is not anchored in a specific time, place or the stuff of physical being. Hints of this hidden relationship occur for those who hear once, are calmed, uplifted, converted or given timely warnings. Others hear regularly and conclude that this superior intelligence is governed by an interior aim, that the relationship has a purpose. Often they are explicitly authorized to act, translating its goals into a visible mission or its words into books.

That much has been established without claiming to know what *it* really is or where it comes from. Speculations about the nature of consciousness—un-, sub-, collective, bicameral, super-, ultra- or cosmic—surround the experience in a fog of abstractions. Calling it *ecstasy, awakening, conversion* or a *peak experience*, even if any of these terms were fully accurate, does not help. They cover the experience like a blanket, maintaining its mystery under a different name. "It was ecstatic" could refer equally well to a vacation in Maui or to a hand-packed pint of your favorite ice cream.

We need simple terms that name the elements and relationships among them, a metaphor hearers would accept as accurate and, at the same time, would act as a powerful new paradigm. What runs through these experiences like a necklace string, so simple and obvious that it is difficult to see?

The selection of descriptors is arbitrary to a certain degree. Different terms are more or less fitting. Reasonable people will make different choices. Let me make the case for *inner teacher* and *transcendent education*.

Inner Teachers Conduct a Transcendent Education

Whether it is called God, Jesus, Daimon, Master, Adept, Guardian Angel, Mentor, ordinary earth names or exotic aliases, the role of the voice is to teach. *To inform* is the first goal of teaching. *To inspire* is a cherished hope of teachers. *Authorization* is the essence of commencement, the call to start one's work in the world. Inner voices come from inner teachers.

---

*Inner voices come
from inner teachers.*

A philosopher refuses to defend himself in court, is convicted, swallows hemlock, comforts his friends and embraces death unafraid. A persecutor of Jesus is born again as a fearless disciple. A 17-year-old illiterate farm girl rallies a demoralized army, raises a siege, crowns a king and defies her inquisitors. A cloistered nun and chronic invalid who wanted most to pray in solitude writes five books and starts 19 convents and monasteries from abject poverty and against the resistance of the ecclesiastic world. A master of all science doubles his prodigious literary output describing heaven, hell and the spiritual sense of the scriptures. A frustrated artist commands an army that conquers Europe. The world heavyweight champion stops boxing and starts a church, then 20 years later regains the heavyweight title. Uneducated blacksmiths and shoemakers write novels, epic poems and music.

We ask how these individuals underwent such extraordinary changes and are told that their inner teachers informed, inspired and authorized them. It is true vocational education—beyond acquiring professional skills and mundane questions of one's livelihood—to our ultimate purpose in living. As Helen Schucman reported, inner teachers conduct a transcendent education.

This is a course in miracles. It is a required course. Only the time you take it is voluntary. Free will does not mean that you can establish the curriculum. It means only that you can elect what you want to take at a given time. The course does not aim at teaching the meaning of love, for that is beyond what can be taught. It does aim, however, at removing the blocks to the awareness of love's presence, which is your natural inheritance.[71]

Power of the Paradigm

Formal power is defined as who has the right to control what. Adoption of this educational paradigm asserts that the inner-voice experience is not a medical process under the control of doctors. It denies the claim of psychiatrists who say that all inner voices are symptoms of mental illness, and that doctors have the responsibility to make them go away using psychotherapy, drugs or electric shock. The educational paradigm also denies the claim of clergy who argue that inner voices are strictly a religious matter, that discerning the source of the voice is the first issue and that the clergy have the true and only criteria.

The inner-voice experience
is not a medical process
under the control of doctors. . . .
[or] a religious matter. . . .

Asserting that one's inner teacher provides a transcendent education, however, means that the experience is a free, private, inalienable right; that this inner development is beneficial; and that worldly authorities should not try to control it.

The experience is a free,
private, inalienable right. . . .

Better paradigms increase our power to describe, predict and control. For instance, Freud's paradigm was simple. Unconscious drives bend our choices and shape our behavior. An invisible reservoir of inchoate forces, forgotten traumas and childish needs bubbles up into our lives surreptitiously in dreams, fears, slips, tics, phobias, prejudices and neurotic behavior. It acts like a hidden personality influencing—some say controlling—the way we deal with reality. Freud's hypothesis helped make sense of the mysterious disappearance of hysteric symptoms when patients remembered forgotten childhood events. It led to greater understanding of how early childhood experiences influence later development; produced new therapeutic methods for liberating adults from the warping constraints of their childhood; and generated new interpretations of topics as diverse as the psychology of humor and the origin of religions. Today, this once radical idea is axiomatic.

The paradigm that inner teachers conduct a transcendent education is equally simple, parallel and powerful: just as unconscious forces can be uncovered, superconscious forces can be revealed. An invisible reservoir of superior information, inspiration and authorization can manifest itself in visions, inner voices, warnings, flashes of insight, pangs of conscience and sudden total knowing. This hypothesis helps make sense of otherwise extraordinary changes in ordinary individuals: conversions, inspired writing, missionary zeal. It leads to greater understanding of how self-transcendence occurs and provides a route to liberation from the anchoring effects of oppression, and ways to triumph over life's tragedies. It offers new explanations for phenomena as diverse as artistic creativity, imaginary playmates and the origin of religions. Today, this ancient idea is still radical even though "inner teachers have conducted an eternal transcendent education" throughout history.

----

*Just as unconscious forces
can be uncovered,
superconscious forces
can be revealed.*

Ariel's Messages

Ariel's messages recorded in this book's dialogue with Dr. Nathanson reflect the best of inner teaching. Inner teachers do not prescribe specific solutions but deepen our understanding of problems, leaving the listener to decide what to do and muster the courage to do it. They respect our free will as individuals, as if God wants each of us to choose our way back home freely and not on the advice or command of an inner dictator. The messages support and empower us by offering a transcendent perspective on our lives.

Ariel is consistently loving, generous and patient, as if she had all the time in the world to assist us on our journey. And in eternity, perhaps she does.

Notes and References

1. The Princeton Religion Research Center, a division of the Gallup Poll organization, reported in *Emerging Trends* (Vol. 7, #5, p. 1) "43% of adult Americans have had an unusual and inexplicable spiritual experience." The results are based on 1,525 adults, 18 and older, conducted in over 300 scientifically selected localities. "One can say, with 95% confidence that the error attributable to sampling and other random effects could be 3 percentage points in either direction."

When the same survey question was asked in Great Britain, by Sir Alister Hardy's Religious Experience Research Unit at Manchester College, Oxford, 33% replied affirmatively.

A similar set of questions was asked by Andrew Greeley and William McCready at the National Opinion Research Center at the University of Chicago. In their *New York Times Magazine* article "Are We a Nation of Mystics?" (Jan. 26, 1975, p. 12ff.), they report that 50% of their respondents said they had had a "religio-mystical experience"; 45% said they had felt as though they had become completely one with God and the Universe; 40% of their 1,500 respondents said they had felt very close to a powerful spiritual force that seemed to lift them outside themselves. In these three different surveys, the affirmative answers range from one-third to one-half of those interviewed.

Of those reporting ecstatic experiences in the Gallup Poll, almost one out of five described the "presence" as an inner voice—guidance, help from God, a guardian or conscience. After examining over 3,000 written reports of religious and spiritual experiences, Sir Alister Hardy found an almost identical percentage of Britons who heard calming or guiding voices, music and other sounds (*The Spiritual Nature of Man*, 1979. Oxford, England, Larendon Press, p. 26).

If one-third to one-half of the adult population has had an ecstatic spiritual experience, and 20% of those heard inner voices, then 7% to 10% of the total adult population has heard inner voices. This figure is consistent with the results of a survey of normal people conducted in England over 100 years ago. Henry Sidgwick found that 9.9% of the 15,316 people interviewed had heard inner voices. (Henry Sidgwick, et al. "Report on the Census of Hallucinations." *Proceedings of the Society for Psychical Research*, 1894, 34:25–394.) Translating these percentages into numbers of current Americans, 7% to 10% means that as many as 20 million adults and an additional number of children have heard inner voices.

For some 85%, the experience of hearing inner voices is extremely positive with highly beneficial consequences. In the *Emerging Trends* report (ibid), 7% said there was no effect; 10% said they "didn't know." Greeley and McCready (ibid) report that only 8% felt "isolation." This also is consistent with Hardy's data.

Greeley and McCready report "virtually all of the respondents have never spoken about their experiences to anyone. When a discussion of statistical research on the subject legitimated talk about it, the revelation came as something utterly astonishing, even to those who know the person well." (*The Ultimate Values of the American Population*, 1976. Beverly Hills, Sage Library of Social Research, p. 23.)

2. Sczarmach, P. E. (Ed.) 1984. *An Introduction to Medieval Mysticism in Europe*. Albany: SUNY Press.

3. Danskin, W. 1858. *How and Why I Became a Spiritualist*. Boston: Bela Marsh.

WHAT IS IT LIKE TO HEAR AN INNER VOICE?

INNER LISTENING

4. Saint Teresa of Avila. 1960. *The Life of Teresa of Jesus*. trans. E. Allison Peers. New York: Image Books, Doubleday and Co.

5. Skutch, R. 1984. *Journey Without Distance*. Berkeley, CA: Celestial Arts. 56.

6. Oliver, F. 1974. *A Dweller on Two Planets*. San Francisco: Harper & Row. 2.

7. Brown, R. 1971. *Unfinished Symphonies*. London: Souvenir Press. 38; Young, M. 1984. *Agartha,* Walpole, New Hampshire: Stillpoint. 30; Guyon, G-M. 1980. *The Autobiography of Madam Guyon*. New Canaan, CT: Keats Publishing, Inc.

8. Matthew 17: 1–8; Mark 9: 2–8; Acts 1: 1–10; Acts 9: 3–9; Underhill, E. 1960. *Mysticism*. New York: Meridian Books. 180–181; Warner, M. 1982. *Joan of Arc*. New York: Vintage Books; Freud, S. 1951. *Psychopathology of Everyday Life*. New York: Mentor Books. 154.

IT'S NOT ME

9. Saint Teresa of Avila. 1960. *The Life of Teresa of Jesus.* trans. E. Allison Peers. New York: Image Books, Doubleday and Co. 231–233.

10. Skutch, R. 1984. *Journey Without Distance.* Berkeley, CA: Celestial Arts. 54, 55.

11. Maclean, D. 1980. *To Hear Angels Sing.* The Park, Forres: Scotland: Findhorn Publications. 28.

12. Lowell, in Ghiselin, (Ed.) 1952. The Creative Process. New York: Mentor/Dutton. 202, 203.

13. Bailey, A. 1981. *Unfinished Autobiography.* New York: Lucis Press.

14. National Public Radio. March 13, 1984. Interview with Ray Bradbury, Herbert Gold and Judith Rossner; Stevenson, R. L. 1912. *The Works of Robert Louis Stevenson. Vol. 16.* London: Chatto and Windus; Harmon, W. and Rheingold, H. 1984. *Higher Creativity.* Los Angeles: Tarcher, ibid.

15. Tribbe, F. C. 1985. Research Report—Musical Composers. *Spiritual Frontiers.* 85, 86.

16. MacLaine, S. 1986. *Dancing in the Light.* New York: Bantam Books. Chapter 16.

17. Rodegast, P. 1985. *Emmanuel's Book,* Westport, CT: Friends of Emmanuel. xxiv.

WHO ARE THEY? WHAT DO THEY SAY?

18. Podmore, F. 1902. *Modern Spiritualism: A History and Critique.* London: Metheun & Co. Volume I. 159–160.

WHAT DO THE GOOD VOICES DO?

PROVIDE SUPERIOR INFORMATION

19. Van Dusen, W. 1974. *The Presence of Other Worlds.* New York: Swedenborg Foundation.

20. These quotations and comments on Socrates are based on discussions found in J. Mishlove's *The Roots of Consciousness.* 1975. New York: Random House. p. 25, and in F. W. H. Myer's *Human Personality and Its Survival of Bodily Death.* 1903. London: Longmans, Green & Co. 95–100.

21. ibid.

COMPLETE UNFINISHED WORK

22. The descriptions and quotations about Chief Blackfoot are based on a tape of National Public Radio Journal #810525, "Chief Blackfoot Returns."

INSPIRE AT TIMES OF DOUBT AND FATIGUE

23. Saint Teresa of Avila. 1960. *The Life of Teresa of Jesus.* trans. E. Allison Peers. New York: Image Books, Doubleday and Co.

24. Dinnage, R. 1986. *Annie Besant.* Harmonsworth: Penguin Books. 66.

25. Pelikan, J. Sept. 18, 1983. "The Enduring Relevance of Martin Luther 500 Years after His Birth." *New York Times Magazine.* 44.

26. Oates, S. 1982. *Let the Trumpet Sound—The Life of Martin Luther King Jr.* New York: Harper & Row. 88–89.

27. Charcot, J-B. 1982. *Christoforo Colombo Marinaio.* Firenze: Giunti Martello. 211.

CONVERT UNBELIEVERS

28. Bunyan, J. 1938. "Grace Abounding" in *Pilgrim's Progress.* New York: American Tract Society. 5–129.

29. ibid.

30. Jaynes, G. April 22, 1985. "In Texas, Spreading the Word," *Time.* 9–11.

31. Gandhi, M. in K. Kripalani (ed.) 1980. *All Men Are Brothers: Autobiographical Reflections.* New York: Continuum. 63.

AUTHORIZE MISSIONS

32. Exodus. 3,4. Revised Standard Version.

33. Warner, M. 1982. *Joan of Arc.* New York: Vintage Books.

34. Saint Teresa of Avila. 1960. *The Life of Teresa of Jesus.* trans. E. Allison Peers. New York: Image Books, Doubleday and Co.

INSPIRE WRITING

EASE

35. Brockmann, R. J. and Horton, W. 1988. *The Writer's Pocket Almanack.* Santa Monica, CA: Info Books.

36. Cummins, G. 1965. *Swan on a Black Sea.* London: Rutledge and Kegan Paul.

37. Bailey, A. 1981. *Unfinished Autobiography.* New York: Lucis Press.

38. National Public Radio. March 13, 1984. Interview with Ray Bradbury, Herbert Gold and Judith Rossner.

39. ibid.

SPEED

40. Boehme, J. 1882. *Theosophia Revelata: Das Ist—Alle Gottliche Schriften.* H. L. Martenson (trans.). Amsterdam: Grafen—Hainichen.

41. Guyon, G-M. 1980. *The Autobiography of Madam Guyon.* New Canaan, CT: Keats Publishing, Inc.; Saint Teresa of Avila. 1960. *The Life of Teresa of Jesus.* trans. E. Allison Peers. New York: Image Books, Doubleday and Co.; Curtayne, A. 1930. *Saint Catherine of Siena.* New York: Macmillan and Co.; Ghose, A. 1985. *Sri Aurobindo on Himself.* Pondicherry, India: Sri Aurobindo Ashram.

42. Quotations from Blake are taken from *The Portable Blake,* A. Kazin (ed.) 1976. New York: Penguin Books. 212–214, 445.

PRECISION AND HIDDEN COHERENCE

43. Saint Teresa of Avila. 1960. *The Life of Teresa of Jesus.* trans. E. Allison Peers. New York: Image Books, Doubleday and Co.

44. Bailey, A. 1981. *Unfinished Autobiography,* New York: Lucis Press.

45. Linton, C. 1858. *The Healing of Nations.* New York: self-published. Podmore, F. 1902. *Modern Spiritualism: A History and Critique.* London: Metheun & Co. Vol. I.

46. Skutch, R. 1984. *Journey Without Distance.* Berkeley, CA: Celestial Arts. 56.

47. Oliver, F. 1974. *A Dweller on Two Planets.* San Francisco: Harper & Row. 2.

48. Guyon, G-M. 1980. *The Autobiography of Madam Guyon.* New Canaan, CT.

49. Tribbe, F. C. 1985. Research Report—Musical Composers. *Spiritual Frontiers.* 83.

50. Halpern, S. (year unknown.) On Dick Sutphen's *Ask the Expert,* audiotape.

51. Brahms J. 1970. In P. E. Vernon, ed. *Creativity: Selected Readings.* England: Penguin Books Ltd. 57.

TRANSCENDENCE

52. Bailey, A. 1981. *Unfinished Autobiography.* New York: Lucis Press.

53. Krishna, G. 1971. *Kundalini: The Evolutionary Energy in Man.* Boulder, CO: Shambala. 226, 227.

54. Brown, R. 1972. *Unfinished Symphonies.* New York: Bantam Books. 2, 3, 27, 28, 30.

55. ibid.

56. Litvag, I. 1972. *Singer in the Shadows.* New York: Popular Library.

WHAT IS THE BEST THAT CAN HAPPEN?

57. The conclusions are based on material from: *Sri Aurobindo on Himself.* 1985. Pondicherry, India: Sri Aurobindo Ashram; Satprem's biography, *Sri Aurobindo, or the Adventure in Consciousness.* 1968. New York: Harper & Row Publishers; The Hadiths compiled by Mohammed ibn Ishaq of Medina, as reported in J. A. Williams. 1962. *Islam.* New York: George Braziller; Balyuzi, H. M. 1980. *Baha'u'llah, King of Glory.* Oxford: George Ronald; Teherzadeh, A. 1980. *The Revelation of Baha'u'llah.* Oxford: George Ronald, Vol. 1; Esselmont, J. E. 1970. *Baha'u'llah and the New Era.* Willmette, Illinois: Bahai Books, 3rd edition; Effendi, S. (Ed.) 1971. *Gleanings from the Writings of Baha'u'llah.* Willmette: Bahai Publishing Trust; Curtayne, A. 1930. *Saint Catherine of Siena.* New York: Macmillan and Co.; *The Journal of George Fox.* 1952. London: Cambridge University Press; R. M. Jones' *George Fox: Seeker and Friend.* 1932. London: George Allen & Unwin, Ltd.; and Swedenborg, W. Van Dusen. 1972. *The Natural Depth of Man.* New York: Swedenborg Foundation, and W. Van Dusen. 1974. *The Presence of Other Worlds.* New York: Harper & Row.

WHAT IS THE WORST THAT CAN HAPPEN?

58. Langer, W.C. 1972. *The Mind of Adolf Hitler: The Secret Wartime Diaries.* New York: Basic Books. 34.

59. Cayce, H. L. 1964. *Venture Inward.* New York: Paperback Library.

HOW DO YOU STAY SAFE, SANE AND HEALTHY?

REJECT TEMPTATION

60. Curtayne, A. 1930. *Saint Catherine of Siena.* New York: Macmillan and Co.

MAINTAIN FINAL AUTHORITY

61. Fodor, N. 1964. *Between Two Worlds.* West Nyack, NY: Parker Publishing Co. 19 ff.

62. National Public Radio. March 13, 1984. Interview with Ray Bradbury, Herbert Gold and Judith Rossner.

63. Hadamard, J. 1945. *The Psychology of Invention in the Mathematical Field.* Princeton, NJ: Princeton University Press. 16.

64. Wolff, L. (Producer) 1995. *The Beatles Anthology,* Apple Corps Limited. (Film).

65. Podmore, F. 1902. *Modern Spiritualism: A History and Critique.* London: Metheun & Co. Vol. I.

STAY AWAY FROM CULTS

66. Prophet, E. C. 1976. *The Great White Brotherhood in the Culture, History and Religion of America.* Los Angeles: Summit University Press. 151, 344.

WHERE DO THEY COME FROM? WHAT ARE THEY?

THE DEBATE

67. Shaw, G. B. 1960. *Saint Joan.* Baltimore: Penguin Books. 16.

68. Jaynes, J. 1982. *The Origin of Consciousness in the Breakdown of the Bicameral Mind.* Boston: Houghton-Mifflin.

69. Quoted by William James in *Varieties of Religious Experience.* 1929. New York: New York Modern Library. 470–471.

70. Underhill, E. 1960. *Mysticism.* New York: Meridian Books. 23.

INNER TEACHERS CONDUCT A TRANSCENDENT EDUCATION

71. *Course in Miracles.* 1975. Tiburon, CA: Foundation for Inner Peace.

Preface

In Search of Guidance

Stevan J. Thayer

I have always, by nature, been inquisitive. Since my youth, I have been drawn to taking things apart and fixing them to understand how they work. This made me a natural candidate for engineering, and I eagerly unleashed my inquisitive nature on course after course, completing a master's degree in electrical engineering from Columbia University. Bell Telephone Laboratories hired me as an engineer (a dream come true) and I began a 15-year career with the Labs. It was filled with interesting projects, lots to learn and discover. For many years I thrived. I was co-awarded a patent for a new use of a computer communications protocol, was promoted to supervisor and managed several new computer product developments. As time went on, the environment at the Labs became increasingly stressful, and I developed several illnesses which required two surgeries. I knew nothing at the time about mind-body connections, that my work environment and stress were in any way connected to my illnesses or that my illness was a message.

The Communion

In 1984, on the evening before my second surgery, I was standing at the window of my hospital room looking out at the sun setting over New York City's Central Park. I was filled with fear as I reviewed all the possible surgical outcomes and their relative probabilities described to me by the surgeon. I wondered if I would even be alive the next day to see the sun set.

Without warning, I was overtaken by the most holy presence. The sensation was one of being outwardly paralyzed, or frozen, and inwardly pushed aside as this presence entered my body. It entered through the top of my head and felt like something thick, like honey, pouring in and spreading slowly throughout my body. I could not stop it and did not want to stop it. For as the presence slowly moved through me, I was transported to the most indescribable state of spiritual ecstasy. I was filled with peace of mind. All my fears were gone. I knew with absolute certainty that all would be well with the upcoming surgery. This understanding all took place in an instant. I stood there transfixed when suddenly the knowledge *this is Jesus* flashed into my mind. I was filled to overflowing with joy. I cannot explain how I knew, but I knew beyond all question that this indeed was Jesus.

I remained in this state of communion for some time. Then as steadily and surely as Jesus had entered me, he left. Even after his presence was gone, I remained elevated in a state of spiritual ecstasy for the entire evening. The surgery did indeed go fine. I healed quickly, returned to work at the Labs and never spoke of my communion experience.

The Transformation

The long-term effect this mystical experience had on my life has been dramatic. In the six years that followed, with tremendous love and support from my wife Carol, I resigned my position with the Labs; began an intensive meditation training program at the Zen Mountain Monastery in Mt. Tremper, NY; undertook and completed numerous trainings in holistic health therapies; completed a program of studies at the New Seminary in New York City; was ordained as an Interfaith Minister; opened a full-time holistic health center called The Center Of Being; and began a full-time ministry of spiritual counseling, energy therapy and teaching. While this mid-life transformation contained many difficult times (or wonderful spiritual growth opportunities, depending on your viewpoint), I have never been as

happy or as healthy as I presently am. My life is filled with meaning. I truly feel that I am now doing exactly what I was placed
here to do. I am living my soul's mission in life.

Experiencing Inner Voices

Much like my initial mystical communion with Jesus, my opening to the ability to hear inner voices and channel their messages
came suddenly and powerfully. Unlike my communion, however, I had been asking to be blessed with the gift of channeling.
I had been deeply inspired by the books *The Starseed Transmissions* by Ken Carey, *Agartha* by Meredith Lady Young and *Seth
Speaks* by Jane Roberts.[1] The messages brought through these
channels spoke to my heart and soul. I devoured them, yet the
thirst in my soul could not be quenched merely by reading these
messages. I had to find out how this channeling worked. I
yearned to have the transpersonal ability to connect directly
with the realm of higher consciousness as these people had done
and receive divine guidance directly.

In the summer of 1990, I had just read *The Mists of Avalon* and
was on vacation in England. One afternoon, while visiting the
town of Glastonbury, I created my own version of the Avalon
spiritual process. In hindsight, it seems a little melodramatic. At
the time, however, it was perfect. I drank water from the Chalice
Well; I climbed the Tor; and while standing atop the Tor, I
looked to the heavens and said out loud, "God, please use me in
your service as a voice of your divine message. Please let me
channel." I expected a clap of thunder, the heavens to part and a

---

1. Carey, K. 1983. *The Starseed Transmissions: An Extraterrestrial Report.* Walpole,
New Hampshire: Uni*Sun/Stillpoint Books; Young, M. L. 1984. *Agartha: A Jour-
ney to the Stars.* Walpole, New Hampshire: Stillpoint Books; Roberts, J. 1972.
Seth Speaks. New York: Bantam Books.

voice to boom out bestowing upon me the power to channel that I had been seeking. Nothing happened. Or at least so I thought.

Several days later, while visiting a small stone circle called Castlerigg in the Lake District, I had my first inner-voice channeling encounter. My years of intensive Zen training had taught me to concentrate my mind's focus in meditation and experience a deep state of inner quiet. I was sitting alone in the circle atop one of the stones, in a deep state of meditation, when I felt a presence approach me. The hair on my arms stood up. I looked around to see who was there but found that I was alone. I asked mentally and with some fear, "Who's there?" I felt a sense of peace surround me, reminiscent of my communion with Jesus, but not nearly as strong or as loving. Words formed calmly in my mind, saying quite simply, "I am the keeper of the stones." The words came easily and quickly, and thus began a wonderful inner-voice conversation with the presence.

The keeper of the stones explained in great detail the use of the stone circle. I found the encounter fascinating, but I completely doubted its authenticity. While my prayer on the Tor had seemingly been answered, the keeper's words had come so easily and quickly that I truly believed that, in my eagerness to channel, I was just making the whole thing up. I expected that if and when I started to channel, I would first receive a word or a phrase and, in time, develop the ability to receive a whole thought and then a series of thoughts. Yet here I was receiving detailed information from the keeper as easily as though I were talking to another person.

Overcoming Doubt

Upon returning home, I joined a psychic development class aimed at helping people develop their natural ability to hear their inner voices and cultivate their channeling gifts. Normally, people joined the group to learn how to begin to channel. I joined fully able to channel, or what seemed to be channeling, with the goal of overcoming my doubt and convincing myself that I wasn't just making up the messages.

In the group, I was repeatedly able to enter a state of prayerful meditation, move my mind aside and open to the messages of what I call *guides* (since they are like inner guidance to me) who wished to communicate through me. I received messages from a wide variety of guides. Each time I opened to a guide, I felt to one degree or another the familiar feeling of peace and love that came as I moved my consciousness aside and received their divine message. The fascinating thing was that the other group members would also feel the increased level of peace and love as the guide entered. The messages always came spontaneously, quickly and easily. I would begin to speak a sentence, never knowing what would be said, how the sentence would end or what the next sentence would be.

The messages were tape-recorded and transcribed. I read and reread these messages and was surprised at the differences in terminology and grammar that each guide used. I was amazed to see that many of the recordings were about things I had no way of knowing or had never thought of before. Also surprising was the fact that, while some messages were 10 to 15 minutes long and their transcription spanned several pages, there was an incredible consistency. Some messages clearly referred to things said pages earlier. Another phenomenon was the fact that I rarely remembered much of what was said. When I read the transcribed material it was like seeing something for the first time.

During the six months I was in this class, I became convinced that the source of these words was "not me," that is, not my normal ego sense of who I am. But if not me, then who or what? I am still not sure of the answer to that question. Since different guides exhibited varying styles of message and quality of energy, it seemed like they were separate beings communicating to me. However, I have always had a sense that they might simply be aspects of my own higher self. (I was pleased to receive guidance from Ariel saying that both viewpoints are simultaneously correct.[2])

Finding Guidance

Over time, I have had the most marvelous opportunity to receive guidance and messages from an increasingly high level of guides. The intensity of the love and energy that I feel when I open to these guides has grown steadily, and the divinity of their messages has risen higher and higher. These guides have helped me to understand the true nature of my personal difficulties and fears. They have shown me a new and more spiritual way to understand life and its workings. Their love and their messages have helped me to heal many of my deepest wounds, to deal with wounds that I haven't yet healed and to find my true purpose in life. I have also been blessed with the ability to receive guidance for many of my clients to support them in their personal journeys of self-healing. As time has progressed, I have felt safer sharing this guidance with larger and larger circles of people.

In addition to personal guidance for my own or my clients' self-healing, these guides have given me extraordinary new insights into healing using the human energy system, and they have shown me many subtle relationships between suppressed feelings and their corresponding energy blocks within the human energy system. I have been able to combine these insights with my years of holistic health experience and use my engineering background to develop a remarkable new holistic therapy system I call Integrated Energy Therapy® (IET). It is my life's joy to use IET to support others in their self-healing journeys of personal empowerment. My goal is to continue to expand and refine the form of IET and teach it to students throughout the world.

---

2. Question, page 301, "Unseen Universe."

Meeting Angel Ariel

In the summer of 1993, several months before I met Linda Nathanson, co-author of this book, I was facilitating an IET session with a client who was having difficulty with emotional and health problems. In the middle of the session, a very high and powerful presence entered, a guide that I had never before experienced. The guide had a profoundly divine quality and immediately brought powerful healing energy through me into my client. We both felt the shift in energy take place. I entered into a state of prayerful meditation, moving my mind aside, and opened to receive any message this guide had for my client. The guide seemed to have a gentle yet strong female quality (while a guide is neither male nor female, my subjective perception of each guide I encounter is usually more male-like or female-like). The guide spoke through me to my client about the traumas in my client's past. The energy and messages were so powerful that both my client and I were elevated to a state of tearful joy.

My client asked the guide, "What is your name?" The guide answered, "We don't have names." My client persisted, "Then what name can I use to call upon you in the future?" The guide answered, "Names will not be necessary, we will hear you and be with you." This did not satisfy my client who persisted, "I need to have a name to be able to know it is you." There was a pause, then the guide spelled out the name *Ariel*.

After that, the guide, who identified itself as Ariel, came and worked through me on a regular basis, bringing powerful healing energy and wonderful teaching messages to support me in my own healing journey and my clients in theirs. I came to understand that Ariel is a special angel who serves God through teaching and healing. Her gift is the ability to help people see beyond their limited, self-centered vision of the world, to help them develop an ever-deepening personal relationship with the divine and to help them find their true purpose in life. While she is glad to support the lives of individual people, as she has done with my clients and me, her larger mission is to reach all people with her truth.

An Angelically Arranged Meeting

I first met Linda Nathanson in January 1994 when she arrived at my office for an Integrated Energy Therapy session. Linda told me about her thyroid problem and her pounding heart. I used my energy therapy techniques to channel energy into her and found that the energy was quite restricted as it passed through her throat center. I have come to understand that the throat center relates to our creative self-expression, and any energy restriction in this area cannot only limit our joyous, creative self-expression but also result in physical illnesses that affect, among other things, the thyroid.

It is possible for me to "read" a person's energy and, in effect, see that person's true nature. In reading the energy of Linda's throat center, I found her to be a talented, driven and energetic person with a passion for writing, teaching and success. I also found that she was unconsciously allowing the limiting experiences in her past to hold her back from the creative opportunities in the present.

Ariel shared many messages and insights with Linda, giving her guidance and encouragement in her new endeavors. In our work together, we "broke through" Linda's restrictions and unleashed her full creative energy. As this happened, Linda's life took on a flurry of creative activity. She developed an entire publishing strategy for a line of résumé books and launched a publishing company called Edin Books. In the process, not only did her thyroid and heart rate return to normal, but she went from lethargy to bubbling energy and joy.

Learning of the Angelic Plan

During our sessions, Linda tape-recorded Ariel's messages so she would miss none of the wondrous information we were receiving. Several months later, she came to one of our regular meetings beaming and handed me a cover-design mockup for a new book called *Interview with an Angel*. "I've had the Ariel tapes transcribed," she said, "and I think we have the start of an extraordinary book. Do you want to continue working as co-authors and bring Ariel's messages to the world?"

This was more than I could have dreamed. I had always aspired to write and share my spiritual understanding of how life works with others. I agreed and we began our work on the book.

There was a slight problem, however. When I thought Ariel's words were just for Linda, I was at ease and could channel them with little difficulty. But knowing that every word I spoke would go into a book, I was so nervous and self-conscious that I could not even connect with Ariel. It took several weeks before I could reach the original level of connection so we could continue our work.

As we began on the book, Linda asked Ariel whether she would consider working with us on such a project. Ariel replied:

We find it humorous that you would ask us if we would be willing to do what it is that we chose you to do.

I was overjoyed to learn from Ariel that meeting Linda, recording Ariel's messages and deciding to write this book were all part of a divine angelic plan in which Linda and I were being lovingly guided. It was not that we were making Ariel aware of our plan; rather, she was making us aware of hers.

The Process

Linda developed a database of questions for Ariel which she did not share with me. Therefore, I could not think about the questions and possibly influence Ariel's answers as they came through to me. Linda asked the questions and often changed subjects several times in a session or returned to questions asked in earlier sessions.

What amazed me was that, when Linda asked an impossible-to-answer question and I was thinking, "How could there possibly be an answer to this question?" Ariel began with complete ease and confidence to provide a grand answer. The answers came through so quickly that I often had difficulty speaking them into the tape-recorder fast enough to keep up with Ariel. After each session, Linda had the recorded answers transcribed and used them to form her follow-up questions. She did not share the answers with me.

After nearly two years of work, we received Ariel's answers to the final questions, and Linda gave me the 300-plus pages of manuscript. I will never forget reading the transcribed material. Since I had only vague memories of Ariel's answers, I was in effect seeing it for the first time. I was overwhelmed. Ariel's messages touched my heart and soul deeply, and I had to pause on many an occasion to let heartfelt tears flow.

In Conclusion

Ariel has become my dear friend, close guide and wonderful teacher. Serving as the voice for Ariel's messages has been a joy and a privilege. Receiving Ariel's messages and sharing them with the world will continue to be an integral part of my ministry. Each time I share Ariel's messages with larger and larger audiences, I face the opportunity to penetrate through deeper and deeper layers of my own fear. Authoring this book is providing me with yet another wondrous opportunity for personal spiritual growth.

A great spiritual master named Jonathan Livingston Seagull said:

> It is good to be a seeker,
> but sooner or later you have to be a finder,
> then it is well to give what you have found,
> a gift into the world,
> for whoever will accept it.

My contribution in voicing Ariel's messages is my gift to you. I hope that as you read *Interview with an Angel*, Ariel's messages not only entertain you but help you to deepen your personal relationship with the divine, attain perfect human relationships, find your perfect form of self-expression and produce a positive transformation in your life.

I would ask, however, that you be discerning and do not blindly accept these or any other spiritual teachings as truth. Please take Ariel's messages into your heart, accept what resonates as true for you and reject what does not. You will grow spiritually in the process.

In Search of Alternatives

Linda Sue Nathanson, Ph.D.

In 1978, I was desperate to avoid a fourth trip to the hospital for a gynecological problem stemming from an intrauterine device that was causing injuries with sometimes fatal results. A gynecologist at Albert Einstein College of Medicine in New York, where I had a post-doctoral research fellowship, told me surgery was mandatory or I could be hospitalized several times a year for the rest of my life. I decided to explore alternatives.

As a former graduate student with a research assistantship at UCLA's Neuropsychiatric Institute, I had met Dr. Thelma Moss, a faculty member doing research in psychic healing. She used Kirlian photography, a technique that captures emanations of light coming from the body (auras). Dr. Moss took Kirlian photos of psychic healers and their patients before, during and after healing sessions. The resulting photos showed a transfer of energy from healer to patient.

With this background and the encouragement of a psychic friend who had introduced me to many extraordinary phenomena (spirit guides, past lives, extraterrestrials and the legitimacy of accessing information from beyond the five senses), I began my search for a psychic healer. To justify the effort in my own mind, I thought of myself as a reporter going after a story. I wasn't pretending to be doing anything scientific; I went looking for a miracle.

I read books on alternative and psychic healing[1] and wrote to five practitioners. Two responded—Etel deLoach and Olga Worrall. I drove to Baltimore to attend a healing session at Mrs. Worrall's church. Weeks later, I returned to Baltimore for a one-on-one healing session with Mrs. deLoach after she gave a lecture on alternative healing at Johns Hopkins University. One month after that meeting, the gynecologist reexamined me and said the pelvic inflammatory disease had disappeared. He used the term *medical miracle* and canceled surgery. The problem never returned.

Fifteen years later, after a sudden and excessive weight loss and a pounding, rapid heartbeat, I was diagnosed with an overactive thyroid. Colleagues with the same diagnosis had endured these symptoms unabated for years despite aggressive medical

---

1. St. Clair, D. *Psychic Healers.* New York: Doubleday; 1974. Kruger, H. *Other Healers, Other Cures: A Guide to Alternative Medicine.* Indianapolis: Bobbs-Merrill Company, Inc., 1974.

treatment. Given my excellent track record with nontraditional approaches, I went looking once more for an alternative and, in January 1994, found Stevan Thayer, a holistic practitioner and developer of Integrated Energy Therapy® (IET).

At times during our IET sessions, Stevan entered what seemed like a self-induced, altered state of consciousness and spoke in a voice not his own, offering knowledge beyond his experience, as if someone else were speaking through him. He said he was accessing information from outside himself and stepping aside "to let the guidance come through."

I viewed Stevan as a gifted visionary and found his information optimistic and insightful, his approach nonintrusive. He said he felt an energy block in the area of my throat—a sign of restricted creative energy—and this was probably related directly to my thyroid condition. He said that I must write to unblock the energy. During one of his altered states, I heard these words:

> You will see that your life has a theme. It is not one of doing for others, for you have the capacity to do that. But it is one of taking your knowledge of how to do it and teaching. . . . Using your tool of résumés, you have the ability—working as hard as you possibly can—to do several hundred résumés in a year. But if you could teach others how to do their own résumés, you could touch tens of thousands in a year.

I was elated with such a prescription. As a successful résumé writer, technical writer and owner of a typesetting and design studio, I had long wanted to write a book on résumés. But there were always perceived roadblocks—money, time, competition, finding a publisher.

Energized, I began writing *Résumés That Sock It to Them!* (in progress), became a contributing author to *A Funny Thing Happened at the Interview* (Edin Books, 1996), invited comedian and author Steve Allen to be the foreword author (he said "yes"), and inspired the creation of a cartoon character to illustrate the books.[2] I continued with the IET sessions and, within weeks of beginning to write, my thyroid-related physiological data were within normal ranges. In essence, the thyroid condition disappeared and never returned.

The Ariel Tapes

I wanted to learn more about Stevan's "other personality." During his altered states, I asked questions, much as I've seen lawyers and psychiatrists do in movies and TV shows about multiple personalities. I began with such innocuous inquiries as "What's your name?"—unaware that I was not the first to encounter Stevan's inner voice. I was told it did not have a name, but if one were needed, the name that seemed to belong to its energy was *Ariel*.

The information Ariel shared with me about my life was fascinating and, in March 1994, I began audiotaping our sessions.

By April 1994, it became clear that in the time it would take me to *find* a publisher for my résumé books, I could *become* a publisher. Resources fell into my lap to support me in this effort.

> Ariel: *It is always joyful when one who has been in a bright room with her eyes closed finally opens her eyes and sees the light. We have tried for some time now to give you what you've asked for, and yet you have been as though with your arms held tight—not reaching out. It gives us such pleasure to make your life easy, to guide you to those who will help you and, in turn, who will be greatly helped by working with you. This simplicity you may refer to or know as* synchronicity.

2. Drawn by Chris McDonough.

You live in a dynamic, rapidly moving mosaic of life in which, when all are following their hearts—not stuck off somewhere in fear or resistance or struggle, but following their hearts—all move like a dance in which you are being guided and led. The dance is enjoyable. It brings you each step of the way to a higher and higher level of your truth. You find partner after partner after partner—some short-term and some long-term—to dance with you.

The words we spoke to you before—that there has never been, nor will there ever be, anything extra in your life— will ring true to you even more. You will see everything you have built, although you may have built it for another reason in your life, has been built to support the very work that you are in the midst of and all the works to follow. Nothing is extra.

Two weeks later, April 29, 1994, I incorporated as Edin Books, Inc., with a corporate mission to publish career and metaphysical titles—books and tapes devoted to personal and professional empowerment. (The name *Edin* was created from my parents' names **Edi**th and **Nat**.) Ariel shared the following words:

Ariel: *If you ever had the desire to stay hidden or invisible, it is well to give up such desire. The truth you've seen. We have watched you make these wonderful discoveries on your own path by letting yourself, giving yourself permission, to dare, to do and follow your heart. And the successes, the synchronicities that you have discovered, the wonderful, wonderful chance series of events that led you to exactly what you needed to see. . . . It fed fuel into your fire of belief, and we can feel by the energy in your heart that you truly believe in yourself now. . . .*

One of the greatest teachings is not so much what is contained in the books but what is contained in the life of the writer of the books. For, in your own way, the very fact that the books exist at all demonstrates that you have applied for, satisfied and received the job you set out to do. And while it went with no formal process—no résumé, no interview, no passage of papers—the essence of what you are asking for is that every person who buys, reads and follows these books is transformed by your work.

The essence of what you are asking them to do is what you have already done. That alone will underscore the success of your work. For authors, writers, teachers who ask their students to go into uncharted territories to which they themselves have never ventured, never succeed.

During the year that followed, I asked many personal questions, mostly about my career. The tapes during this early period chronicle one human journey—the genesis of a publisher and a publishing company.

An Angel Sighting

My questions to Ariel continued to be personal until Stevan told me about someone who had had a startling experience of *seeing* an angel named Ariel. I began to wonder. Was Stevan more than a visionary? Was he being used to give voice to a being from another dimension? Was I—a nonreligious, Jewish research psychologist—talking to an angel? I felt myself for the first time considering the possibility that there could be an intelligent life form to whom Stevan was connecting psychically. I went to the scientific literature and the popular media to see if such a phenomenon had been documented.

Science Meets Religion

With the help of the Parapsychology Foundation's library in New York City, I searched for experiences like Stevan's. The investigation revealed numerous literature reviews, theoretical models, experiential reports and laboratory research. They tended to focus on the experience or physiology of the receiver of the information (the channel). Regarding the *origin* of the information, the literature includes the following definitions:[3]

- "An unspecified source outside conscious awareness"
- "A source that is said to exist on some other level or dimension of reality than the physical as we know it, and that is not from the normal mind (or self) of the channel"
- "Knowledge that lies beyond conscious awareness"
- "Some sort of intelligence, the nature undefined, whose purpose is to promote spiritual teachings and philosophical discussions"

Conferences held by the Parapsychology Foundation, Foundation for Research on the Nature of Man, Institute of Noetic Sciences and the Scientific & Medical Network show the scientific sophistication that has come to the area of inner-voice research. For example, a conference called "Beyond the Brain: New Avenues in Consciousness Research" was held in Cambridge, England, in the summer of 1995. Leading researchers

3. Harman, W. and Rheingold, H. 1984. *Higher Creativity: Liberating the Unconscious for Breakthrough Insights.* Los Angeles: J. P. Tarcher; Klimo, J. 1987. *Channeling: Investigations on Receiving Information from Paranormal Sources.* Los Angeles: J. P. Tarcher; Kautz, W.H. and Branon, M. 1987. *Channeling: The Intuitive Connection.* San Francisco: Harper & Row; Hughes, D.J. 1992. "Differences between Trance and Channeling and Multiple Personality Disorder on Structured Interview." *The Journal of Transpersonal Psychology,* 24(2), 181–192.

and scholars explored "contemporary research on states of consciousness, transpersonal psychology, nonlocal aspects of mind, and the search for a broader scientific framework for the study of consciousness."[4]

The Public Embraces Angels

On-line searches of newspapers, magazines and *Books in Print* revealed over two thousand references to *angels*, with articles in such mainstream magazines as *Newsweek*, *Time* and *Life*. A division of the directory publishers, Gale Research, Inc., published a book called *Angels A to Z*.[5]

Television presented interviews or reenactments of reports of angelic intervention—"Angel Stories" and "Miracles and Other Wonders," both on The Learning Channel (TLC); "Unsolved Mysteries" on NBC (with reruns on Lifetime); UPN's "The Paranormal Borderline," Fox's "Miracles and Visions: Fact or Fiction" and "Miracles and the Extraordinary: A TNT Larry King Special." CBS aired a weekly angel drama called "Touched by an Angel." NBC had a talk show called "The Other Side," which showcased interviews of people with paranormal experiences.

A search of the U.S. retail market revealed 194 stores that carried angel items. A Gallup Poll reported 72% of Americans believed in angels.[6]

Even case law has addressed whether copyright protection is available for the work of an author who channels the expression of a spiritual entity. According to Attorney Jonathan Kirsch:

4. *Noetic Sciences Bulletin,* Spring 1995, 4.
5. Woodward, K. "Angels." *Newsweek,* December 27, 1993, 52–57; Gibbs, N. "Angels Among Us." *Time,* December 27, 1993, 56; 58–62; 65; Colt, G.H. "In Search of Angels." *Life,* December 1995, 62–65; 67–72; 76; 78–79; Lewis, J. R. and Oliver, E. D. *Angels A to Z.* Detroit: Visible Ink Press,™ 1996.
6. McAneny, L. *Gallup Poll Monthly,* January 1995, 14–17.

The basic question to be answered in determining whether copyright protection is available for the work of an author who "channels" the expression of a spiritual entity is whether the spiritual entity can be regarded as (a) a fictional character created by the author, or (b) a person that exists apart from and independently of the author.

If the spiritual entity—i.e., an angel, a ghost, a spirit, etc.—is merely a character created by the author, then copyright protection is available. "[I]t is clearly the prevailing view that characters per se are entitled to copyright protection." *Nimmer on Copyright*, Sec. 2.12, citing *inter alia*, *Walt Disney v. Air Pirates*, 581 F.2d 751 (9th Cir. 1978).

If, on the other hand, the spiritual entity is presented by the author as a "person" with an objective existence of its own, then the author cannot claim to own a copyright in the words and expressions dictated or channeled through [the channel] by the spiritual entity. . . . The question has been addressed in two cases. . . .

The Oliver Case

In *Oliver v. Saint German Foundation*, 41 F.Supp. 296 (S.D. Cal. 1941), plaintiff was publisher of a book titled *A Dweller on Two Planets*. The author of the book (whose name was Oliver) claimed that his book was a factual account "dictated to him by the spirit of a previously deceased person," that is, a spirit from another planet known as "Phylos the Tibetan." Oliver did not claim to have written the book and said that he acted only as the "amanuensis" for the spirit Phylos. Defendants in the Oliver case were an author named King and the publisher of his book. King, too, claimed that his book consisted of words that were dictated to him by the same spirit who dictated Oliver's book. The court refused to permit the publisher of the first book to sue the author of the second book for copyright infringement on the grounds that both authors might well have received dictation from the same spiritual source.

The Silva Case

Another, more recent case, also suggests that two authors may encounter and describe the same spiritual entity without infringing on each other's copyrights. Plaintiffs were Charles Silva, author of a book titled *Date With the Gods*, and his publisher. Defendants were Shirley MacLaine; Bantam Books, publisher of MacLaine's *Out on a Limb*; and ABC, which broadcast a TV movie based on the book. The court ruled against Silva and specifically held that "Silva's copyright in *Date With the Gods* cannot bar MacLaine from describing interviews she had with others and her own experiences."[7]

From Moses to MacLaine

It was evident that Stevan's paranormal experiences were not unique. Wanting a historical context for the phenomenon of receiving guidance from an unseen source, I contacted the winner of the Parapsychology Foundation's 1994 award for parapsychological literature, Dr. Alfred S. Alschuler, who graciously agreed to write a paper on this subject. In a comprehensive and scholarly essay, Dr. Alschuler traced the history of famous people—from Moses in biblical history to MacLaine in Hollywood—who have been guided in remarkable ways by what they perceived as an inner voice, an entity beyond themselves, a spirit guide, an angel. His powerful presentation became the introduction to this book.

7. Kirsch, J.L. Esq. Kirsch & Mitchell, Attorneys at Law, personal communication, Jan. 4, 1996.

The Interview

It occurred to me in 1994 that if I am really talking, through Stevan, to an intelligent being from another dimension, I could go beyond personal issues and get some potentially powerful answers to more global, controversial, seemingly unanswerable questions on such topics as angelic encounters, abortion, extraterrestrials, past lives, death, alternative healing, AIDS and many others.

Interview with an Angel consists of Ariel's answers to these questions distilled from 50 hours of audiotape obtained over two years, from 1994 to 1996.

Unlike research that focuses on the nature, physiology or life of the channel, and more than a mere transcription of one-way pronouncements, this book reveals a dynamic dialogue, an unconventional conversation between a research psychologist and a nonphysical life form that said it was using the human's questions as a platform for communicating divine information to the people of Earth.

> Ariel: *Those burning questions that come from the soul are the ones we seek, for those are the ones through which we can most effectively do our work.*

The answers are optimistic, comforting, controversial, sometimes jolting, consistently insightful. While the intent was not to criticize any group, the entity said it would have no problem "shaking belief systems."

For Those Seeking Alternatives

A series of medical emergencies forced me to consider an alternative approach to treatment. (Ariel tells us that illness is often a persuasive alert by one's soul to get us back on our life path.) By opening up to a medical alternative, I found it easy to be open to other kinds of alternatives—professions, philosophies, lifestyles, attitudes, religions. And my life has changed during the course of this project, evolving from local résumé/technical writer to international publisher and author.

If you question traditional views, if you seek alternatives, you will find support and insight within these pages.

Ariel: There has never been a time like the time that you presently exist in, in which so much opportunity is available.

Stevan and I are leaving the laboratory research on paranormal phenomena to others. Our purpose is communication—to share the messages we have been given as willing and eager participants. We are adding our experience to the wealth of anecdotal evidence that supports the existence of information from beyond the five senses.

It is our hope to reach people who are looking for alternatives in their lives—spiritually, philosophically, vocationally, medically. We are sharing with you another point of view about our world, our selves, our destiny—the words and wisdom of an angel named Ariel.

Invitation

Prologue

In January 1994 Dr. Linda Sue Nathanson, a research psychologist seeking a medical alternative, met Rev. Stevan Thayer, a holistic practitioner and developer of Integrated Energy Therapy® (IET). At times during their IET sessions, Stevan entered a self-induced, altered state of consciousness and spoke in a voice not his own, offering knowledge beyond his experience.

In time, Linda came to believe she was in a dialogue not with Stevan, but with another "personality," identifying itself as Ariel, to whom Stevan had "connected." Linda began asking questions of this other personality in much the same way she saw lawyers and psychiatrists probe multiple personalities in movies and television programs. Ariel said, "We plant the knowledge, the knowing, in his [Stevan's] mind. . . ."

Directing her questions, then, not to Stevan but to a nonphysical intelligence beyond Stevan's conscious awareness, Linda began by asking for permission and cooperation in compiling Ariel's words and wisdom into a book.

✳

LINDA: I would like to ask you questions the way an explorer meeting an unknown life form would ask and then put your words in a book. How do you feel about that?

ARIEL: We find it humorous that you would ask us if we would be willing to do what it is that we chose *you* to do. Your desire to ask us questions is the reason you were specifically selected. We cannot inject into someone's mind the questions, the probing, the desire for knowledge. We selected you because you have these questions. You have a burning desire to know and a way of thinking that tries to organize your thoughts, the world and even the angelic realm into a sense of order. This is so inherently the basis of who you are that this work is easy for you.

We wish to convey much information, but we cannot convey information to a mind that does not already seek it. So, of course, this information is readily available to you whenever it is appropriate for you to ask.

We wish to convey
much information. . . .

LINDA: Are there certain categories of questions you would like me to focus on?

ARIEL: We place no restrictions on the category of questions. We have chosen you to ask the questions because you, by the very nature of your mind, create an inquiry that will enable us to answer what we wish and in a way we wish. We will always utilize whatever question you ask to give the message we wish to give.

---

*We will always utilize
whatever question you ask
to give the message
we wish to give.*

❋

LINDA: **Would you answer questions about the meaning of Bible stories?**

ARIEL: There will be times when you will ask us questions which we will rebuke or refuse to answer because they will take you far afield from the main current of your soul's flow. This question that you ask now is in the flow of your life, and it would be our pleasure to address such questions with the following understanding.

It is not our mission to create any disharmony in life. It is not our mission to attack, make wrong, criticize or condemn even the most incorrect thinking.

We will attempt in many ways to have you understand the limitations that your language and your mind have for perceiving the things of this realm. In what you call your *history*, many have attempted to create a "best understanding," using the models and constructs of the mind's logic at that time, to fit things into categories and compare and contrast them as the human mind is so aptly designed to do. These models were accurate and adequate ways of understanding this realm from the perspective of the evolution of the human mind at that time.

---

*It is not our mission to . . . criticize . . .
even the most incorrect thinking.*

At each point in your time that we convey our wisdom, we must always work within the limits that human consciousness has evolved to and convey understanding in words and images which can be comprehended at that point in time. We wish you to take the words that we offer you now about such biblical references as yet another way from a more current perspective (in your view of time) to convey an understanding that is still flawed by your limited ability to perceive things of this realm. It is our hope that our answers to such questions will allow an expansion and a shifting of your consciousness that will allow you to better understand this realm and its workings. Those who come after you and ask similar questions will receive our wisdom in a way that is appropriate to their minds' evolution at the time they ask.

While our work is entertaining and while we will be happy to provide entertaining reading for those ready to take it in, our words always seek to provide permanent change for those who have experienced them, a change that opens up an inner light, redirects the soul and brings someone back to the very path of his own life. Our objective is to put information into the minds of those ready to accept it.

Our words always seek to provide . . .
a change that . . . brings someone back
to the very path of his own life.

With these words said, biblical questions would be very useful, helpful and joyful for us to use in sharing our wisdom with you.

We can tell from your questions and the activity of your mind that you have started to understand the reason you and Stevan were selected to work with us. Make no mistake that you two are

a force that will guide the revelation of our words to people who
are hungry to hear and hungry to read them.

----

*You two are a force
that will guide the revelation of our words
to people who are hungry to hear
and hungry to read them.*

Those people you know now and those you have not yet met
who will receive our information as part of this process do not in
and of themselves have your capacity to ask and to probe. People like Stevan have gifts to receive our messages but do not yet
have the strength and discernment to reveal their gifts on their
own. You, while you do not yet allow yourself to receive our
messages directly, are devoid of such fears and in fact eager to
present a wakeup call to those ready to hear it.

The work is ready to be done by those on this side whenever
you two are ready to begin on that side.

※

LINDA: **There are books on the market today that are by or
about angels. Have you or those in your realm helped write
these other angel books?**

ARIEL: Some books have been inspired and communicated from
those in this realm, yes. Others have evolved to clarify the
human models for interpreting the words that have come from
this realm.

The phenomenon of heightened awareness and desire for
knowledge about angels that you have been experiencing for
some time is, in part, the work of this realm. We have, as always,

attempted to bridge and convey and interact with the human mind and human consciousness.

The . . . desire for knowledge
about angels . . .
is, in part,
the work of this realm.

But do not interpret the current abundance of material or the thirst for that material as any increase in the information sent or the desire to send information from this realm. Rather, it is an evolutionary opening to being able to communicate with this realm and receive information directly. It is also the thirst, in the hearts of those who have evolved to the point of believing in this realm, for more and more knowledge to fill an uneasy emptiness that grows within the human spirit.

The evolution is quite apparent when viewed from the perspective of your history. Your species has reached a peak in its ability to create and produce. You have evolved socially from working with mere hands to working with crude machinery to working with refined machinery to working with advanced machinery. You have evolved even further in terms of working with knowledge created by the minds of humans in advancing technology. You have developed the ability to process, manage, control and communicate information at higher and higher levels of complexity with faster speeds and more efficiency.

Your species has reached a peak
in its ability to create and produce.

You have changed sociologically your dynamic of family so that every force that can work and earn is working and earning, with both partners actively engaged in expanding the world of technology and manufacturing. Your world of form has reached a point of maximum level. Your desire has always been to find fullness, meaning and purpose for living a life within the human realm. And the world of form has served its purpose very, very well within your evolution.

However, it is a little hard to describe the phenomenon taking place. It is akin to having scaled a very high peak, spent a great deal of effort and much, much ingenuity, craftiness and perseverance to attain such a height, only to reach the top and wonder: Is this all there is?

The world in which you abide is nearly at such a peak. As more and more people attain the pinnacle of their efforts and stop to reflect, they begin to understand that there is indeed more. Not more from the world of form and the realm of human creation, but more from moving beyond the limitation of the human ego to undertake more soulful tasks and obtain more soulful nourishment.

---

*As . . . people attain
the pinnacle of their efforts . . .
they begin to understand
that there is indeed more.*

Many people in your world have followed this historical path and neared the peak of what they may do, create or manifest. This has created an opening of consciousness which permits human minds to be open to and hungry for angelic knowledge—knowledge that even several years ago in your time would have been viewed with very skeptical eyes as a hoax or a fraud. Those who dared to talk about or even seek knowledge from the realm that you call angelic would have been considered on the fringe of your society.

An opening of consciousness . . .
permits human minds
to be open to and hungry for
angelic knowledge. . . .

Human desire to satisfy its growing hunger for spiritual knowledge within the soul has caused angelic communication to enter your mainstream of life. And as a result, not only will more and more spiritual knowledge be conveyed and published, but even more will be sought. You will see that the popularity will not diminish until souls themselves have had their hungers satisfied.

LINDA: **Your powerful words are in conflict with some religious and societal ways of thinking, and one of your premises was that you did not want to criticize or make any group wrong. Please comment.**

ARIEL: Make no mistake, we are not opposed at all to shaking belief systems. We have done so for what you call centuries. All we ask you to know in the core of your heart is that there is no right and there is no wrong.

We are not opposed at all
to shaking belief systems.

What we give you will be at best an approximation of truth that your mind and your consciousness can handle at this moment. When compared to an approximation of truth perceived earlier in your time, it may be in conflict; it may create controversy. Our goal is not to raise so *much* controversy that the message is ignored, but to create the right level of controversy such that the message is sought out.

When compared to
an approximation of truth
perceived earlier in your time,
it may be in conflict.
It may create controversy.

LINDA: I expect that Stevan and I will get some criticism once this book is published because there will be people who don't agree with these words. Can you give us some advice about how to address our critics?

ARIEL: There are several pieces to your question. It is our fervent objective to offer truth, to offer understanding, but in no way to make any belief system or any person wrong.

One tenet of human experience is free will, the ability to freely guide yourself in your own path toward your own destiny. There is also divine will, which works to guide you. One of the joys in experiencing life is to bridge divine will and free will into a unified harmony.

*One of the joys
in experiencing life
is to bridge divine will
and free will
into a unified harmony.*

It is our fervent desire that all who read these words take them into their hearts; experience them; see how, with free will, the words resonate within their belief system. It is our desire that those who do not agree with or harmonize with the words we have spoken simply reject them, quickly and completely. It is our desire to allow these people to follow in their own process to determine the eternal spiritual truth which does resonate within their own experience.

It is our desire that these words reach those people who are open to and resonate with these truths, and will use these words to spark and cultivate a sense of inner growth and nurturing. It is our desire that these words feed and nurture the souls that are hungry for them.

*It is our desire that these words
feed and nurture the souls
that are hungry for them.*

As for the vehicles expressing these words at this time—the one who speaks [Stevan] and the one asking questions [Linda]—it is quite part of their karmic path and a necessary step in their spiritual growth to face the possibility, but not necessarily the actual experience, of criticism or questioning or verbal attack.

The basis of offering our words, which can be experienced as controversial by some, is an essential truth. Within your [Linda's and Stevan's] experience of our presence, there is a firmness, a depth and a commitment of heart that will withstand any human query or controversy. The core truth that you have found in our work with you cannot be shaken.

If you [Stevan and Linda] do not possess the faith that what we are doing is true and that what we have spoken is right, then it is best to keep what has been spoken private. Let it be an interesting experience, an exercise of personal healing and growth.

However, it was no chance happening that you two, your souls, have united for this purpose and this task. Once your personal trust and faith in the energy and the dynamic of what has been spoken is sufficient, you will find that judgment or criticism will bear little consequence as you express this truth to the world. You will move forth in the light of your truth, and you will not be affected by the doubt or fear that could arise from others.

You will not be affected by
the doubt or fear
that could arise from others.

✳

LINDA: **Regarding the sharing of information, Stevan and I have discussed at great length ways in which we could bring your words to the public. Our work on this project is not simply a personal experience for either of us, and we will use our resources to reach as many people as we can.**

ARIEL: We would not have chosen the two of you for this work if we thought that you would not share it. The only question has been how long it would take before it was shared.

LINDA: **Is that a question for me?**

ARIEL: It is an observation. You two both possess within you a fear of expressing these words. You both possess karmic histories which contained what you would judge as negative experiences resulting from expressing such truth. You will not be led into re-experiencing the karmic past. While there may be some who challenge the authenticity or truth of your work, there will be far more who will amplify the truth and the authenticity and who will praise the expression of such work. The karmic healing which will take place will far outweigh any karmic resistance to or repetition of your past.

Angelic Life

Anatomy of an Angel

LINDA: **Do you have the basic five senses—sight, hearing, smell, taste and touch?**

ARIEL: The simplest answer to your question is, "No, we do not." The senses you refer to are quite specifically designed to bring knowledge from the world in which you live through these various forms of perception into the consciousness that is occupying and alive within the human form. Such forms of perception are not available or needed in the realm from which we speak.

The closest parallel to what you have described as these organs of perception would be a state of *knowing* versus a state of *perceiving*. One *perceives* in order to acquire enough information to logically determine or intuitively infer truth about the environment and the world one abides in.

The realm from which we speak is a state of consciousness in which *knowing* is the method by which information about the environment is determined. All that is needed to be understood in the state of pure consciousness is simply known; it is simply available. There are no barriers of individual or separate entities to hinder the unity which pervades the form from conveying this knowing everywhere.

---

*The realm from which we speak
is a state of consciousness
in which* knowing
*is the method by which information
about the environment is determined.*

This knowing is not limited to this specific realm, for there are many within the human realm who possess this state of knowing, who have ability beyond the five senses that you describe.

These people have the ability of pure knowing, or cognition, that is impossible to obtain through the five senses.

There are many
within the human realm . . .
who have ability
beyond the five senses. . . .

There are numerous cases of communication by knowing that happen in ordinary life by ordinary people. Through the bond of love, for example, a mother will instinctively know when a child is in danger. Or an individual without any possible input from the organs of perception will know that something has just happened to a loved one. Or, as the phone rings you may know that it bears bad news, and when you answer, it does bring bad news. This *knowing* is not questionable; it is a fact transcending all limited sense organs.

There are many who use this ability in seemingly less spiritual matters of business negotiations, stock markets, even gambling, where beyond all the facts and every bit of available data, there is a knowing of what will happen and lives are guided by that knowing. This rare, momentary or possibly gifted ability of a few within the human realm is the pervasive means of understanding within this realm.

This . . . gifted ability of a few
within the human realm
is the pervasive means of understanding
within this realm.

❋

LINDA: **Were you ever in human form?**

ARIEL: It is difficult from your perspective to understand the answer. We will express it in a way not entirely accurate but understandable. We are many, and some within the collective, what is called *we*, were in human form. There are many who have not yet had the experience of inhabiting a human form and others who never will. Of the ones who have had that experience, many remember a great deal of it and know the limitations of the human form.

Of the ones who have had
that [human] experience,
many remember a great deal of it
and know the limitations
of the human form.

There is inaccuracy in our answer, but again, we cannot find words that can help you understand this dimension. It is not as though there are many of us here, because in reality there is only one of us. In reality, in the world of humans too, there is only one.

This *one* takes different forms. It might help to think of electronic communication signals. You are surrounded by hundreds and hundreds of broadcasts by radio, TV and cellular telephones—communications in many, many forms. They are all happening simultaneously, thousands of them surrounding you. A specific device—telephone, radio, television—might pull in one signal at a time, and you would think it was the only one, that it was separate and distinct from the others. Yet they all exist simultaneously and they are all the same thing. When you perceive us and the signal you have come to know as Ariel, it is a similar phenomenon.

LINDA: So Stevan and those gifted people like him can tap into this signal?

ARIEL: As a receiver would, yes. And that vibration [Stevan], although it is hard to describe, is perfectly suited for his present ability to receive.

LINDA: I'm interested in learning more about what you refer to as your realm, your world, your compatriots.

ARIEL: Another contrivance, another set of words for you to understand what is not understandable. The realm we speak from is a realm that is consciousness not encumbered by ego and not attached to a physical body. Words that are not accurate but might help your understanding are: we are souls that have not attached to a physical form.

We are souls that have not attached
to a physical form.

Many times in order to help people understand this concept, we have described a hierarchy ranging from the lowest form to the highest form. Many of your faiths have such a hierarchical view of this realm. From our perspective, they are not valid for there is no perception in this realm of "better than" or "worse than," "higher than" or "lower than." All just *is*. But as we are brought through and experienced by those in your realm who serve as bridges or channels between here and there, there is a human interpretation of "higher vibration," "lower vibration," "closer to God," "further from God," "good," "evil." This human interpretation leads to a conclusion that there is a system. And from your perception, it is correct. But it is not what is true from our perspective.

*

LINDA: **Are there many of you in your realm?**

ARIEL: This is a very difficult question—are there many of us in our realm? It is only you, in your identification of self as separate and distinct from all other living beings and creatures, that tries to project upon this realm an idea of separate and distinct. And again, while it is not true, there is an element of truth to it.

It is not true that we are separate and distinct, which is why for the purpose of communicating to you we never speak in singular terms [as *I*]. Although a label, a name, a feeling, an energy, an image is often conveyed to the one who brings through messages, they are purely for the purpose of helping that individual, not as a statement of true or singular identity.

Your ranking, systematizing and categorizing hierarchies of realms of angels, using names, labels and identities, are in a way inaccurate. We have communicated to the human mind over time and in such form to be helpful. We have presented an image, which people through different times and places have consistently seen. This has fostered human interpretations of our identity as separate and distinct, differentiating this from that, one from the other. It is more of a tool to try to make that which is incomprehensible to the human mind partially comprehensible. For if we could not be comprehended, we could not speak and work and guide and teach and help. And we could not direct your evolution spiritually.

_____

We have communicated
to the human mind
over time. . . .

_____

Make no mistake, the energy of this realm is available to everyone. There are more than enough (call them angels, guides, helpers, guardians) to serve, help and teach every single person on this planet—and a hundred times that many. But only those people who are ready, who have grown, who are open, can be reached.

_____

The energy of this realm
is available to everyone. . . .
But only those people who are ready . . .
can be reached.

_____

❊

LINDA: **Could you elaborate further on the nature of the angelic realm?**

ARIEL: Again, it is impossible to find the right words or metaphor to describe it to you accurately, for your mind is not capable of grasping the truth of our reality. But it would help to use an analogy as an approximation that would allow you to see it more clearly.

If you take one of your devices, a prism, and subject it to sunlight, it will array a beautiful rainbow of colors on the wall. Technically each of the colors (blue, green, red, violet, etc.) appears to be separate and distinct. To your eyes, you can see the red and notice it's different from the blue or the yellow. You will find that each color, in and of itself, does not really exist except as a vibration, except in your perception. And yet, any prism taken across any beam of sunlight will always produce a spectrum of colors that you will recognize.

What we are is more like sunlight. When you look at the sunlight, it's one uniform thing. There's no blue over here and red over there. Neither one is higher nor lower. Yet your mind naturally wants to separate them as higher vibration versus lower. That is what happens when the human mind tries to perceive this realm. The mind is like a prism. Since it cannot perceive the entire spectrum at once, it must separate and work on a small section, an infinitesimally small part of what is available in the realm from which we communicate. It does so within the model it is comfortable with.

The mind is like a prism.
Since it cannot perceive the entire spectrum . . .
it must separate and work
on a small section . . . of . . . the realm
from which we communicate.

For all of your history, those who have been open to our communication have connected with small fragments of this realm. In so doing, human traits such as names, personalities and characteristics have evolved, very much like our metaphor of color.

A collection of people from various cultures or backgrounds, even across various of your time periods, who view the color red and then write about it will have a similar experience. Likewise, minds that connect to and tap into the bands of consciousness, much like a radio receiver tuning in frequencies of a radio spectrum identified as Ariel, will (within the limits of their own distortion) experience the same being, the same vibration, the same words, the same essence. You will see, however, that you have many historical records of angels by different names, seen over many periods of your history and described with many seemingly contradictory characteristics—the same voice, the same name and the same presence seen in one case as male and in another case as female, in one case as good and in another case possibly as bad.

These interpretations, labels or descriptions are not ones we have applied, but ones that you have applied. When people tap into a specific range of consciousness and bring through that information, they place on it their own judgment, their own idea, their own interpretation of what they have seen or heard. As a result there appears to be, as viewed from the human mind, an entire realm of infinitely many beings of all descriptions, with many, many names and of many hierarchical rankings.

Indeed your own communications systems have such rankings with what you call VHF and UHF television, AM and FM radio, higher and higher frequencies, all seeming to be different, each having its own personality. Any two people with the proper receiver can tune in the same station on a specific frequency and find the same material. Yet in reality, it is all vibration; it is all one thing. It just has been fragmented for different purposes. Similarly a channel—an individual, who speaks, sees and communicates with the angelic realm—is at that moment looking through a very narrow band in a way that the channel's mind can comprehend.

A channel—
an individual, who speaks,
sees and communicates with the angelic realm—
is . . . looking through a very narrow band . . .
that the channel's mind can comprehend.

But do not confuse the picture of that one small segment with
the totality of what exists, or even as an accurate representation
of the totality. A channel will consistently see the image over and
over, each time appearing the same, just as a color in the spectrum looks the same each time. But remember, it is the human
mind that acts like the prism to separate this realm into perceiv-
able segments that can be comprehended. And, unfortunately,
at this point in the evolution of the human mind, the ability to
grasp the totality of this realm, or in the words of your religions, the totality of God, the totality of Allah, the totality of the
Tao, the totality of the Father, or the Mother or the Goddess, is
not possible.

It is unfortunate that, through your history, sometimes people have focused more on the messenger than on the message itself. And yet you will see that throughout all time, the message
has never changed.

You will see that throughout all time,
the message has never changed.

❊

LINDA: **The message of what?**

ARIEL: The message of love.

✳

LINDA: **What elements, what living things or nonliving things, compose this "unity" that you talk about?**

ARIEL: There is great importance to your question for it underscores, again, the need to describe the indescribable in words that your mind may comprehend. By attempting to use your words to answer your question, we hope to further your understanding of this important matter.

There is nothing you can think of—nothing of substance, nothing without form, nothing in the form of energy or vibrational waves—that is not part of this whole, this unity. It encompasses everything. The building blocks themselves are made up of the very substance of the world in which you abide. It includes everything that contains consciousness—both consciousness that is discernible and consciousness that you have not found ways to understand and appreciate. These living things that you mentioned, such as people, animals and plants, matter of various chemical elements, as well as this terminology you have of extraterrestrial life, are all part of this unity. But so are those of this realm, angelic expressions of consciousness which do not abide within a physical form, and even more subtle expressions such as thought are all part of this infinity or unity that we have tried to describe to you.

There is nothing that you can think of . . .
that is not part of this whole, this unity.

✳

LINDA: **Is there apparatus we can put in this room that would detect your presence?**

ARIEL: It is very difficult to answer because the question asks many questions. If we use, as many spiritual teachers in your world have, the image of your humaness as a wave on the ocean, the wave takes form [birth]; it lasts for a while [life]; it moves [the journey]; and then it disappears, returning to the ocean [death]. All along, the wave was the ocean. But it's easy to see the difference between one wave and another. They are each distinct. Each wave is like a person. Each distinct. Each arising out of nowhere. Each moving through a process they call their life's journey. And each returning through a process called death to the ocean.

Your question would be much like "How could I, while living deep in the ocean, build a machine out of water that could measure water?" There is nowhere within the world you live in—the universe you live in—that is not what you call *God*. You yourself are made of God. You yourself are created in God's image, not this physical form, but the image.

Find the thing within you that is there when you are alive, that isn't there when you die. Weigh yourself. You stay the same before and after death. Measure yourself with every one of your instruments and it is the same. No molecules have left, yet you're dead. Something is not there. What we are . . . is that something.

Find the thing within you that is there
when you are alive,
that isn't there when you die. . . .
What we are . . . is that something.

Many of your traditions have labeled it with the word *soul*. It is accurate enough to fit this description. Soul is the essence, the substance, the energy that is God.

LINDA: **And that's what makes us alive?**

ARIEL: Yes. It is what gives life to all form. It is the thing you call consciousness—the spark of awareness.

LINDA: **Have you been around for centuries?**

ARIEL: The question underscores other questions. It is important for you to understand that there has never been a time before which we did not exist, and there will never be a time after which we do not exist. But equally important, there has never been a time before which you did not exist. Nor will there ever be a time after which you will not exist. And we do not mean the identity which you have acquired in this journey and in this life. We mean the essence, the life force itself, which is the one thing that directly experiences pure cognition, that piece of you that is life itself. That is the *you* we refer to.

There has never been a time before
which we did not exist,
and there will never be a time after which
we do not exist.

LINDA: **Are there different types of spirit guides, angels, ghosts of departed humans, etc.?**

ARIEL: Your question aims at the heart of the matter. Because there are two different perspectives from which to view your question, there are two different answers.

From our perspective there is no difference in terms of the experiences, the beings or presences which are being encountered. But this is from our perspective that all things are from one pervasive vibration and, in truth, are not separate.

However, the question you asked was from the perspective of the separate human mind which, in order to exist, is forced to segment its experience of reality into distinct, compartmentalized ways of viewing life. And from that perspective, there are indeed different experiences.

Many of your scholars and authors have categorized the divine realm with words such as "celestial hierarchies" or "celestial realms." These words indicate a rank or structure, in some cases almost like a schooling system in which one progresses through higher and higher grades until one attains graduation. Again, the limitation of your language combined with your mind's inability to comprehend our realm while rooted in your concept of separateness makes it difficult for us to explain that such a view is in one sense true and in another sense untrue. The truth is that this unity, this life force vibration that makes up or manifests in all life, has within it the entire range of possible experience.

The part of your understanding that would see a hierarchy from a lower form of celestial being all the way up to the most high form of celestial being is really the way in which the human mind works, with its insistence on partitioning, segmenting and categorizing. It's the way the mind structures a variety of vibrations (or souls) which have evolved to different places of vibrational attainment, or different levels of spiritual growth. It is the way the mind experiences them in their place within this fabricated hierarchy of the human mind. As perceived from this realm, it does not exist. However, as perceived through the filter and distortion of the human mind, it does exist and has been experienced repeatedly by many people through what you call history.

So, in your example, someone encountering the presence of a soul no longer inhabiting a body, a soul which has not attained (from the human perspective) extremely high levels of refinement or vibration, would indeed view it (from that perspective) as lower in its divinity or celestial rank than an encounter with a soul which has evolved substantially further and attained higher and higher levels of divine vibration in its journey. And yet, from the underlying perspective of the pervading unity of the universe in which you abide, there is in truth no difference other than the vibrational characteristic. They are all part of the same eternal vibration.

※

LINDA: **Are all vibrations beyond the human mind "angels"?**

ARIEL: The term *angel*, as you apply it, is used to denote a vibration beyond the normal human experience. It denotes a vibration of life essence and life energy, a vibration of high and most divine spiritual presence. In some of your hierarchical frames of reference, it is used to denote one which is closer to God than to the human experience. So it depends on how you choose to use this label of *angel*, which is artificial.

A possible interpretation is: an angel is everything in the realm which, on a vibrational level, exists between the human experience and the concept of unity or God. With this definition, everything in this realm could be viewed as *angel*.

But other definitions have been used. These definitions require a certain "high" level of vibration to be labeled, from the human perspective, with the term *angel*. And yet the underlying essential truth is that all colors in the spectrum of light are indeed nothing but light. It is only when viewed through a prism that one wonders whether red is higher or lower than yellow, or questions at what point along that spectrum they become invisible.

And once they are invisible, are all the colors the same? Are all colors above the line of visibility the same, or are some higher and different from the lower ones? Just as it might possibly seem unimportant to worry about all the colors in the spectrum of light above the point of visibility, it is somewhat like the question, "Are all beings beyond human conscious awareness angels?" Do you follow our example?

LINDA: **This is a tough concept to understand and I'd like to address it again at a later time.[1]**

Close Encounters

LINDA: **For those of us who have no direct sensory awareness of your presence, can you give us hints about how to tell when you are trying to communicate with us?**

ARIEL: It would be unfair to say that there are many people who have no direct awareness or ability to communicate with us, or knowledge of such communication. The more accurate observation is that while such communication takes place frequently, the human mind will often not acknowledge the origin or importance of such communication. There are so many ways, in settings far less formal than we are communicating now to you,

---

1. Questions on this topic are presented in "Unseen Universe": page 301, "The Unity" and "The Search for God," page 313.

in which we touch and connect to the lives of those we wish to direct or guide—those we wish to help.

There are so many ways . . . in which
we touch and connect to the lives of those
we wish to direct or guide. . . .

Many categories of human experience are caused by angelic communication. The first is *intuition*—that is, a simple decision made in the mind for no specific reason and without much logic, often a quick or chance kind of choice, which turns out to be pivotal in its impact on your life.

Examples in this category of our connection could be quite simple, such as driving to a certain destination, suddenly taking a different route for no specific reason and finding out later that the original road was closed with a tremendous delay. By making this seemingly chance choice, you saved considerable time or effort. Or a seemingly chance experience of having someone pop into your mind and you choose to call while you're thinking of it. Then you find out that it was particularly important you called. In the case of a business call, for example, it was made at exactly the right time, and the business connection you wished to make was very successful because of the timing. Or, in the case of a friend, that the friend was in desperate need of hearing from you at that time, and your "chance" call brought a message or connection that was very important.

These types of seemingly spontaneous connections are all, at their basis, communication in which we have projected an idea, a thought or an image toward a mind that is not ready to receive refined communication from this realm. As such, it is not perceived at the time as anything special. Nor is it identified even after it occurs as anything special, for the ego will work to deny the importance of such chance events or communications.

---

*Seemingly spontaneous connections are all . . .
communication in which we have projected
an idea, a thought or an image
toward a mind that is not ready to receive
refined communication from this realm.*

If the ego were to acknowledge the importance and the power of such communication, then the ego would have to admit that there is a part of your being that is beyond its grasp and beyond its boundaries. This threatens ego, so such occurrences happen quite often without the person acknowledging or thinking too much about its source. The underlying source for such communication, such spontaneous bits of intuition, could be, as your poets have described, an angel whispering in one's ear.

The second category of our communication is *insight*. Sometimes we utilize the form that you call *dream state*. In the midst of your sleep, complete pictures, sometimes very literal and sometimes quite metaphoric, arise in the mind, giving beautiful understanding of a direction to be taken, beautiful solutions to problems to be solved or wonderful new insights and strategies where the person previously seemed hopelessly stuck and blocked. This beautiful state that you call dreaming is a wonderful and ripe opportunity for communication of insights, and we utilize it to guide, steer, direct and offer information to the mind that is ready to accept it. However, there is often difficulty in such cases. For once the information is brought into a normal ego state of consciousness, the individual must understand the sometimes metaphoric communication before he or she can actually utilize the information. That is beyond our ability to influence.

*Dreaming
is a wonderful . . . opportunity
for such communication. . . .*

A third way in which we lovingly attempt to guide and open a person's consciousness to our information is through *revelation.* Usually this is done at times in which a person is most frustrated or most stuck in a mental process or most frightened by some impending decision or choice. These are times when the normal mind, with its ego-control, is weak. Mental states of frustration, fear, feeling stuck with no solution possible, bring the ego to its knees. When the ego's control over the mind is weakened, our ability to communicate with you is greatly increased. In such moments, someone may suddenly have a flash of awareness in which the missing key element is seen, an entire strategy unfolds or an understanding of a path or solution is seen in clear detail.

*When the ego's control over the mind is
weakened, our ability to communicate with
you is greatly increased.*

Sometimes, in these moments, the solution itself cannot be conveyed to the mind but a key link or element can be. As a result, we lead a person to suddenly think of a colleague or friend who may help, and indeed that colleague or friend has the answer we have been trying to provide. Or suddenly a book may flash into one's mind as a possible source of the solution, and when the book is opened, there is the answer we've been trying to direct the person toward.

For people who have a more open consciousness, we have a fourth way to guide: through *images* and *words* as we are doing now. In these cases, when guidance is sought, when understanding is requested, the information can be brought through not only to help in the specific context of the request but also to teach more broadly. We try at every opportunity not simply to solve problems or make life in your human journey easier, but to help guide and direct so that your soul may move through its growth as efficiently as possible.

> *We try at every opportunity . . .*
> *to help guide . . .*
> *so that your soul may move*
> *through its growth*
> *as efficiently as possible.*

Sometimes in our guidance we see where specific information would save tremendous personal effort but deny much needed soul growth. In those cases, the information is not provided. This is not to say that information is withheld to the degree that one would have to struggle or suffer. The purpose in this wondrous, most precious experience of being human is to evolve and grow, to learn who you are—not just who you've defined yourself to be, but who you are on the most spiritually high levels— and to develop your personal relationship with the realm from which we speak.

LINDA: **There are moments when a person feels struck by an idea or gets an answer to a question or has insight into a problem. Is that an angelic communication?**

ARIEL: If we may, we will use your question to answer a broader question. There are times when the human mind seems to have an extrasensory experience. This may be a cognition, a knowing of something that is beyond its mere logical grasp, something that does not proceed by linear, rational thinking. It may be anything from a marvelous creative insight, something spontaneously flashing into consciousness, to a creative act in which a painting seems to paint itself or a story seems to write itself. It may also take the form of experiences in which something is known to happen just before it does happen, such as thinking of someone and having the phone ring with that person calling you.

These and thousands of other human experiences like them are all moments in which one experiences a state of mind beyond the normal ego. At these moments, one taps into the higher state of consciousness which is always available and yet sometimes rarely encountered.

Again, as we have explained in answers to earlier questions, when one moves beyond the ego state of mind that normally considers itself separate and distinct, and moves into this realm of consciousness where there is no separateness, no distinction, all is essentially and infinitely "one."

There are two models which human consciousness has used to explain this higher state. Both are correct and incorrect at the same time. One model defines this experience as extending upward to a higher dimension of oneself, loosely termed *the higher self* or *higher consciousness*. The other model defines it as reaching beyond conscious awareness to the angelic realm which conveys divine information downward [to physical beings].

You have asked, is "feeling struck" the interjection or communication of an angel to the consciousness of the person who receives the inspiration? In truth, both models—the model of reaching up to a higher dimension of mind and the model of an interjection down from an angelic being—are correct. The truth is, the human mind is simply accessing a part of what has always been there but is rarely connected with. Nothing new has been added. Simply what is there is being used—very much the way the mind of the one speaking at this time [Stevan] is accessing beyond any sense of self and connecting to the wisdom we inject by forming thoughts that he then speaks.

This too, this connection, this reaching out, can come spontaneously in moments of wonderful creative work. Sometimes it comes at moments of frustration and desperation, whether it be the creative work of the artist or the business executive who in a brief moment suddenly sees what was there all along but was invisible to the eye or the mind. You could say that in those moments, an angel has whispered into that person's ear and has given the insight. You could also say, as correctly, that the mind has reached beyond its normal boundaries, even if for a brief instant, and found a higher state of consciousness in which all of the answers reside.

_____

An angel has whispered
into that person's ear
and has given the insight.

_____

❋

LINDA: Is there a difference between our own thoughts and angelic guidance?

ARIEL: Yes, it is quite correct that there are differences between thoughts and angelic guidance. The difference is in the origin of the spark of creative energy that produces what ends up to be a thought.

The primary difference is whether or not the thought is one which is self-perpetuating. In other words, whether the thought is one which then creates another, which creates another, which forms what you might call a train of thought or some visual image in your mind that plays out over time as you allow the mind to follow it. These trains of thought or images are often very self-centered. They are orchestrated and directed by this phenomenon we refer to as *ego*. These thoughts place you as the chief character in the scene. These are thoughts that are directed to help you ac-quire more, to help you look better, to help you feel better. They are scenarios or images of fantasy playing out in which you are the hero or heroine others admire or envy. These very self-focused and self-serving thoughts are produced and directed by the ego.

The thoughts which are influenced or sparked by this realm are very different in nature. Often there will be a physical sensa-tion upon receiving a revelation, that is, a thought inspired by the divine realm. The revealed thought will not just be a mere mental experience. When the thought arises in the mind, it will often have with it a feeling of the heart opening tremendously. This will produce a feeling of great warmth in the area of the heart center of your body, a feeling of great peace, tranquillity and harmony. If the mind's activity had been one of struggle and fear, when the revelation occurs there is a sense of certainty and safety in knowing that all will be well. If the revelation relates to a person, when that person is thought about there's a feeling of tremendous connection and warmth in the heart center for that person. When the revelation is an inspiration for an idea on a project or a strategy to solve a very difficult problem, tremen-dous levels of excitement follow—far more so than any normal ego-based thinking would produce.

Thought inspired by the divine realm . . .
will often have with it a feeling of
the heart opening tremendously.

❋

LINDA: **Can you tell us why those in your realm have such an attachment to humans on earth?**[2]

ARIEL: We struggle with the word *attachment*. We have expressed before that there is a common unity between all life, including us in the realm that you label as *angels* and you in the realm that you label as *human*. From an angelic perspective, we are the same thing as human. However, because of this phenomenon of the human mind that you call *ego*, it cannot be stated that you are the same thing as angel.

From an angelic perspective,
we are the same thing as human. . . .
It cannot be stated that you
are the same thing as angel.

We do not have your idea of separation. We do not see the world through your filter of the ego mind. So this phenomenon you call our *attachment* to helping and guiding would be hard for your ego-filtered mind to understand. But if we were to pose a question for you to think about, you might have your answer.

We might ask you: Why do you have such attachments to your own life, to your own possessions, to your own creations, to your own identity? The answer which would normally spring forth in your mind is "because." But since we are not separate from you, our answer, too, is "because." If you determine why you answer "because," then you will understand why we have such an attachment to you.

---

2. Question from Dale Weinberg, Eastchester, NY

LINDA: **The language barrier among humans does not seem to be a barrier in your realm. You communicate with and reveal information to people of all races and all languages. Can you tell us why language is not a barrier to you?**

ARIEL: We do not use language. Our method of communication is quite simple, yet inexhaustibly complex to try to describe in words. The paradox is that we do not speak to humans. We allow access to us by a human mind which has a limited ability to join us in what we have termed *knowing*. This is the prerequisite, the requirement, for a mind to be able to serve as this metaphoric radio, television or other form of receiver for the vibration of communication which we convey.

The words spoken through Stevan's voice are not his words, yet in a way they are his words for we plant the knowledge, the knowing, in his mind. The thoughts or words that Stevan uses to convey the knowledge we have given him just seem to arise from the depths and recesses of his own mind. This is analogous to a daydream that you might be having yourself. You could follow and analyze the words that we are revealing (if you could do so without interrupting the flow of their creation), and they would very much sound like your own thoughts and your own ideas. What we do is simply connect, that is, enter into a state of resonance with the consciousness of one like Stevan and communicate a knowing of that which we wish to convey.

What we do is simply connect . . .
with the consciousness of one like Stevan
and communicate a knowing. . . .

The knowing is within the mind of the receiver. It is brought through a process—very similar to a directed daydream—from the recesses of the mind that forms the knowing into a linear set of words or images.

These words and images are created by the mind of the human receiver, not by the consciousness of the angelic sender. However, the words approximate the knowing or the knowledge that has been communicated. This is why there is something of a "personality" to each of the human voices we use to convey our knowledge.

Some people will use certain terminology that their minds easily fabricate, whereas others would not use that same terminology. It is also why several channels or scribes, however you prefer to label them, convey our messages using different words, different structure, different style and possibly even different metaphors.

While the style may differ, they all possess the identical knowledge and truth. It is also why several people who have a link to the same vibrational band or the same angelic being [such as Ariel] will convey the same knowledge, but with many different spoken or written personalities. The various personalities are not a reflection of this realm; they are a reflection of yours.

The various [angelic] personalities
are not a reflection of this realm;
they are a reflection of yours.

❈

LINDA: **Why is it that some humans can see you with their eyes and others cannot?**

ARIEL: Once this established connection has been made and a mind-to-mind transfer of knowledge has been achieved, the latitude the human consciousness has to express or interpret that deep knowledge or knowing is vast. There is no mystery to the process. Once the unconscious mind has linked with the knowledge, the conscious mind and the perception of the individual can receive it.

The conscious reception in one case may take the form of words which are spoken, as is happening at this time for you through Stevan. In the mind of another, rather than words, the conscious reception may take the form of visual images which the mind fabricates through the organ of the eye, and these images appear absolutely real and, in some cases, with astounding detail for the perceiver. Some may perceive with eyes closed and some with eyes open. The truth is that the mind is creating the image, based on what has been known. The mind creates the image to allow the consciousness, or the ego, to see what has been conveyed through the process of knowing.

In some cases the mind will receive what it knows as words or thoughts. In other cases, the person hears words from outside of himself, as though someone were speaking with a voice from outside. In some cases, it is more of a feeling, a vagueness without words or images, but a sense. In some cases there can be a sense of touch or of physical sensation, a bodily sensation. These are all simply ways that the human mind informs itself of what it knows. Because the knowing happens at what you call a subconscious level, it must be brought to the conscious level to be perceived. So, it is a way the mind tells itself what it has already obtained. These words have rambled somewhat, but we hope they are descriptive of this phenomenon.

Words or thoughts . . . or images . . .
are all simply ways
that the human mind
informs itself
of what it knows.

※

LINDA: **If I were able to see you, would I have the same vision of you as others who see you?**

ARIEL: No, not necessarily. To help clarify, consider the following example.

If you heard a beautiful passage of symphonic music at the same time that another person heard the same passage, while technically the vibrations and frequencies sent out from the instruments are identical in both cases, the soulful experience of the music might touch one heart and one soul differently than it touches the other. And while you both heard the same music, when you talked about it, when you described it, when you tried to put it into human terms, you would likely have very different viewpoints on what was heard.

We are no different. We cannot be fully understood nor described nor categorized by the human frame of reference. Our appearance is subjective, fitting within the heart and soul of the viewer. An image as seen by one is personal—it is an interpretation of that which cannot be interpreted. And while there may be distinct similarities amongst people who perceive our form, energy or words, there will likely be (and throughout your history have been) variations on what is seen, what is perceived.

Even in the world around you, when you see a color and someone else sees the same color, while the frequency and vibration of the color didn't change, you might each have a different interpretation of its hue or its vibrancy or the sensation. Drinking a glass of wine, two people have a different viewpoint on how it tastes. This is the dilemma.

We cannot be fully understood . . .
by the human frame of reference.

LINDA: Regarding the concept of knowing, and the information you have access to, do all parts of your unified realm tap into the same information source?

ARIEL: Your question refers to "all of us." In the unity that abides in this universe and the unity that is experienced within this realm, there is no concept of *all of us*; there's one. There is one consciousness, one pervasive life force or (and we use these words cautiously) one mind that exists.

As to the source of information—the source is God. We have access to this source (as do you). However, we in this realm are open to receiving information through knowing while you are more limited in your ability.

As to the source of information—
the source is God.

LINDA: **What elements, what living things or nonliving things, compose this "unity" that you talk about?**

ARIEL: There is great importance to your question for it underscores, again, the need to describe the indescribable in words that your mind may comprehend. By attempting to use your words to answer your question, we hope to further your understanding of this important matter.

There is nothing you can think of—nothing of substance, nothing without form, nothing in the form of energy or vibrational waves—that is not part of this whole, this unity. It encompasses everything. The building blocks themselves are made up of the very substance of the world in which you abide. It includes everything that contains consciousness—both consciousness that is discernible and consciousness that you have not found ways to understand and appreciate. These living things that you mentioned, such as people, animals and plants, matter of various chemical elements, as well as this terminology you have of extraterrestrial life, are all part of this unity. But so are those of this realm, angelic expressions of consciousness which do not abide within a physical form, and even more subtle expressions such as thought are all part of this infinity or unity that we have tried to describe to you.

There is nothing that you can think of . . .
that is not part of this whole, this unity.

LINDA: **Given what you are telling us about the oneness of all, when we feel joy or fear, do you experience emotions as we do?**

ARIEL: No, this is not correct. These things you speak of as feelings—such as joy, fear, happiness or desperation—are particularly and uniquely human. They are what makes the gift of a human life so precious and so powerful.

If you could only experience these feelings without attaching to them, without judging them, without trying to manipulate which ones you would have and which you would not have, you would find that you are living in an environment that is rich beyond description, filled with these experiences you call feelings. And yet, so much of your effort is spent manipulating these feelings, running from the ones that are distasteful and running toward the ones that are wonderful. You manipulate the very chemistry of your mind with substances that numb unpleasant feelings and allow pleasant ones to continue. Or even, most tragically, numbing all feelings, denying the joyful ones to avoid the unpleasant ones.

The only common experience we have in this category called *feelings* is the feeling called *love*. It is broader than this label describes, but it would suffice to say that the common denominator in feelings between the realm of angel and the realm of human is the feeling you call *love*. Love is the eternal common link. When we refer to love, we do not refer to the experience of lust, or love in a sense of attainment or getting something from someone, but full, open, heartfelt love which may come in many forms.

-----

*The only common experience . . .
is the feeling called* love.

The human journey is filled with opportunities to experience this common feeling, this thing called *love*. It can be love of a beautiful mate, a soulmate. It can be love of a parent or a friend. It can be love of an animal, a pet. It can be love of work. It can be love of nature or love of art. And it can be love of the divine, love of an angel or love of God.

So rich and so broad are the ways in which humans can experience love that it would be indescribable. Yet so infrequent are the times in the human experience that love is present. All too often it is denied because of all the other feelings, and activities derived from those feelings, that the ego creates. The necessary element in order to find this common link of love which we experience is quiet, to be still, to have the activity of this ego mind cease its incessant longings, judgments, fears and frustrations, and to simply be still. And in that stillness, even if for but a brief moment, you will experience our realm, you will experience the feeling of the love that we feel.

LINDA: **Are there different kinds of love?**

ARIEL: There is one kind of love, but there are many doors that you can pass through to have that experience.

There is one kind of love,
but there are many doors
that you can pass through
to have that experience.

LINDA: **How do those in your realm feel about us when we are angry, annoyed or have negative feelings?**

ARIEL: A wonderful question. You are not intended to be superhuman. You were chosen because you were human. We in this realm will dance with joy as easily in seeing you outrageously angry as in seeing you outrageously happy. For your anger and happiness are both expressions of your aliveness.

We in this realm will dance with joy
as easily in seeing you outrageously angry
as in seeing you outrageously happy.

The only thing that could bring despair or frustration in our mind would be if you are stuffing, avoiding or hiding feelings, not being true to what you are feeling, or in some way trying to numb your feelings. Because then you are blocking the flow of life and the gift of your aliveness. It's the same flow of life that creates raging anger that creates outrageous joy and laughter. Either way, it is still very alive in you. Being human, and not having attained sainthood yet, you are totally entitled to fits of anger, jealousy, fear. It would be unnatural for you not to have them.

LINDA: **Could you share with us who you've communicated with from our past—names that we might recognize from the Bible or from our history?**

ARIEL: We read into the question a possible confusion in our identity. From your perspective, there are many, many other angels, many other colors in this infinitely wide rainbow, who have also spoken to, touched the souls of and lifted the spirits of people throughout time.

*We have worked . . . with those
who can influence . . .
an entire culture, as well as those
who can influence their own lives.*

We have not limited communication to prophets or saints or religious scholars, nor have we limited communication to statesmen and spokesmen or great leaders of nations. We have worked in many capacities and in many ways with those who can influence an entire race, an entire culture, as well as those who can influence their own lives. Enumerating the communication would be untenable, and the scope is infinitely wide. But trust in your heart to know that there has been no significant leader—political, religious or in any form throughout time—who has not been touched by the message and by the grace of our work.

*There has been no significant leader . . .
who has not been touched by the message
and by the grace of our work.*

LINDA: **Please consider two instances from the Bible. One is Moses receiving the Ten Commandments. Another is Noah receiving instructions on how to build the Ark. Were these examples of communication from your realm?**

ARIEL: These are indeed examples of the love and the power this universe contains, the love and the power that God has for those navigating the spiritual journey of being human. Most of what we have attempted to convey to you in our recent words relates to your climb out of the ignorance created by your having eaten from the Tree of Knowledge, and your climb toward union with God.

What these stories, in their own way and in their own manifestation, show you is the effect of the love and power and glory of God reaching down (as it might appear to you) to touch you and to touch your lives and, in these cases, to touch the spiritual evolution of mankind. These are most blessed examples of the compassion and the love that we are constantly at a loss to describe. They underscore the power and the force that this love can have. While it is indeed the task within the human mind and the human experience to move into communion with God, it is also God's love and joy to move into communion with you.

While it is indeed the task
within the human mind . . .
to move into communion with God,
it is also God's love and joy
to move into communion with you.

These times you have described are the most powerful representations of that communion experience where, in support of the unfoldment of the divine plan of spiritual evolution within the realm of human, the intercession of God directly to man took place. The knowledge conveyed, through the process of knowing, is recorded in these two stories as well as in many other places and many other forms within this most holy of texts.

Please read them again, not looking for the human mind's attempt to understand the paranormal, but to see the diversity of the ways in which God may reach and touch your heart, your soul and your mind. Look also at the compassion, the glory and the effect that each of these occurrences has produced.

There are many references, from a human perspective, to far

less dramatic expressions of this God-to-human communion. It is within the realm of possibility that in your own life's experience, especially as you evolve further and further and reach higher and higher in your quest to know the divine, that the divine, of its own accord, may reach down with the most indescribable of graces and bless you with a communion that you may not even have been seeking, and in that communion infuse you to the core of your being with love. And, if it is important that you, at any specific point in your life's journey and in the journey of human evolution, be used in any way in service to the divine, you will be filled with everything you need to carry out the tasks you will be instructed to do.

> *If it is important that you . . . be used . . .*
> *in service to the divine,*
> *you will be filled*
> *with everything you need*
> *to carry out the tasks. . . .*

You have seen, beyond the holy and sacred scripture of what you call the Bible, stories in other holy and sacred scriptures of similar events in which, even in cases where great resistance to communion was offered through the human mind and its fear, the loving mercy of God reached down from this realm into yours, touching the consciousness of an individual with such force that the communion could not be prevented.[3] These cases all lead to tremendous change in a very positive and a very uplifting unfoldment of human spiritual development.

---

3. Such as the experience of Mohammed discussed in the Introduction, pp. 44–46 [Ed.]

LINDA: **It is very special to have this kind of contact.**

ARIEL: We know not whether you speak from our perspective or your perspective, but what you have said is very true from our perspective. What you do not see is that while you perceive this to be a gift we give you, there is no way to describe the extent and the magnitude of the gift you give us.

We search long and hard for those with the skill, with the openness, the tolerance and the daring to work with us. It is rare indeed to find someone like yourself who matches what is needed. The relationship we have formed is eternal.

What you do not presently see is that at some point in a future time, it is we who will be you and you who will be us. You may think only in terms of this lifetime and what you will accomplish during its momentary experience. But be very clear, everything learned, everything done, everything experienced in this, what you perceive as this lifetime, will move you into this realm that we exist in, and at some future point, from this place where we speak, it will be you speaking to us as we inhabit bodies. The work does not end.

LINDA: **Did angel visits occur in our history? And is there some significance to the current proliferation of reported angel encounters?**

ARIEL: There should be no surprise and no confusion over what is transpiring. And, yes, it is indeed true that what you call *history* has shown many examples of such connections (or communion experiences), of seeing, hearing or being touched in the heart and soul by angels. These have been the experiences of great mystics and advanced saints and sages of all spiritual traditions. But it is all quite straightforward and easy to comprehend.

There have been times in the process of the unfoldment of human spiritual evolution where it has been necessary to literally take the presence of the divine and bring it into human form such that it could be seen, touched, felt and believed. There are many masters who have taught on your planet who have been touched by this realm. Sometimes it comes in the form of a momentary direct experience and other times for an extended communion experience.

In the tradition of what you call *Christian* alone, or even in the earlier part of the Judaic origins, there are those—Abraham and Moses—who were in a state of such total communion and heightened awareness with the divine that what they brought back and shared with others came with such conviction and had such authentic energy around it that it transformed the nature of the evolution of the race.

Still later, an individual you know as Jesus of Nazareth lived in such long-held close communion, extending day after day, that there were no skeptics. There was nothing but either total admiration and love or the other natural human reaction, total fear.

After that, throughout time, those who removed themselves from the world of the ordinary and perfected through various, very rigorous disciplines and training the advancement of the communion experience with spirit, were able to be touched by the grace. Many, many such people have written profound mystical doctrines. St. Teresa, with her works from Avila, is an example. Others who are seen painted with their golden halos and their wonderful insights have been canonized. But the shift of the planetary consciousness has come to a point—and you are right in the middle of it and will be a significant part of it— where the mystical experience will become ordinary. You're at a point in what you call time where, in the not too distant future, it will be an ordinary experience for the vast majority of people to communicate directly, to see or to speak, with angels.

*In the not too distant future,
it will be an ordinary experience . . .
to communicate directly . . . with angels.*

But for now, a chosen few have been communicated with to help teach others and to bring others to the point where they, too, can see, hear and understand. These words that we are giving you now are designed to help you in that process. It is not predictable at this point how quickly the evolution will happen, for there is human free will involved. But it could be a very short time.

There was even divine guidance in the form of this tradition that you call *Christianity* and something referred to as a *second coming* of this being Jesus of Nazareth, known as Christ. The prophecy is accurate. The interpretation is not.

The second coming, if you would like to call it that, is what is happening right now. It will not come in a physical form and it will not come to a few people. It is a planetary and global evolution of mind moving at a very high spiritual vibration, bringing people's awareness up and out of their five sensory receptors into a greatly expanded state of consciousness where the communion experience with what you call the *Holy Spirit* will come as a natural and normal phenomenon. As this happens, it will bring about an enormous easing of fear on the planet and a tremendous opening to love and joy. Free will will remain very much a part of the human experience, but it will be free will guided to expressions of love, joy, health and harmony.

*The second coming [of Christ] . . .
is what is happening right now.*

Your work [and Stevan's] has always been to guide people—to move people beyond their limit of "self" expression into a more glorious unlimited unfoldment. While it will take diverse forms, you will play an instrumental role in helping people evolve, helping people unfold. And you will bring this guidance through you in a wide variety of forms to help people in their evolution.

It is wonderful that you [Linda] have selected the title *Edin* [Edin Books]. You will see how many, many ways you do things without knowing how profound they are at the time. Although you [Linda] may choose to spell words differently [Edin vs. Eden], the planetary cycle, again from this somewhat mythological Judeo/Christian description, starts in Eden, starts in a sense of total grace and total innocence, in total communion with the divine, and journeys away.

However, there is the journey back. The end result of the planetary transformation and the human race moving toward spiritual unfoldment will be a return to what has been known as Eden. But not with the innocence that was once held. For nothing that has been gathered along the journey has been lost. The knowing and the knowledge of what the journey has brought, through the unfoldment of human evolution, will bring it back to that garden, that grace, that unity.

The end result
of the planetary transformation . . .
will be a return
to what has been known as Eden.

❋

Life Passages

Marriage and Divorce

LINDA: What is your view of marriage?

ARIEL: We have two answers. Marriage, as you see it, is an after-thought. Marriage, as we see it, is what happens first. It is what happens the moment two people see each other, the moment two souls connect to each other.

From our realm, it is something that can be seen with great ease, for the light that shines forth is very bright. Neither soul gains anything. There is no missing piece provided by the other. But there is a power—an energy, like electricity—that one soul ignites within the other which allows that soul to come alive. When true marriage happens (marriage as viewed from this realm), two souls find each other, and with no effort whatsoever, they bring alive within each other that power, that force. You tritely call it *love*, but it is far more than the word you understand. These two souls bring alive the possibility of the fulfillment of each soul's destiny through the very process of their meeting.

There is a power . . .
that one soul ignites within the other
which allows that soul to come alive.

What *you* call marriage is more a formalization for those within government, religion or family to proclaim and legalize that which has happened long before any such celebration occurs. It is a most joyous and a most sacred experience, for it is a triumphant celebration that two souls have found each other and, in that finding, unlocked the potential to live the lives they came to live.

> *From our realm,*
> *[marriage] . . . can be seen*
> *with great ease,*
> *for the light that shines forth*
> *is very bright.*

✳

LINDA: **What is your view of divorce?**

ARIEL: Divorce, as you see it, is also an afterthought. It is first seen from this realm. The light that shines forth from the joining of two souls dims. The power that each person has to support the other in the fulfillment of their lives' and souls' destinies ends.

> *The light that shines forth*
> *from the joining of two souls dims.*
> *The power that each person has*
> *to support the other . . . ends.*

It would not be possible for us to describe fully why and how this happens. It is clearly visible from this realm when it does. Factors that we often see are too much distress, too much interference from the mechanism of personality or ego. The ego creates more fear, distress and disruption than the energy of the union of two souls can compensate for. The fear blocks out the power that the meeting of two souls can manifest within a life. And without that power, without that spark and that divine flow being active in their lives, the light that shines forth from the united being of these two souls is very dim.

Sometimes the light shines forth for a period of what you call time and then is dowsed or cut off by the interference of the ego. Other times in the ever-changing, ever-evolving flow of life as you know it, a soul is meant only to join with another for a period of time, so long as that divine spark stays alive. For some, that spark grows more powerful throughout an entire lifetime together. In other cases, after time together has passed and tremendous growth has occurred, there is a natural plateauing, or ending, of this power that each has to evolve and grow. As a result, the energy begins to dim. There is a natural ending of the union. Later, as you see it, divorce occurs, but it has already happened well before the legal, religious or societal action that you label *divorce* takes place.

Thinking the answer was complete, Linda asked a new question but was interrupted by Ariel who offered the following statement.

ARIEL: We wish to add a statement to our previous answer before answering your new question. The resistance of the one who is speaking [Stevan] did not allow the information we offered to come through. However, upon our insistence, the information will now come through.

Within the framework of many of your Christian religions, and in the sentiment of many other religious celebrations of what you call *marriage*, there is a phrase that expresses the truth but also misses the truth, depending on its interpretation. The phrase commonly used is:

That in this union between man and woman that we call marriage, what God has joined together, let no man put asunder.

When viewed from this realm, it is the highest-level statement of truth. Using the limited vocabulary and models you possess, the statement, "What God has joined together" is a simple way of saying what we have tried to describe as the union of two souls and the light that shines forth from those souls.

It is not appropriate for anyone to try to interfere with that union, for the spiritual magnitude of what has happened is not of the realm of man. However, that phrase is often used to try to keep together for human purposes that which, from this realm, is clearly seen as God no longer joining two souls together. For as that spark, that light, of the two souls dims, it is clear that God no longer joins them together.

So, while this phrase uttered in many a union celebration is accurate and true, it is often interpreted to mean that once the human celebration of marriage has taken place it can never be undone. And, from this realm, that is not true.

✳

Career

LINDA: What would you say to people who are struggling in their search to find the right profession or who are unhappy in their jobs?

ARIEL: We would begin by saying, "Congratulations!" Congratulations that there is an awareness of this unhappiness, this being stuck within one place while yearning for another, or being in between places and looking for the place that will bring fulfillment. This is a most marvelous time in the journey of a soul within a life. For it signals that there is movement afoot, that a process of change is taking place, that stagnation is being avoided.

It signals that there is movement afoot,
that a process of change is taking place,
that stagnation is being avoided.

It is an unpleasant time for most because it unearths the deep uncertainty that the human ego has at its basis. It's a time filled with fear and doubt, which is the playground for the ego to create pain and problems that seem to have no solution. It is also a playground for the soul, for the spiritual dimension of the being to rise up and to grow. For change itself is one of the most powerful spiritual growth mechanisms that the human experience has available to it. So, it is a time of great celebration that very positive and powerful movement is happening within the life of that individual. That individual must know at the deepest level that tremendous soul growth is taking place.

As to how to move through the change, how to move into finding the fulfillment of the soul's destiny in terms of its work, in terms of what has been called its right livelihood or perfect expression through work, each human being possesses a guiding compass. The capacity of the heart, if left unencumbered by the doubts, criticisms and limitations of the ego mind, follows very much like the primal instinct of animals that you might consider the lower species. Animals have within them the instinct that allows them to migrate, allows them to find perfect expression of living environments, allows them to find perfect fulfillment of feeding environments.

Each human being possesses
a guiding compass.

So, too, the human soul has a power (even beyond what you have marveled at in the animal kingdom) of instinct. The human soul has the ability to navigate directly as an arrow finding the center of a bull's-eye and find perfect expression which matches divine purposes in life, matches emotional fulfillment and intellect developed. It will also serve as the jumping-off point, the springboard from which all future unfoldment and development will occur.

Your society has spawned a simple expression of this phenomenon in the marvelous work *Do What You Love, the Money Will Follow*.[1] This title encapsulates the essence of our words, for doing what you love, following the expression of the heart, following the compass that exists within the very center of your being, allows you to literally play and enjoy and revel in that which you do.

The chief protagonist here is the ego, which will often attempt to subvert and convince you that it is not possible to make enough money to live on, prosper and be safe doing what you love. You must work hard, suffer and slave.

But this is simply an idea of the mind, not a truth or a reality of the marvelous world in which you live. For the very thing that you love the most, the very thing that would make you so excited and so happy to be doing that it would seem too good to be true, is the very thing that the divine has for you to do within this life. It is the very place within the indescribable mosaic of the life and the flow of your universe that you were created to fill.

---

1. Sinetar, M. 1990. *Do What You Love, the Money Will Follow.* New York: Villard Books.

The very thing
that you love the most . . .
is the very thing
that the divine has for you to do. . . .

When you are in that piece of the mosaic, that is where you belong. The feeling of joy, the feeling of rightness of your livelihood, the creativity of your expression will be at its maximum level. Hence, you will be the happiest you can be; you will be the most spiritually fulfilled you can be; you will be the healthiest you can be; and you will be the most prosperous you can be.

The human challenge is to read the heart's compass and find what it points to. Very often there will be much soul growth and development needed to journey in the direction of this compass and become the piece of the overall mosaic of life you were created to be. While the ego often looks for instant gratification, the soul enjoys the richness of the journey, for every step along that journey brings increasing aliveness.

The human challenge is to
read the heart's compass
and find what it points to.

✳

Death[1]

LINDA: **What do souls do between dying and coming back in another body?**

ARIEL: Your question has many questions embedded within it. First, it presupposes that a soul *will* come back in another body. Second, it presupposes something is done, that is, an action is taken. We will begin to explain the process.

The connection that we have with the one speaking [Stevan] is fading, but we will use it for as long as we can and ask to have the opportunity to continue our answer at another time with you.

Death is a process that is not instantaneous, not as the soul perceives it. Although there are many indices that your medical community can define which constitute the moment of death, the soul does not instantaneously disconnect from the physical body at a moment of death. Death is simply the ceasing of the metabolism and the physiology of the body which the soul has been associated with through the journey of the life. It is the beginning of a sequence of what you might consider *steps* which take place.

The first in this sequence of steps is an experience in which the vibration of the individual begins to change. The lower end of this vibration, this connection to the gross physical body, begins to be dissolved. The process is not instantaneous. It varies in this framework you call *time* and depends on the individual soul's degree of association with its physical identity.

This aspect, however, that you know and that we have loosely called *ego*, does cease to exist within a short time after the experience you call *death*. But the soul itself simply begins to disconnect its physical association with its vehicle, with this

---

[1] In the first public presentation of these words from Ariel (February 9, 1996), at Linda's request, Rabbi Jerrold M. Levy delivered excerpts from this chapter as part of his eulogy to Linda's mother, who died before this book went to press.

body. It stays in a higher, less associated or less connected vibration within the proximity of this physical body for a period of time and can often be experienced or felt by those who had especially strong heart connections with the individual. It may feel to them as though the individual is still present, even though the physical body has ceased to function in its aliveness.

The detachment from the physical body which has served as the vehicle for the soul's journey in a life varies in time and could take from what you call minutes to what you call hours. During this time, consciousness is present. It is not consciousness as you understand it, as viewed through the filter of your ego, but the consciousness as we understand it from this realm.

This begins several phases, depending on the degree of connection or attachment to the physical life experience. Next, after separation from this physical vehicle or body has taken place, there can still be a very strong connection, especially to those whose hearts have intertwined—to loved ones, to family members, as well as to areas of energy that embodied love or a heart connection, including physical dwellings, structures and houses.

After separation from
this physical . . . body . . .
there can still be
a very strong connection . . .
to loved ones. . . .

There is a process of moving away, of clearing the strong heart connection which can still be present as this phase begins. While the soul does not want to stay connected to this physical vehicle, this body, there can be a very strong soul-level desire to stay connected to the sources of love it has experienced. Very much as with the physical body, there is a need to distance, to separate, in a manner of speaking, to say "Goodbye" and bring resolution.

The unit of measure of what you refer to as *time* is quite variable in this process. There is no simple formula we may give you, for the duration might span from hours of your time to years of your time.

The phases which follow are very complex and there are many possibilities of evolution. We will deal with these in our next communication with you.

Ariel's answer continued two weeks later.

There is really no adequate way to delineate the remainder of this process since this delineation is, again, a phenomenon of the way the human mind works, attempting to compartmentalize things that cannot be compartmentalized. At the core of this journey, moving further from the association of the physical body and more into the state of complete unity, is a process of heightening the energetic vibration or the energetic rate of the essence that we speak of as *soul*. This process involves refining or removing from the soul-essence the remains of the association with that specific physical body and with the specific energies of those who have been so close and so loving.

The period of what you call time that this may take varies greatly. Depending on the person, the situation and the fluidity of the process, it is possible for pauses to occur in which past connections are refined and resolved.

※

LINDA: **When the soul is in close proximity to its physical body shortly after metabolic death, is this a time for a loved one to be aware of the soul's presence?**

ARIEL: A soul may stay for a period of your time, around those whom it has much love for and has received much love from, as the process of distancing or detachment takes place. This is often felt by loved ones still abiding within the physical body who feel, even after the death of a dear one, a sense of her presence. They may even feel a shiver or a chill or a sense of knowing that the one they loved so much is still nearby. And, in these times, even for periods of what you call days or weeks after the experience of this metabolic death, a presence of such loved ones can still be felt.

> *A soul may stay . . . around those*
> *whom it has much love for. . . .*
> *This is often felt by loved ones. . . .*

This is not a figment of the mind filled with wishful thinking. This is the actual process that transpires as the soul lets go, not only of the physical body but of the deeply heartfelt bond (as best we can place it in your words) that it has created with other souls still abiding within physical form. This phase sometimes takes longer than the first phase of distancing away from the physical vessel whose metabolic functions have ceased.

The speed or period of time that it takes is not predictable. It in no way reflects the degree of love or lack of love, but a highly individual soul-process of growth. And when the separation or the letting go of that attachment to the love connection, to the source of love, is resolved, the soul then moves further away.

As this progresses, the soul essence moves further and further from the vibration of human form into the state of unity where it becomes a part of the realm from which we are speaking to you now.

LINDA: What does the soul do after it moves away from its loved ones and its physical body?

ARIEL: The process that is taking place, that underlies all of these phases we have described, is a movement of consciousness away from the self-identified perspective that the soul lived through in its association with the physical body (what we have labeled *ego*) into its true association with the unity. It is not an instantaneous phenomenon in your reference of time. It evolves at the pace and in the method that a specific soul requires. It is, in essence, a forgetting of who you were and a remembering of who you are that moves gradually, as all that was known from the framework of a specific life is gradually released, and all that is known throughout this universe, throughout this realm, is remembered.

> *It is . . . a forgetting*
> *of who you were*
> *and a remembering*
> *of who you are. . . .*

LINDA: **Is it reasonable, then, to state that a soul departs from the deceased physical body and becomes absorbed by the unity you speak of?**

ARIEL: We inevitably use far too many words and never come close to describing what you are seeking to know. Allow us to use a metaphor, which we have used in many cases with many people we have attempted to teach, that may satisfy your desire to know more than we can tell you. If you equate the soul in the physical body to the solid form of water, namely ice; and you equate to the liquid form of water the steps or phases of the soul's transition out of the physical body; and you equate this [angelic] realm to the gaseous form of water, namely steam—in any of its forms, the substance that you call water is what we equate to soul.

At death the vibration begins to rise, much analogous to the vibration of water with temperature beginning to rise. Over time, and depending on the vibrational change and the characteristics of what you call atmosphere, the ice will turn to liquid, then to gas and will eventually disappear. Yet the water is still water. The part that we cannot convey adequately to you is that with water, the molecules dissipate. The soul, although rising in vibration and "moving from solid to liquid to gas," has consciousness that maintains essence even though the physical form is not solid.

LINDA: **Does the soul remember who it was, the life it had as a human, the people who loved it?**

ARIEL: As it moves away from the physical body with which it has such a close association, yes, it does remember. In this phase, the soul is drawn to, and often moves to be with, those who have been the recipients of its love and the sources of its love. Again using our analogy of water, as the soul moves beyond liquid into gas, the love, the vibration of love that has been received throughout the life, is in essence kept and preserved.

The one thing you get to take with you when you leave the physical body is all of the love you had gathered during your life. Pain, fear, guilt, hatred and similar feelings are still somewhat present in this liquid phase that we talk to you about, but they do not pass into the state analogous to steam.

The one thing
you get to take with you
when you leave the physical body
is all of the love you had gathered
during your life.

LINDA: **I watched a TV show called "Angel Stories," and there was a young man who had lost his sister and was angry. He asked why his sister who had so much promise should be taken by God. He described a communication with an angel who said that sometimes God takes the brightest flower in the garden. The man did not ask why. I ask, first, is this true, and if it is true, why?**

ARIEL: Once again, your question has within it a belief, a statement, which we would like to address first.

The very nature of the question speaks of a concept you have that a human life, that the human experience, is the most important aspect of consciousness as viewed by what you call God. We wish to be clear that human life is an indescribably rich opportunity for a soul. The infinite complexities of the magnificent sensory and intellectual treasure of the human body with its array of sensory experiences—smells, tastes, touch, sights, sounds—and indeed its thoughts, are a most precious gift.

But your question, the way it was stated, has the belief that this is the most important of what you call God's manifestations. No matter how bright or brilliant, no matter how promising or loved a person is in a lifetime, if her soul moves from that lifetime to join the unity of the divine, make no mistake that she is called, moved, to something far more important—not only for the evolution and the growth of the specific soul that is having the experience of death, but in the infinity of this universe, in the complexities that you cannot even begin to fathom of this realm and the workings of this force that you identify as God. It is only the loss that it represents in the lives left behind that is clouding the ability to see what is really happening. If we look from the perspective of that particular soul, what you label as this "premature, untimely, unnecessary, uncalled-for death" is indeed signaling the most high honor that a soul may have.

If her soul moves from that lifetime
to join the unity of the divine . . .
she is called . . . to something
far more important. . . .

All the motivation for the question you raised, and that infinitely many people have raised after having lost a loved one, is basically, Why? Why do I have to live without the person I have loved and who has loved me? Why do I have to have this person removed from my life? Why can't I enjoy this wonderful, loving person more? It indeed comes from a form of selfishness. And it is completely mistaken, because the glory and the honor that a soul has in being called from human form back to this realm, there are no words in your language that could describe the honor and the magnificence that act contains.

※

After the end of this session, we talked about our feelings and sensations while receiving Ariel's message about the death process.

LINDA: **I spent the past hour of our work listening to Ariel's answers with chills in my body. And you spent the time speaking Ariel's words through your tears. What were you experiencing that made you cry?**

STEVAN: *Something magnificent and extraordinary happened. I don't even remember what question you asked. As Ariel was answering, I received a visual image. What I witnessed—what I think so many people who have had near-death experiences perceive—was basically a conically shaped beam of light. In other words, a tunnel. The focus was entirely on what was inside of it. It became absolutely brilliant the further I looked into it. The level of love was indescribable. I can't even put a label on it. As I projected my awareness further and further toward the brilliant end of the tunnel, the level of love present was so overwhelming I could not contain the tears. It was almost like a state of love and joy at the same time, and yet I did not have a sense of passing into the light beam. I just had a sense of looking into it, being an outside observer.*

I think what Ariel was doing, and again words fail, was providing me with an experience. So to try to answer your question, I was basically given the experience of looking into that tunnel.

LINDA: **Is this the first time you've seen that?**

STEVAN: *Yes.*

LINDA: **You feel you were seeing what people who have near-death experiences see?**

STEVAN: *Yes, but there was one difference. From the little reading I've done on this subject, people report a sensation of moving into that tunnel and traveling through it, whereas I looked in but I didn't enter it.*

✳

Suicide

LINDA: **Could you share with us an example of the karmic result of suicide?**

ARIEL: We regrettably cannot give you an example or simple formula that you seek. This experience, this phenomenon that you know as suicide in which an individual, a soul, feels trapped in what we label *hell* with no escape, no possibility of exit, is perhaps one of the saddest experiences of the human condition. It, along with this phenomenon you so easily label as *war*, is the most difficult to fathom from this [angelic] realm of perception.

Suicide . . . is perhaps
one of the saddest experiences
of the human condition.

The pain, the suffering that we see inside the consciousness of one who quite ironically so fears death that he takes his own life to avoid his fear, is very, very difficult to witness. It is extremely difficult to be impotent in helping, supporting or preventing a person intent on suicide. For the very consciousness of one who is so lost, so separate, so isolated, so trapped inside his own fear as to consider suicide is unreachable. There is no connection, no opening through which we can touch his life.

There is no . . . opening
through which we can touch his life.

The karmic consequence of suicide, the future experience as well as the journey from the ending of metabolic life away from that physical body toward the unity, is indescribably complex and cannot be modeled in a way that you would understand. There is no linear or pre-ordained way that you can predict what will transpire, for the process of projecting the karmic consequence of any act from one lifetime to the next is highly individual. Each soul's journey is absolutely unique and distinct, and the overall dynamic process that you know as life, so complex and ever moving and changing, is unpredictable in a sense that could be fathomed by the human mind.

LINDA: **Are there words that a fellow human could share with someone contemplating suicide?**

ARIEL: A person contemplating suicide is in a state of mind, a state of consciousness, that is so desperate and so trapped that he is difficult, at best, to reach by those in this realm or in your realm. The mind's very isolation, its very separateness, its very self-feeding state of fear causes the person who is experiencing it to reject help, support or guidance from others. An added difficulty is that seeing and experiencing someone who is so troubled, who is so on the verge of despair, is very difficult for others to witness, for it taps into their own primal level of separateness and exacerbates their own levels of fear.

The ego's goal is to reassure itself that it is indeed separate, it does exist, it is an individual and unique entity. In the case of a person contemplating suicide, the despair, the degree of separateness and the experience of the depths of hell created by the ego have grown without bound. The ego has succeeded in creating pain, struggle, confusion and fear. It has reached a point of utter collapse.

Just as we are ineffectual in breaking into a mind that is so totally closed, you too may be ineffectual in breaking through. However, as the ego becomes overwhelmingly lost, the possibility exists in that moment, if the consciousness can just let it in, of opening up through prayer and petition, through beseeching of divinity, of unity of God, for grace. At that moment, the most powerful of mystical unions and shifts can take place. Prayer and the opening to this realm is the one true solution to the problem—not the prayer of simply reciting rhetoric or going through routines or mindlessly chanting, but earnest, heartfelt prayer petitioning for help.

As the ego becomes overwhelmingly lost . . .
the most powerful of mystical unions
and shifts can take place.

The moment in which the separate self feels the height of its separateness and its fear is ironically when it is most available to meet the divine directly. For in that moment when the entire magnificent house of cards the ego has created—which is now so ominous and so overwhelming that death is the only escape—is ready to collapse, the ego could move aside with such force that overwhelming grace would fill the individual.

In that moment we could literally infuse the love and the magnitude of our realm into the very heart of this person near suicide and, in that moment, completely heal all of his fear. The challenge is to find the mechanism, the way, the words, the support, the encouragement that will allow that final collapse and that final reaching out to take place. For unless a human consciousness reaches to the divine, as in prayer, the wall of fear cannot be penetrated.

Unless a human consciousness
reaches to the divine,
as in prayer,
the wall of fear
cannot be penetrated.

Birth

LINDA: At what point in the development of a human fetus does the soul enter a human body?

ARIEL: We delay in answering the question because our overriding objective is to provide light and knowledge—to allow people to see great insights from our perspective without attacking, making wrong or in any way condemning those who have other viewpoints. We feel a great deal of sensitivity to the question you have asked, for it has been a subject creating much pain and much controversy and much karmic energy in the experience of your recent times.

The specific area in which we have great sensitivity to answering your question is the tremendous plight of healing and karmic energy that is being enacted upon judgments of abortion and ending the life of a fetus while inside its mother's womb, and the raging controversies in some belief systems over the point at which a soul attaches itself to the fetus.

We will address this question at another time when we have prepared a way of answering which will both satisfy your question, your need to know, and satisfy our objective.

✳

Linda asked Ariel a related question months later.

LINDA: **What happens before a person is born? Can you describe the journey from the celestial realm back down to a newborn baby?**

ARIEL: As with the process at the other end of the journey of the life, we simultaneously cannot describe it to you and yet will attempt to describe it to you.

The essence that we referred to as *soul* is, in your terminology, eternal. The soul evolves by learning, growing, being loved and learning to love. There are many complexities to a specific way in which growth occurs before birth. The soul works with others embodied in human form who will ultimately go by the title of *parents*. The soul reaches a level of understanding or, if you will, communication, which the potential parents are often unaware of. An understanding is made as to the joining of that soul with the others through the process that you call *birth*. Prior to the actual conception of the most indescribable miracle that you call a child, everything is in perfect accord with the soul.

_____

The soul works with others
embodied in human form
who will ultimately go by
the title of parents.

_____

However, everything is not necessarily in perfect accord with the personalities and egos of the parents and others involved. It is often very difficult for those in the role of parents to experience, for example, an early death of the physical body of their child, whether it be through what you call miscarriage, fetal death or the termination of pregnancy by natural causes or by externally influenced causes such as abortion.

We wish to convey none of your human judgment on the rightness or wrongness of these actions for this is not our domain. But we wish you to know in your heart, from the perspective of soul, that these are not random experiences. These are no different a growth opportunity, a spiritual lesson, a divine experience, than living (in your frame of reference) a great many years, a full life, and the physical body dying of what you call natural causes.

Specific souls in their evolution and growth require different experiences. Each experience is complete for that particular soul at that particular time. There are no experiences extra, no experiences missing.

✳

LINDA: I remember your awareness of the sensitivity regarding *when* the soul enters the human body and I wasn't trying to again ask the abortion-related question. I was trying to get a picture of what goes on in the celestial realm before birth, similar to the way you were describing the time after death.

ARIEL: It can be crudely equated to reversing the process that we described earlier. The stage of water as gas in our analogy is equated to this absolutely miraculous interrelationship of the souls involved.

As the soul destined to be the child connects to the physical body—beginning at this point of conception where the miracle of new life is rapidly expanding—the soul moves through the phase we described as liquid earlier, and into more and more association with the physical vessel which is growing and expanding and developing. As the physical body grows, this fetus grows and develops. The phase moves more into the solid, and the soul attaches more and more of its connection and identity to this physical being, able to radiantly live within the physical vibration, yet maintaining extraordinary clarity of connection to this realm.

LINDA: The soul's involvement in the birth process sounds like a gradual strengthening of the connection accompanied by a gradual departure from the celestial unity. Is that correct?

ARIEL: This is essentially correct, yes. The movement between the physical and the divine realm is not (in your reference of time) instantaneous, either in leaving or entering. It is a process which, as your phenomenon of time takes place, moves at a rate dependent on the particular soul and the particular circumstance.

Life on Earth

Health

LINDA: Do people get sick because they are not going according to the universe's plan for them?

ARIEL: Sickness is very complicated. It is so misunderstood by people. Sickness can be a warning—a warning that you are living far from your truth, a warning that you are ignoring tremendous feelings, especially fear and stress. But sickness can also be the weight one lifts. There are sicknesses, illnesses, that are diagnosed in order to wake someone up—to snap him out of being so stuck, so imprisoned in fear; to awaken him in a spiritual sense to a higher part of his life. The ego has many ways it can be coached or coaxed into growth, into sharing the limelight with its divinity. Fear of sickness and death is a very, very powerful force.

LINDA: We use the term alternative healing or alternative medicine to refer to nontraditional methods of healing the body. Do you have a comment on the value of these approaches?

ARIEL: In truth, all the approaches you speak of are alternatives. Each one is an alternative to the true focus and the true mechanism of healing. To understand this answer, it is important to know what is being healed. All of what you consider needing to be healed, all "dis-ease," or disharmony of the human body, mind, emotions or spirit, are simply manifestations of human beings' limitation in connection to the unity of this universe in which they live.

All are manifestations of ways in which this idea of separateness that humans insist on having is allowed to run too freely and allowed to take such importance that it cuts off the person from his true source. It is the true source, the harmony and connection to the unity of this universe and the energy therein, that is the source of all health and hence the source of all healing.

It must be understood that any healing that takes place happens within the individual. All healing, no matter in what form, is what you might label *self-healing*. All of these things that you describe are, in truth, alternatives to self-healing—the true form of healing. Each one has its perfect place. This is why each one has been created. Sometimes when the individual has been distant from his very source for a significant length of time, such disharmony or disease will manifest within the physical body or the emotional body to the point where intervention, outside help, is needed.

---

*All of these things
that you describe
are, in truth,
alternatives to self-healing—
the true form of healing.*

In truth, all intervention is a support to self-healing. All intervention, whether it be from what you label *traditional* or what you label *alternative* or even what you label *spiritual* forms of healing, are simply devices that allow the person to be brought back within the range where this self-healing can take place.

Even when a surgeon removes material from the body or reconnects tissue to itself, these are simply mechanical acts, acts that are in and of themselves great marvels and, in some cases, great mysteries even to the ones who are performing them. But it is ultimately the person who heals, who takes that support and within whose body the soul manifests the knitting together of the tissues, the muscles that have been severed by a surgeon's scalpel. The more that a healing mechanism can support the natural union with the nature of the soul's harmony and the connection to unity, the more it will support the person in his self-healing.

The more that a healing mechanism
can support the natural union
with the nature of the soul's harmony . . .
the more it will support the person
in his self-healing.

Each being, each person, has a natural affinity or openness to a certain method of healing. Each method of healing provides a technique that is supportive for certain people. As a result, in this marvelous mosaic of life, there is a healing approach, a support, a tool, for every type of person. What will work for one may not work for the other. But, in all cases, the most important healing happens not at the surface level where symptoms are fixed, but at the deepest level where the source of the problem is corrected. And that can only happen deep within the individual.

There is a healing approach . . .
for every type of person.
What will work for one
may not work for the other.

You have seen too often how a disease will appear. It will be eradicated by the most complex of medical science procedures, only to reappear after a period of what you call time. The symptom was treated but the problem was not dealt with as part of the medical procedure. Likewise, within the world of what you call alternatives, symptoms are sometimes corrected and yet the underlying problem remains, so in time the symptoms reappear.

The more that a therapeutic approach combines dealing with a manifest symptom that is visible and interrupting the harmony of the person's life while balancing the person's true inner nature with the unification of his spiritual connection, the more that approach will provide a total solution of supporting true and permanent self-healing within the individual.

LINDA: Do you have a comment on organ replacement such as heart, kidney and lung transplants?

ARIEL: These are extensions of the alternatives that we spoke of earlier. They are most remarkable and marvelous ways in which you can correct the symptom of that disharmony or disease within a soul as it has become manifest through the physical vessel called its body. But they are again simply methods used to undo temporarily the damage done by the real disease within the person. Such procedures give the soul more time to correct and heal the real problems.

---

*Such procedures give the soul
more time to correct and heal
the real problems.*

Sometimes, when a person experiences a near-fatal heart attack or faces death because a donor organ is not available, a deep, deep healing of the core problem can take place within the person. And then miraculously—or so you think—the donor organ appears. That soul is never the same again. In these extreme situations, the soul is often pushed to its very edge. It is a time of great inner reflection, often a time of great growth, spiritual union and connection. And it is sometimes the very facing of one's mortality that is the catalyst for the final healing of that which needed to be healed at a soul level. The organ simply allows the physical body to continue that soul's journey for a period of time in which the real, deep, deep inner spiritual healing can unfold in that life.

It is sometimes the very facing
of one's mortality
that is the catalyst for the final healing. . . .

LINDA: **When somebody receives a major organ transplant such as a heart or kidney, do they also take on some physical or personality characteristics of the donor, perhaps through cell memory?[1]**

ARIEL: There is that capacity, and yet it is much the same as what we tried to describe in the process of death. If you will recall, in the early stage of the process of death there is a clinging at some level to the physical body, a clinging to the deep association with the physical vibration that the soul has known. This clinging is supported by the life in the cells themselves which contain what you may call an imprint, or a pattern, of the essence of many of the physical embodiments characteristic of that soul.

Even though the soul may have disassociated or disconnected from that physical being, the life within that organ, tissue

---

1. Question from Kathi Dunn, Hayward, Wisconsin.

or cells being brought into serving another soul in another body can often convey what you might call transient or temporary phenomena—phenomena that are more closely associated with preferences of ego—likes, dislikes or mannerisms. It is not a merging, not a taking of the essence or part of the essence of one soul and adding it to another, for this cannot occur. But you have seen in the reactions of those who have experienced such transplants that certain likes or dislikes which were common to the ego expression of the donor can manifest overnight in the recipient.

It is not a merging . . . of the essence . . . of one soul
and adding it to another,
for this cannot occur.

❋

LINDA: **If people learn not to fear death because they believe death is not an ending but a next step, perhaps they may not feel the need to spend thousands of dollars for medical intervention in their last weeks of life trying to buy yet another day of life. Do you agree?**

ARIEL: Again, the question within the question. The person who spends hundreds of thousands of dollars or depletes an entire life's savings attempting to maintain life for another week, another month, another year can be perfectly in accord with his experience. That particular soul operating in perfect truth and perfect harmony may be doing exactly what it is divinely guided to do. Do not underestimate the value of it. We are cautious in the words we use to describe this for we do not wish to make death trivial.

Death is not an option to placate and satisfy ego preference. Do not look at life as a suit of clothes the soul wears. If you dislike a particular suit of clothes, you change into another which you like better. And if that one doesn't suit you, then it is changed again. We have seen all too often in cultures that believe in reincarnation—widespread cultures that you would call *oriental*—that when children especially, who are not spiritually mature, find that they are not pretty enough, that they inhabit a body that isn't beautiful or they have parents who are not wealthy or the circumstances of their lives are not what they wished, they wanted better—they simply kill themselves, hoping to come back in better circumstances.

Do not look at life
as a suit of clothes the soul wears.

This is a total misunderstanding. Human life is absolutely the most precious gift that you have. Death is only to be surrendered to when, despite your desire to stay in your body, to stay alive—even if for but another breath—you hear, you feel, you sense the will of God and you are called from your experience of being human. This is the time when surrender to death should take place.

Each person who has faced this moment knows beyond words, beyond ideas, that it is her time. For she is being invited and beckoned into an ever increasing level of love, passing into what your human mind might see as an ever increasing brilliance of light, moving to levels of love that you, from your human perspective, have never experienced. Such death is simply a letting go and a moving toward or moving into that love. The death that we spoke of before as suicide is not an invitation into this love, not of the form we are speaking now. It is an escape from the hell of a specific life.

And as difficult as it is for those who must watch impotently or helplessly a loved one suffering in pain with disease, make no mistake, souls do not grow and evolve based on what's comfortable or uncomfortable. Through the pain of cancer, the spiritual growth within the heart and soul of that very being who is afflicted can be immeasurable. And so long as that soul knows—knows in its heart that it is not its time—then working and struggling and fighting to stay alive can produce the most powerful evolution. And yet at the moment that the soul knows it is being beckoned and called, invited and embraced by the open arms of this divine light, it simply lets go of its human form and is drawn into the invitation that God creates.

---

*So long as that soul knows . . .
it is not its time—
then working and struggling and fighting
to stay alive
can produce the most powerful evolution.*

LINDA: **What is the purpose of epidemics like AIDS or, from an earlier century, the bubonic plague that wipe out large numbers of people?**

ARIEL: The purpose of such, what you call catastrophic epidemics, is multifaceted. We can attempt to explain to you some of its purpose. However, some of it we cannot, for there is nothing in your conceptual model that would enable you to understand it.

The piece that is most easily understandable is that throughout your concept of time, such outbreaks have brought devastation of such proportion that they could not be ignored. Likewise, throughout your time, outbreaks of tremendous love and joy, tremendous healing and harmony have occurred. In both cases, they are events that cannot be ignored and thus make a permanent change in the lives of all who witness them. Epidemics of disease cause an enormous fear and sense of frailty to be experienced by people who are aware of and potentially exposed to these diseases. As a result, they serve as a vast opportunity to grow spiritually, to grow into an unfoldment of more of their lives' purpose.

Oftentimes people as a collection, what you might call cultures or societies, evolve away from their truth, away from their spiritual essence, and are locked into living a life based on the fulfillment of the ego. Epidemics of the magnitude you have spoken about serve to awaken. They awaken consciousness, awaken souls from their slumber and their misguided lives.

Whenever [a catastrophic] event . . . occurs,
know that the population is being asked to change.

Not only the ones who are touched by the disease, but also those who witness it, can be freed from the backwater eddy they existed in and propelled back into the very flow of their lives. Whenever an event, either positive or negative as you may judge it, occurs, know that the population is being asked to change. It is being invited, if not forced, to wake up from its stagnation. The growth of your species and the spiritual unfoldment of your entire planet always moves forward from such disasters.

The growth of your species . . .
always moves forward
from such disasters.

✳

LINDA: But AIDS started out in and continues to target the homosexual community in particular. Is there a reason?

ARIEL: The community you speak of, the one you label as homosexual, this community above all required a tremendous call to awaken. The souls of these people have been afflicted with much pain—in part from society, in part from the church and in part from government. Within this group called homosexual, there are those who are in the perfect expression of their souls' nature within this life. They experience the light of love shining forth most brightly when they are in a relationship with another soul who happens to be inhabiting a body of the same gender. This group has been stifled, condemned and, as a result, lived out of harmony with their true souls' nature.

They experience the light of love
shining forth most brightly
when they are in a relationship with another soul
who happens to be inhabiting a body
of the same gender.

The virus of HIV and the complications and life-threatening consequences known as AIDS served as an unavoidable call to stop the self-destructive behavior of suppressing their truth and to bring forth the life-promoting behavior of these people. Many a soul has come into positive fulfillment of its life's purpose by contracting this virus which indeed can, what you may think, end its life prematurely.

This virus is not a punishment. This is not an attempt to further execute what ego consciousness has already so perfectly executed against this group. This is a very personal and direct invitation for every member of the homosexual community, as well as members of the heterosexual community, to wake up to who they truly are and to express that to the world. It serves you no purpose to know in your heart what your true nature is, to know in your heart what brings you closest to the divine, to know in your heart why you came here and what you are supposed to do, and then to hide it, to fear it, to feel guilty over it.

Now indeed this virus, while seen by some, from an ego perspective, as the perfect expression of punishment upon a condemned group, is in truth the most magnificent of blessings upon a group that required such a force to help them avoid self-condemnation and holding back self-unfoldment as they have been doing. What will follow from this wakeup call will be a powerful and positive shift in the consciousness, in the hearts and in the souls of the entire population of your planet.

This is a very personal and direct invitation
for every member of the homosexual community,
as well as members of the heterosexual community,
to wake up to who they truly are
and to express that to the world.

✳

Homosexuality

LINDA: **The gay community seems to have special challenges in their lives, both societal and medical. What could possibly be the nature of their experience from the past that is leading them to have the challenges they are facing today?**

ARIEL: The unfoldment of this energy that we are labeling karmic is not what your mind would call linear in that an infinite variety of circumstances or needs could lead to the experience that you label homosexuality, complete with, in some cases, its great difficulties and great struggles.

There are, from a perspective of the spiritual soul-level journey through a lifetime, many situations that can inflict what an ego might view as pain and difficulty, yet what a soul may view as enormous opportunity to develop, expand, learn, grow and evolve. You have identified a category that is visibly challenged.

Also visibly challenged are those who have an experience of sexual abuse, incest or rape; those who have been abandoned at birth through a process of adoption; those who have a physical handicap; or those who have a mental handicap. The opportunity to have difficulty does not even require any external form, for you need not look far to find those who, from an emotional or a physical standpoint, have everything that the human spirit could ask for, and yet their lives are filled with struggle and challenge.

There are many ways in which karmic unfoldment can manifest at a specific point in your time and space in a life that, possibly through its difference and possibly through its commonality, is filled with rich opportunities for tremendous soul evolution.

LINDA: **Is there a karmic root to homosexuality?**

ARIEL: Everything that is experienced in human form is influenced by, a reflection of, or a result of karma. This experience that has been labeled *homosexuality* is no different from the experience labeled *heterosexuality* in terms of its karmic consequence or karmic manifestation and unfoldment. In truth, you are extremely fortunate to abide even for a brief time inside the vessel that you call a human body.

Everything that is experienced
in human form
is influenced by,
a reflection of,
or a result of karma.

This most rare and wonderful experience is indeed nothing more than karma manifest in a physical form at a juncture of what you refer to as time and space. So, all that ever has been within your human world and all that ever will be is a continuation of the unfoldment of this karmic energy at each point in time and space. Your very life is one such time/space point of karmic unfoldment.

So, yes, this homosexuality, heterosexuality, asexuality or any form it takes is a juncture point and is a most glorious unfoldment of karmic life. It is only the ego's judgment of one unfoldment in comparison to another that would cause anyone to miss viewing the unmistakable truth as truth.

It is easy when living in human form, with so many rich experiences, so much sensory information, and with the illusion of yourself as separate and distinct from all others, to be overwhelmed. And, all too often, this state of being overwhelmed can cultivate fear. When fear is combined with the idea that you are a separate individual, different from all others, it is quite easy for you to be drawn to those whose karmic unfoldment along your time and space experience is similar to that of your own.

Your wonderfully cute idea of "safety in numbers" is an attempt that those with similar karmic unfoldment make to overcome the fear created when they are overwhelmed by the human sensory experience. As such, they sometimes view with judgment those having a karmic experience, an unfoldment different from their own, as being worse than or better than their own. The unfoldment is no better or worse. There is no good or bad other than that which you apply to it.

᠁

Tragedy

LINDA: **So many people have tragedies in their lives. Is it all part of growth?**

ARIEL: It is again only you with this idea, this ego, that labels events as *tragedy* or *miracle*. If you could see them as we do, without judgment, with a very broad perspective, and with the truth of how this process of incarnation works, they are simply experiences. As an example, to one person, drinking a cup of coffee can be a treat, tasting delicious, aromatic and savory, while to another it can be a cruel form of punishment, tasting bitter, strong and vile. It is the same coffee in both cases, just the human judgment is different.

Consider the person whose house is destroyed, the person whose child is killed, the person who suffers terribly the loss of his loved one to cancer and is filled with pain over the loss. Metaphorically, these can be viewed as very heavy weights on a barbell. In these situations, the ego of the afflicted person did not consciously choose to lift that barbell. But make no mistake, the soul specifically planned the experience.

It is as though the soul could choose for you to build muscles, but the ego doesn't know about the plan. And one day you are forced at gunpoint to lift incredible weights, which you do, and the muscles grow. The only difference is that if the ego knew about it and agreed to it, it would be harmonious and filled with pleasure. If the ego didn't know about it and thought it was being done *to* you, you would be complaining bitterly, seeking retribution. And yet in the end, the same amounts of weight would have been lifted and the same muscles would grow.

Nothing is by accident.

The burden of inhabiting a human body is that the ego believes that it controls the universe. It believes that it is God. And it sees these things—the accident, the misfortune, the missed opportunity, the betrayals, all these things that are judged as negative— as punishment or misfortune, as *bad*. Indeed, to the soul, it is no more a misfortune than the weightlifting metaphor.

There is nothing that you experience in life, that your ego judges as good or bad, that is not something that you yourself, at a soul level, have specifically requested. Nothing is by accident.

Environment

LINDA: **Do you have comments about the effect humans are having on the health and longevity of our planet?**

ARIEL: First, we would like to offer some guidance to those who are so powerfully affecting, in what you categorize as a negative way, the health of the planet, and that is quite simply to be very careful. The planet you are dwelling on is quite capable of defending itself and will defend itself if brought to a point of endangerment. There is no need for concern about the planet.

What is often (again in that myopic viewpoint of the human mind) not recognized is that the very planet upon which you live is, in essence, a living being. It is filled with the consciousness of the unity of God. It operates in ways that are only beginning to be understood by the human mind through more advanced scientific observation. It has operated in such a way far longer than those who are attempting to profit from its resources and who are ignoring its well-being have lived on its surface. It will operate in a self-healing way, maintaining balance, long after they are viewing, from this realm, what has been done.

The Earth is a most precious element in your lives. It is a living being very much as you are a living being. And yet it is designed by its Creator to fulfill, for an indefinite period of time, every need, every physical, emotional and energetic need, that every human being dwelling on its surface could ever want. If it were not for the fear-based need of the human ego to stockpile large quantities of energy—either as wealth, food or other resources—for potential future use, everything would be far more in balance than it is at this time.

*The Earth . . . is a living being
very much as you are a living being.*

If you look to the realm of nature, the realm of animals, there is always stockpiling, always the need for pulling together abundance and for defending territories to guarantee sufficient food. But it is all in balance, for even those who, in dormant periods you call *hibernation*, stockpile foods, the very stockpiling, in many cases, leads to the inadvertent planting and growing of many trees from seeds and nuts that were buried away and misplaced or forgotten. It is all part of a renewal plan where nothing is harmed and everything flows in perfect accordance with everything else.

Yet, there is little that vast sums of money can accomplish

when they sit in computer memory or in vaults. If it were flowing, as it was designed to do, it could correct all of the imbalance and all of the harm that acquiring it has caused to this most precious and loving of beings that you inhabit. But make no mistake, you have even developed some basic, albeit somewhat naive, understanding of what we are speaking of—a phenomenon that you call *Gaia*—and yet. . . .

LINDA: **Gaia? I don't know that word.**

ARIEL: If you research, you will find theories about the operation of Earth as a living being that have been labeled with this name we have given you. And yet it is far more complex than what has been understood. What has been understood is, in essence, correct, but this Earth upon which you live will tolerate only so much destruction, and when it becomes threatened, when its own survival is at all at risk, it will eliminate the source of its danger, as do all living beings.

---

*Earth . . . will tolerate
only so much destruction. . . .*

This is not intended to prophesy doom or gloom, but is simply a statement of pure fact that, while you are not critically close to causing such a reaction from this living being, this Earth, you are seeing in your own lifetime some of the effects of the devastation and the consequences the Earth will produce to counteract such devastation. If, in the long term, it comes down to a test between the survival of the Earth and the survival of what you know as humans, the Earth will survive.

If . . . it comes down to a test
between the survival of the Earth
and the survival of . . . humans,
the Earth will survive.

❈

LINDA: Can you give us an example of the Earth defending it-self? What would we see?

ARIEL: The human organism is rather fragile. The Earth has total ability to regulate its atmospheric conditions. It has tremendous ability to regulate the temperature on the surface that you live on. It has a great deal of ability to control how much of its surface is covered with water and how much with land. It has great freedom to control environments that you label as tropical or desert. Humans have very little tolerance to changes in these factors. And these factors are not permanent, not guaranteed to remain as they have been. The Earth as a living being has the ability to control and manipulate these factors, and if the very survival of the Earth were ever threatened by the destruction, greed or selfishness of humanity, factors would be changed such that humanity would not be able to survive on its surface.

If the very survival of the Earth
were ever threatened . . .
factors would be changed such that
humanity would not be able to survive
on its surface.

❈

LINDA: **Cataclysmic geographical changes have been predicted by the end of this century. Do you share this expectation?**

ARIEL: There are many in your realm and in our realm who experience truth through a filter, depending on the height and degree of their vibration. The ones you speak of channel wisdom and divinity through clouded filters. They are the doomsayers, the prophesiers. Prophecies of cataclysmic events have existed, have raged, for all time. What they speak of is so focused on fear, so focused on the negative, that it comes through as unspeakable disaster, calamity. And yet others who take the same information and bring it through in love and in clarity see changes happening, but without the emphasis and with nowhere near the intensity that these doomsayers use. They see that any change you might judge as negative is all part of a very positive process of evolution and growth. So that's the long answer.

The short answer is "no." The cataclysm they talk about will not happen. But, yes, changes will happen to the Earth that will make part of what they say true. But the intensity will not be the same as what they speak of.

> *The cataclysm they talk about*
> *will not happen.*

LINDA: **But many of the predictions, especially those of Nostradamus, have come true. Please comment.**

ARIEL: What we wish you to focus on is not the accuracy of prophecy but the motivation of prophecy. Prophecy can have one of two underlying motivations—love or fear.

Even in your time, there are some who prophesy the negative, who publish books, who publish guides, who even have

survival techniques on where to go and how to avoid the cataclysm that they see. You must discern whether their motivation
is one of enlightening, helping and saving others or making
money and gaining power out of their fear and out of other people's fear that resonates with them.

We have chosen you to share our message because your goal
is not one of instilling fear but instilling strength. Yours is not
one of disempowering others by your knowledge of the realm
that others cannot yet touch, and scaring them so they must follow you. Yours comes from giving them a gift that will empower
their lives and make them strong. Throughout all time, there
have been both types of uses of this power.

LINDA: **Do you see the shape of the United States changing
and California and other states falling into the ocean?**

ARIEL: No. This is a prophecy based on fear-driven interpretations of oceans rising.

LINDA: **One of the great mysteries of our planet is the Bermuda
Triangle, an area off the eastern coast of the United States that
seems to swallow up ships and planes. Are there any insights
you could share with us about this phenomenon?**

ARIEL: We wish to once again remind you that our goal in answering your questions is to teach understanding and to convey
knowledge that is important for us to convey. That is part of our
mission, if you will. While there is much you have asked in your
question, only part of it do we choose to answer.

The most important aspect of this phenomenon you describe
as the Bermuda Triangle is the opportunity it creates to evoke

the challenging element of human consciousness called fear. Since it is a phenomenon not understood fully by the human mind, it is—like many other such phenomena—filled with fear and confusion.

It serves as a metaphor for much broader questions that manifest in many, many aspects of the human journey: how to take that which is intellectually not knowable, intellectually unfathomable, and produce from that a sense of understanding or knowing that will allow you to navigate in your life. Each of you has at one time or another in your journey encountered your own personal version of this phenomenon. You have encountered times in your life when devices you use to navigate don't function, times when confusion exists, times when your bearings are lost. These are times when tremendous fear can be generated. These are times when you enter into your own personal Bermuda Triangle. At these times, all ego-based navigation tools that you rely upon begin to fail. These are times destined and directed toward cultivating the aptitude of discernment [i.e., determining God's will for you] and the aptitude of knowing that which transcends this sense of separation [i.e., making contact with a higher consciousness].

You are each equipped with many inner tools which, until you are called upon to use them, you may not even know exist. And when in your own life, in your own journey, you find yourself entering into one of these Bermuda Triangle–like domains where the basis of navigation of your life fails, it is a time in which you are being not so subtly asked to discover and use your tools and talents in a way that will allow you to navigate safely. Appreciate that upon returning from such experiences, the tendency is often to revert to the more self-serving ways of navigating in your life. However, all knowledge gained at the level of soul is permanent and is not forgotten.

We appreciate that you asked a question about a specific phenomenon of your world's geography, and we even read into your question words you did not specifically ask about portals and gateways to other realms and dimensions. It is not in our interest to speak on those matters.

Animals and Plants

LINDA: There are what we call lower forms of life on this planet such as animals and plants. How do they fit into this mosaic of life?

ARIEL: Watch where you go. Again, there is no such thing as a higher or lower form of life. Life is life. There are different ways life expresses, different forms it takes, different levels of its own ability to perceive itself. But the moment-by-moment awareness of the present, the consciousness that exists in you, is identical to the moment-to-moment awareness that exists in a flower.

LINDA: You made a reference about man thinking he owns the animal kingdom.[2] Could you elaborate on that comment?

ARIEL: The specific point was to underscore the incorrect illusion of superiority in terms of the ability to follow one's divine direction in life. The very fact that man uses animals in so many ways—for pleasure from pets, for food, skins, antlers or other such physiological components that are prized—man seems to have developed a perception that these advanced forms of

---

2. Question, p. 264, "Our Selves"

consciousness known as animals are less important, less advanced, and are to be possessed, owned and done with as seen fit. Animals are often superior to humans in following the divine direction of their lives. They are open and willing to have instinct guide them in their life's journey. They are connected to the source of love of the universe and often demonstrate that love to each other.

Animals are often superior to humans
in following the divine direction. . . .

LINDA: I have pets I love. I give them a home. Is that a misuse of power?

ARIEL: The very nature of your question is your answer. You care for them. You feed and shelter them. But most importantly, you started with the principal operative—pets that you love. When an animal is given to and is openly received from this beautiful energy of love, that is not a violation of power or an imposing of will.

The actions that we speak of are where animals are controlled, dominated, killed, used, treated as material elements without love. It may be love of the money they produce or love of the specific elements that they may provide, but without a great deal of adoration or love for the specific animal.

LINDA: Do you communicate with animals?

ARIEL: The communication that exists between this realm and the category that you refer to as animals is very difficult to describe, for animals are in many cases unencumbered with the traits of personality and ideas of separateness that humans are encumbered with.

There is an ease, a simplicity, what we have referred to, in your words, as *knowing*. A communication takes place from the one universal mind of consciousness of this realm—imparting knowledge or understanding directly to the realm of animal. It is not filled with the translation into words, images or ideas that are more prevalent in the human interaction.

We have attempted in the past, in answering other questions, to use the concept of instinct with which the animal kingdom is so blessed in its ability to perceive and obey. There is a great deal of guidance and communication that takes place from this realm to the group that you have referred to as animals.

LINDA: **What happens when an animal dies?**

ARIEL: Simply put, it is not possible for us, in words and ways that you could really understand, to share that, and that said, we will attempt to use your words and ideas to convey this information.

The process is not dissimilar to the one that has been described in terms of human beings. The elements are very similar. The life force essence, or soul, of the particular animal is rooted and bonded in its connection to the physical body. And as we have attempted for human understanding to fragment pieces of a continuum into identifiable steps, there is a parallel with the animal world.

The first is this disassociation, or letting go, of a very, very close energetic attachment to the physical vessel that has been the source of such beautiful reception of information through the sense organs, and has been the vehicle through which much experience in the physical world has taken place.

There's also, as you yourself are aware, a great deal of love that animals are capable of giving, not only to each other of the same species, but even to those of other species.

Safety in the animal kingdom is of paramount importance in the ability to love and be loved. When there is safety, there is little encumbering the divine connection in the form of separate personality or separate sense of self. As a result, the level of love, especially to others of its own species where it feels a high degree of safety and association, can be extremely profound. In fact, it can even exceed in many cases the degree of love that can be experienced between two members of the human species. Just as in the continuing process of letting go that is experienced within humans, the process within the realm of animals involves letting go of the attachment, the connection, that is experienced heart-to-heart between members of groups or families of that species.

There's . . . a great deal of love
that animals are capable of giving. . . .

As this continues, there is less of a process of movement into the unity of this universe because there was less of the concept of self as separate and distinct. So the process, although it parallels the human in nature at a high level, has many specific subtle differences which are very difficult to describe in a way that your mind could comprehend. We hope this has helped answer your question.

✳

LINDA: **I look into my dog's eyes and wonder if an animal has a soul.**

ARIEL: We run into difficulty using your language and conceptual models to describe these aspects. Yes, in their own way, animals have souls. It is difficult to describe the nature of that soul as to its differences from the nature of the human soul.

But within this group of beings that you refer to as animals, each one has a spiritual essence attached to its physical being. Each one is in divine communion with God, but without ego-based concepts, names or labels for this experience. Each one is the embodiment of holiness in a physical form and the energetic essence—the connection to the divine—is brought down and attached to the physical body of the animal. It is correct to call this *soul*.

Many have used the terminology *group soul* or *collective soul* when referring to the soul of an animal. These people are attempting to model, using the human need to partition, that which does not readily fit the concept of partitioning or labeling—because an animal's consciousness has no ego. Their souls are not as separate or distinct as those of humans.

And yet, this indeed is not true, for all life essence has, in the realm of spirit from which we speak, the ability of unity simultaneously with distinctiveness. In other words, from your realm, you see souls merging with God yet keeping their own identity. And yet the paradox your mind has such problems grasping is the ability to be both totally unified and individual at the same time. We wish we could impart this knowledge in such a way that it would make sense to your mind, but it cannot be done.

❋

LINDA: **Your answer reminds me of when I was a little girl. I would ask my father questions and he would tell me, very much like you are telling me, that there are some things beyond my grasp that I will understand someday. Is there a parallel here?**

ARIEL: In a matter of parallel, the words that would often be offered to you are, "You will understand when you are older" or "You will understand when you grow up; then you will know." In a manner of speaking, quite simply put, you will understand and you will know after you have died.

You will understand and you will know
after you have died.

✳

LINDA: **Does a flower have a soul?**

ARIEL: Again, the word soul has many meanings based on its history and usage in your culture. In its truest and most pure sense, yes. But the soul of the plant does not have a self-identity. It does not know time. It does not know itself as being different from another plant. It does not label itself as prettier or better or worse or uglier than the next plant. It lives in this spontaneous cognition of moment-to-moment awareness, allowing pure creativity to unfold through it and manifest in it to, what a human might call, its heart's desire—each one manifesting a little differently according to its own true nature.

You may pray or think kindly toward a plant and its soul will respond. For the energy of love, the energy of God, can be given and communicated, sent and received, amongst all living things, even plants.

You may pray or think kindly
toward a plant
and its soul will respond.

LINDA: **Why did the dinosaurs die off as a species?**

Linda presented this question at the very beginning of the dialogue with Ariel when she was first starting to believe she had access to information from a source beyond Stevan. This question was followed by a long silence and then Stevan spoke.

STEVAN: **What I'm getting in response to your question is basically a block. I'm not receiving any information from Ariel.**

After a few minutes of silence, the connection was restored.

ARIEL: You [Linda] have a quest to understand, to have knowing, be it what happened to this species or what happens in your own life. It is not so much the answer that is important, but the process of acquiring the answer. And for many souls in your time, the process of acquisition of that answer is externally focused. "What happened to them?" is part of a process of developing the answer to the question "What is happening to me?" or "Who am I?"

And while for many lives your dinosaur question and its answer are important to their particular souls' journey, this question, although interesting, has no bearing on your particular life and your journey. There are many, many such questions on your planet, and each one has a select group of souls devoted to finding the answers. The answers, once they come, will be entertaining to you but will be *transformative* to them.

✳

Law

LINDA: **Do you have an opinion on the death penalty as a punishment in our criminal justice system?**

ARIEL: We don't have opinions. Humans have opinions.

We have words that we wish to offer surrounding this. You have several forms of death penalty in your culture. The one we think you spoke of refers to those perpetrators of violent crimes against society who are executed in prison. There's another form of death penalty that your society enacts. You call it *abortion*. Those two are so vivid, but there is a third, less vivid form of death penalty that occurs regularly.

The third category is one that is purposefully suppressed, taken out of the normal stream of conscious thought. It is the death penalty enacted toward those who are not wanted by society, those who are homeless or financially destitute.

So many people live with such abundance and affluence, choosing not to share but to hoard or save their abundance. The resulting by-product is a penalty of death for those who, for a myriad of reasons, cannot sustain life on their own. This indeed is a third category of penalty leading to death—specifically, the penalty of being outside the boundary of normal society.

In all cases, there are two facets in conflict. One is the soul-level facet—a facet of spiritual truth and spiritual unfoldment within a lifetime. There are, from a soul perspective, no mistakes, no errors. There are no chance happenings. Nothing is extra and nothing is left out. So from a perspective of a soul's evolution, these events that you label as penalties in your question are indeed not penalties as viewed by the soul. These are simply events.

There are, from a soul perspective,
no mistakes, no errors.
There are no chance happenings.
Nothing is extra
and nothing is left out.

The events, while they may have tremendous emotional content from the perspective of ego, are simply a transitional step, a piece of growth that soul experiences. And this is true whether it is a soul that inhabits a womb for a short period of time, bonding at a very, very deep level with its mother prior to its life in the physical form being terminated, or it belongs to a soul of one who has committed crimes deemed to be punishable by penalty of death.

These souls may be in a process of working through the karma they have created or are creating to be worked on in the future. The ultimate termination of the body's physical life as the result of that karma through a form of death penalty is the soul's own way of growing and evolving as part of the experience.

The judgment, the labeling and the tremendous passion we see that you have around this issue is important. It underscores the mixed nature of who you are. For if you were entirely the spiritual essence, entirely soul, there would be no judgment on these or any other aspects of life. All would just be, just as it is.

If you were, on the other hand, all ego without any soul or connection to the spiritual nature of your identity, then all would be simply judgment, simply right and wrong, simply what society or what group opinion at any point believes to be right or wrong. Life would be meant to be lived simply within the narrow confines of the established truth of right and wrong that has been agreed to at any moment in time by the people of your community.

And yet, you are neither one of these things completely. You are, indeed, the most precious and complex blend of ego and soul. As such, you are meant to grow through the tension and struggle that exists in the interface between those two worlds. These issues of such profound importance take on tremendous passion where people literally are willing to risk their lives in order to support their beliefs in the rightness or wrongness of these capital punishments. Even for those people who are so inflamed and so passionate on either side of this argument, it is part of their souls' growth, part of their spiritual journey.

So, we hope this information has answered what you sought in terms of an opinion, and we hope that it helps you understand the power and the importance of the topic you raised.

LINDA: **We have an elaborate criminal justice system and, yet, sometimes we feel that it doesn't work. People who are innocent are sometimes found guilty and people who commit terrible crimes go free. Some of us have a tough time understanding that. Could you give us something more than just "it's part of their path?" Could you help us understand how that comes to be?**

ARIEL: The dilemma you raise has many flavors, facets and forms in the world of being human, and it would be the work of an entire volume to accurately give you knowledge on this very complex question. But let us give you a beginning of an answer.

The crux of what we have tried through many answers and in many contexts to share with you is the dilemma that in human form you are given a gift—the ability to discern, to judge, to evaluate, to compare and contrast—which is the most precious of gifts and what separates you from other species in your world. However, when used incorrectly, it gives the ability to set one group against another, one viewpoint against another, us against them. There are many forms. Your judicial system is one of them. Your governments are another. Your international peace-keeping organizations are another. Your churches are another. Your societies are another.

Ways in which the human need for right versus wrong, good versus bad, innocent versus guilty are played out are part of the unfathomable challenge and unfathomable gift of being human. You are faced with the most interesting tightrope to walk. On the one hand, each of these systems has a very important purpose— to bring about ethical, moral and harmonious actions of its participants, such that they may carry forth in a harmonious and guided way the fulfillment of each individual's life mission and goal. And, up to a point, they each support that purpose. However, simultaneously, they each can and often do take a life of their own where they serve as a vehicle to condemn, persecute, judge, punish and alienate, or bless, exonerate and honor the various members.

The action that you have seen is clearly beyond the ability of a simple system of justice to keep people in a path where they may live in a spiritual way and yet cope with the frailties of their humanness. However, your judicial system is not alone in its shortcomings. Even in the name of God, many have enacted trials which were primarily displays of pride, grandiosity and ego. If you would look back at certain famous trials throughout your history and discern what part of them were performances for the benefit of the actors and actresses playing to the audience of viewers, and what part of them were to apply the law, you will find, in some cases, very little law took place.

We must remind you that you are trying to understand justice from the standpoint of the separate ego self as it works with the laws of religious, judicial, governmental and international systems. And, from that standpoint, you see only a portion of what is transpiring. From the perspective of your soul, you would see more expansively the laws of karma working in these situations. You would see that each thing, whether you judge it as good or bad, right or wrong, is in perfect balance and perfect accord with the unfoldment of karmic energy.

You must also understand that while laws created by people are often changed and modified with time, the laws of karma are eternal and unchanging.

❋

Visionaries

LINDA: Is there a difference between what we call *psychic* information and *channeled* information?

ARIEL: The difference is a human difference—in the eye of the beholder. The conceptual model used in obtaining and understanding the information brought from a realm which the ego cannot claim as its own has many forms. In different cultures and even within different religions, there are acceptable models that enable some people to feel comfortable in receiving such communication.

In the case that you have described, one who channels has the idea that she is communicating with a being, a disembodied spirit, that could take any number of forms—an angel, a spirit guide, an ancestor, a deity of one form or another, a deceased loved one or, indeed, even a creature other than human. These are simply images of human fabrication which attempt to explain where information beyond the limits of the ego's cognition comes from.

A psychic does not utilize a model of an external being, rather, she uses a model in which her powers, her ego, her definition of self is beyond the normal realms and therefore her powers and abilities are beyond the average human's abilities.

It is purely a matter of semantics, of the definition of one's self, that changes from one model to the other. And yet even within the realm of those who use a label of psychic, they often communicate with a disembodied spirit, a departed family member or loved one, or someone from a realm beyond human who is invited to join and speak and share. So, from the perspective of this realm, the models that you have presented are in truth all the same fundamental reality. The differences, again, are in the eye of the human beholder.

The differences . . .
are in the eye of the human beholder.

❋

LINDA: When I asked about death and suicide, Stevan cried as he spoke the words of your answer.[3] Was he feeling emotions from your realm?

ARIEL: Please don't confuse these emotions that you see Stevan experiencing as he speaks our words as any form of distress. Questions we answer that create an outpouring of love, an outpouring of compassion, an outpouring of heartfelt longing to reach and be of service to those who suffer in such torment cause these emotions that you witness.

The tears or other emotional reaction of the channel [Stevan] at this point are simply a consequence of the tremendous energy we wish to convey through this [Stevan's] voice and through these words. You may call it our desperation to provide light or

---

3. Questions, pp. 163–175, "Life Passages"

to provide insight to those who are so troubled and so blind to the reality of the very life in which they live. If we could literally move inside of this being [Stevan] and speak directly in a way that could be heard by all, it would be done. But we can trust this treasure, our most precious gift, these words of wisdom to you. We trust that through your publications so many will read and receive our gift.

We can trust this treasure, our most precious gift,
these words of wisdom to you.

LINDA: **People who have a conscious connection to the spiritual realm seem to have one of two paths. They either become authors of books or patients in mental hospitals. Could you comment?**

ARIEL: The primary difference between those who your language would label as mystics, seers or visionaries and those who would be labeled as psychotic, schizophrenic or mentally unstable (and hence possibly institutionalized) is the degree of social acceptability of the framework in which the mysticism is contained. Both the mind of the mystic and the mind of the psychotic reach a similar level of consciousness. Both are capable of tremendous spiritual seeing; both are open to the realms of vision, hearing, feeling or understanding.

The primary difference is the degree to which their experience can be integrated in a socially acceptable and manageable framework within the context of the ego. In the case of what one might call the mystic, the integration is well balanced and socially acceptable. And even within this range, there are those who are judged as more subtle or sedate and those who are judged as more esoteric or even flamboyant in their presentation of what they have seen and what they have understood.

On the other hand, there are those who do not integrate their mystical experience with the physical world, who do not safely journey between the higher realms of consciousness and the ordinary realms of consciousness, and become lost. Or even those who escape to the higher realms and either choose not to or are unable to return in a balanced and integrated fashion. These people are seen and labeled as having one form or another of psychosis.

It is not the insights, knowledge or level of understanding that is the difference between these two groups of individuals. Rather, it is the degree to which the experience can be brought back and incorporated into the whole being, back into the ego of that person.[4]

Not all people who reach out and connect to our realm and integrate the divine information they receive into their lives are, as you say, authors of books or giving lectures and speaking. For,

---

4. A research study (Hughes, 1992) offers support for Ariel's answer. The study examined differences between the experiences and backgrounds of a group of channels and subjects identified with multiple personality disorder (MPD). The results showed that:

> Channels cannot be characterized as suffering from psychogenic amnesia, psychogenic fugue, depersonalization disorder, somatization disorder, depression, borderline personality disorder, or schizophrenia. . . . They seldom have histories of substance abuse, physical abuse or sexual abuse. (p. 187)

Such personality characteristics and histories were present in the MPD population. According to the research, it is widely recognized that the etiology of MPD is childhood trauma from severe and repeated physical and sexual abuse. In contrast, participants in channeling classes believe that experiencing altered states of consciousness promotes personal growth and development. It is very often a skill that is learned by adults with no history of physical or sexual abuse.

Hughes, D. J. 1992. "Differences between Trance Channeling and Multiple Personality Disorder on Structured Interview," *The Journal of Transpersonal Psychology*, 24(2), 181–192.

in many people, this is not in accord with the purpose of their soul or in alignment with the abilities of their ego. Those who do write or speak about such matters are doing so because it is what they must do.

✳

Tradition

LINDA: **Religious holidays. Are they manmade creations?**

ARIEL: While you use the term *manmade*, there is nothing within your realm that is other than God-created. The most accurate description could be *man-influenced*.

The divine force of the Creator has by its very nature put into motion the journey of your own existence, which is to come to know personally and intimately your Creator—to put it succinctly, to find God in your lifetime.

Religious holidays are timeouts. They are time away from delusions, "busyness," your ideas of self-grandeur and self-importance. They are a time to seek God rather than seek ego. They are mandatory and are instilled by the very Creator of the cosmos. In accordance with this creation, spiritual or religious traditions of all types, labels and denominations include a time to stop the activity of self and to spend time with the Creator—to spend time getting to know personally, intimately and deeply this thing you label God.

The ego seeks to adapt this plan to make seeking God a smaller and smaller and smaller piece of your routine as you devote more and more time to what is really important to the ego—pride, accomplishment, money, fame, fortune, building an eternal version of this creation you call your *self*.

All religious holidays or religious days—whether they be a regular Sabbath based on your system of a weekly or a daily time of prayer or a yearly holy day—are reminders of why you are truly here. It is often easy to become so self-absorbed and self-involved that you forget your true mission, which is simply to personally and deeply encounter and know God. And through that meeting, that encounter, that knowing, to place yourself—body, heart and soul—into service of this divine presence.

Religious holidays are timeouts . . .
reminders [of your] true mission, which is . . .
to encounter and know God.

If you follow that simple truth, you will find yourself receiving more—more glory, more abundance, more joy, more passion, more health, more of anything that your wonderful judging, labeling ego could possibly fathom. Your heart's desire will come true, and it would appear as though miracle after miracle is happening in your life.

Every day that you become aware that you are alive should be a religious holiday, for the very fact that you *are*, that you exist, is perhaps the most divine miracle of all. And if that were not enough, simply look around you. The very fact that this infinitely complex world that you live in exists is surely a miracle. And if that still is not enough, look beyond the speck that you exist upon, your Earth, and look into the infinity of the cosmos that you spin within. And if that is truly not a miracle, then you have a death grip on yourself—you do not have any space for divinity or spirituality in your existence.

Every day that you become aware
that you are alive
should be a religious holiday. . . .

❋

LINDA: Can people choose their own way of acknowledging their creation?

ARIEL: Again, it is very human to worry about a form, to worry about a method or a process. It is even more human to compete—my process is better than your process; my form is better than your form; I follow the only true, authentic way and all the others are wrong. It is a subterfuge, for you become so hopelessly lost in the process that you forget the goal. You work very hard thinking with great piety that you are making wonderful progress. Meanwhile you are stuck in quicksand.

The method by which one finds the path to
meeting . . . God . . .
is unimportant.
The meeting is all that matters.

The method by which one finds the path to meeting face-to-face, heart-to-heart, soul-to-soul, this divine, this God, is unimportant. The *meeting* is all that matters, for it produces knowing, beyond the realm of who you believe yourself to be—the meaning of God in your life. This is why you are here. It is all that matters. The rest is entertainment. The process, path, discipline, religion, teacher, church, synagogue, temple, mosque has very little importance so long as it is the one that nurtures you, teaches you, prods you and propels you toward your goal.

---

*The process . . .
has very little importance
so long as it is the one that nurtures you,
teaches you, prods you and propels you
toward your goal.*

※

Prayer

LINDA: **Is prayer a way to initiate contact with your realm?**

ARIEL: Prayer is a most powerful tool. We cannot, even if we speak to you for days, begin to underscore the virtue, value and extraordinary power that this thing called *prayer* can give you.

Most simply put, in order for you to pray, your ego must at some level admit, at least indirectly, that there is something to pray to. This is the key to the power of prayer. When you pray, your ego acknowledges that there is something outside of its boundary, outside of how it has defined itself, that exists. And not only does that something exist, but it can provide help in the form of guidance, healing, understanding or in many other forms that your ego needs. So your ego reaches out beyond its frame of reference and asks this something for help. Whenever this happens, your ego is in a state in which it has lowered its defenses.

The ego's defenses are most often lowered out of fear. We see the vast majority of prayers being offered in times of tremendous fear, and the activity of prayer forgotten in times of tremendous strength. But in these moments of fear, the power of the action of prayer, which takes place in the opening created by the person reaching upward, can be met by our reaching downward. It is this "crack in the ego's armor" that enables us to flood inward with energy, with consciousness, with thoughts and images. It is also a time in which we may support, in an indirect fashion, prayers of petition which ask for something, and work to direct the answer of such prayer to take place.

Prayers are powerful, transcendental units of energy based on thoughts that are directed outward. They are the building blocks of what takes place in this experience you know as this universe.

Prayers are powerful,
transcendental units of energy
based on thoughts
that are directed outward.

You are blessed with many powerful, powerful teachers who put ideas into words that are understandable. One such teacher [Deepak Chopra] has been inspired to state that the very matter of this universe in which you dwell, the very essence of the matter it is made of, responds to thought. It is true. It is also true, in that same line of thinking, that the universe is made from thought. The universe has been created through what you loosely term *thought*. It is an entire structure of life, of matter, that responds to thought. It is created and creates itself simultaneously, ever evolving, ever changing.

Prayer is a way with which the mind may reach out to interconnect with God and join in this process of creation. Prayer should be used constantly, not only in times of need based on fear, which is such a limited use of such a powerful tool. Prayer should be utilized also in times of great joy, fullness and gratitude.

Prayer should be used constantly,
not only in times of need. . . .
[but] also in times of great joy,
fullness and gratitude.

Be aware that the ego will reject the utility of prayer. The ego will not wish, especially in times that it is feeling strong, to admit that there is something beyond it that could be helpful in the setting or situation. As a result, the ego will simply forget to utilize the action of prayer.

It has been a great help that religions, within the structure of life and family, incorporate prayer periodically and ritually throughout the day. When praying is done in a fashion that is more than rote, it is of extraordinary benefit. Praying at regular points throughout the day—at meals, upon arising, upon retiring, at the end of work, at the beginning of work, in gratitude for something marvelous that has happened, as the sun rises, as the sun sets—is a very powerful tool to overcome the resistance of ego in utilizing this most powerful gift.

The most powerful form of prayer
that you can offer
is one in which you pray
that the willpower of your own self . . .
could be brought into alignment with . . .
the will of God.

The most powerful form of prayer that you can offer is one in which you pray that the willpower of your own self, the willpower of your ego, or your self-will, could be brought into alignment with the will of the universe, the flow of life, or as some have labeled it, the will of God. Pray that your will and God's will could be brought into perfect unity and alignment, and that by aligning these wills, that the will of God could be enacted and brought forth into your life. For in that moment, you release all restriction and restraint and you allow yourself to flow beautifully with the harmony and flow of life, perfectly on course, guided and aided. This indeed is a prayer that we would request that you offer many times throughout the day.

We thank you for your question.

❋

Extraterrestrial Life

There are hundreds of billions of stars in our own galaxy. . . .
There are hundreds of billions of galaxies. . . .
No self-respecting scientist would claim that
we on Earth are the only life in the entire universe.

—Dr. Neil DeGrasse Tyson
Acting Director, Hayden Planetarium
NBC Nightly News, October 30, 1995

I believe that these extra-terrestrial [sic] vehicles and their crews are visiting
this planet from other planets. . . .

—Astronaut Colonel Gordon Cooper
Excerpt, letter to United Nations
proposing a committee to explore
the UFO phenomenon

Headline News, July 8, 1947: The Army Air Forces has announced that a flying
disk has been found and is now in the possession of the Army. Army officers say
the missile found sometime last week has been inspected at Roswell, New
Mexico. . . .

—Frank Joyce, Radio Announcer, KGFL Radio
Roswell, New Mexico, July 8, 1947
"The Roswell Incident," 1995, Discovery Channel

An eyewitness of debris recovered from the Roswell crash site described
the material she saw: *"He would wad it up in his hand. When it hit the table, it*
spread out just like water with no wrinkles."

—Frankie Rowe
"The Roswell Incident," 1995, Discovery Channel

I think the pressure that comes to bear on the government from whatever rea-
son they withhold information is certainly getting more and more and more. . . .

—Astronaut Colonel Gordon Cooper
Paranormal Borderline, May 7, 1996
Interview on his 1950s UFO sightings

It's pretty clear that various government agencies have information and evi-
dence of alien contact they refuse to release . . . and we've a right to know. . . .

—Jonathan Frakes, Host
Paranormal Borderline, May 7, 1996

Visitation

LINDA: Is Earth receiving alien visitors?

ARIEL: If your question is, "Is Earth experiencing living beings of consciousness that are not indigenous to the population that you know as resident on your planet?" the answer is "Yes."

The whole phenomenon is of great curiosity as viewed from this realm. So great is your need to feel separate, to feel cut off from the unity of the very realm in which you abide, that the idea of life forces, especially life forces that could possibly equal or exceed your capacities, becomes threatening to you.

We sense fear in you about the possibility of other realms of beings, other planets that have life forms on them, life forms that have marvelously complex systems of life as does this planet you call Earth. If you could simply put down the fear of the unknown and fear of loss, projecting the potential to be harmed or hurt by these other beings, then you could view it more from your soul than from your ego. You would be able to understand and fathom even the smallest amount of the complexity of the universe in which you live—the complexity that your mind cannot grasp. You would comprehend the complexity of the unity that exists amongst all beings that inhabit all realms and all spaces in this universe.

There are many, many places that you call planets, many environments that you call ecosystems. Yours most certainly is not the only such place in this universe. And yet, so necessary is it for your own sense of safety (being such a species of conquerors) that any thought that you do not have dominion over all around you produces much fear.

The thing you miss, and the thing that has not been understood because of this fear, is how much love exists, not only within your own world but in other worlds. The great potential for connecting and communicating with other forms of life which have the same essence, the same one truth, the same ability to be loved and to love, is being missed.

The great potential for . . .
communicating
with other forms of life . . .
is being missed.

❊

LINDA: **Is alien visitation a new phenomenon or has it been going on for thousands of years?**

ARIEL: Again, the question appears to have a question within it, or at least a statement of belief within it. Please note that it is so common for the human mind to believe that the piece of the entire cosmos in which you exist, a tiny particle on an outer edge of a galaxy, is the center of all creation. You seem to think that all life, all creation around you, is focused on you, subservient to and lesser than you.

The question of when did this visitation start or how long has it been going on presupposes that, in some sense, you were here first in your concept of time. The question, "When during the evolution of the beings you know as humans did alien visitation begin?" presupposes somehow that this has evolved during *your* development. It has not.

These beings
have . . . visited . . . Earth. . . .

These beings have existed far beyond the realm of what you understand as time and have, as you put it, visited the place you know as Earth throughout that span of time. They are, in a sense, waiting until you evolve enough to open your hearts and welcome them into your world.

But that will come only after you have evolved to such a place of openness of the heart and communion with the divine that you can safely welcome these beings into your world. For humans are still, even to one another, so frightened and hostile that it appears at times that we are looking upon a planet filled with wounded, hungry, scared, savage beasts.

They are . . . waiting until you . . . welcome them into your world.

And yet shining through everywhere, gleaming momentarily from many a heart, are the acts of kindness, compassion, love and caring that will become more and more prevalent as your growth continues. And, if you are fortunate enough, not only will you be able to communicate with this realm that you call angelic—from which you can safely feel the love without experiencing your wall of fear—but you will also in time be able to experience the love, the offerings, the gifts of knowledge and wisdom that these other beings you label as alien can bring to you.

❋

Contact

LINDA: We see news reports that people claim they are taken away and examined by beings from other planets. Is there any truth to their experience?

ARIEL: An analogy might help us to answer your question. Imagine that you had found a wounded, scared, hungry animal, one that you might know as a dog or a cat, one which inherently can be quite friendly and quite loving. But because of its situation, its wound, starvation and terror, it is quite vicious.

And yet you know if you could only find the way to allow it to let you help, you could heal its wounds, you could help its hunger, give it shelter and nurture it to safety. But when you reach toward it, all it sees is threat. If you are not careful, you will be attacked, bitten or clawed. You are feared. The opportunity for you, from your more advanced ability to help and heal every aspect of this frightened, wounded creature, will go to waste. For you cannot find the way through its terror. You cannot find the place to comfort it and help it.

This is basically the situation that these beings face. For, make no mistake, they feel tremendous dismay, having the ability to heal and help fix the wounds, sores and mishaps that humanity faces. They have love to share, shelter to offer and guidance to give as part of the connections you label *abductions*. So, too, would the scared, wounded, hungry, frightened animal label as abduction any helpful hand that would reach in and pick it up, attempting to support and help it. Even the most loving gesture could easily be seen as harmful.

They have love to share,
shelter to offer and guidance to give
as part of the connections
you label abductions.

Now, in the case of our analogy, animals do not possess this ego that is so hard to work through, and hence they will more readily adapt to the love and the outstretched offering of kindness. And while it may initially scratch out of terror, an animal will soon accept the gift that is being offered, and it will be greatly healed from the experience. Mankind is not at that point. The ability to drop the fear and open the heart has not happened. But it will, in time, as evolution continues.

LINDA: **There are reports of unexplained animal mutilations using a laser technology beyond our scientific capability. In such cases, there is no physical evidence such as footprints or tire tracks near the dead animals to support the presence of human intervention. Is this an example of an alien encounter?**

ARIEL: The whole topic is encumbered by a most human characteristic. While on the one hand you strive for comfort and safety in all aspects of life, you simultaneously need and thrive on creating fear through a process you call *sensationalism*. The specific phenomenon you speak of, in many cases, is created by humans to exacerbate or increase the fear around the perception that other life forms are malicious, savage or harmful.

In many cases, you as a species utilize the lives of animals, for the betterment of the entire race of people, through experimentation. This experimentation often leads to crippling or death of the animal being experimented upon.

Some . . . reports . . .
popularized in your media
do contain accuracy . . .
and do reflect the technology . . .
that such beings possess.

It should come as no surprise that in an effort to find how to reach out, how to succeed in conveying the love, the knowledge and the wisdom they have, these beings would try to acquire more knowledge about the operation and the complexities of your world. Accordingly some, but not many, of the myriad reports popularized in your media do contain accuracy. These events are inexplicable by your present limited knowledge of technology or science and _do_ reflect the technology, science or capacity that such beings possess.

As to your reference to _alien encounters_, please do not confuse the experience as the human understands it with the theory as to how it happens. There are many, many explanations and ways in which one from this realm, or realms similar to this, may intercede into a human consciousness. A person may experience this intercession as coming from an external force, possibly in a spaceship, or with many of the similar characteristics that people report. It is not always what it appears to be.

LINDA: **Despite your explanation that these advanced beings have humanitarian intentions, I would like to feel that I am not in jeopardy.**

ARIEL: In terms of your fear of what human consciousness experiences as abduction, it is not on your journey.

✳

LINDA: How can we extend a hand of friendship to aliens?

ARIEL: You cannot even extend a hand of friendship to each other on your own planet, so it is unreasonable to expect that you could welcome these life forms that you label as aliens. The truth is that you are not ready. The vibration, the spiritual evolution of the entire system, the Earth itself, the animals and the humans that abide on it, are not ready to extend the openness of heart, the consciousness or the deeply loving embrace that is needed to welcome such connections to other and indeed higher forms of intelligent life.

Those who have tried to approach humans with their love, knowledge and greetings have faced tremendous hostility. They have experienced great risk to their own survival, and in many cases have been, in your terms, killed. It is not time yet to expect such loving and open dialogue of the heart.

Within your media, the very nature of the term *alien* brings forth in most minds the fearful image of a cold, calculating and heartless being. Please remember, such an image is one created by the human mind through a wall of fear, and when that fear is present, no love whatsoever can be experienced.

What people are perceiving are not the true characteristics of these beings. Rather, it is the inability of the perceiver to see anything but his own wall of fear.

In your movie, *E.T.*,[1] although the physical form was not an entirely correct representation of truth, the essence of the portrayal

---

1. *E.T. The Extra-Terrestrial* (1982 film). Directed by Steven Spielberg. A 10-year-old boy befriends an alien stranded on Earth. The movie is described as "a warm, insightful story of childhood innocence, frustration, courage, and love." (*Leonard Maltin's Movie and Video Guide 1993*, New York: Signet, Penguin Books, p. 366.)

of an alien being was more correct in terms of the compassion and the heart energy and the love that is truly present.

You as a species do not have the capacity yet to live primarily from the heart, to feel and experience the unity on a regular, ongoing basis. You do not experience the God-essence that is the basis of all life. These beings—the ones with the capacity to reach out and request a welcome from you—*do* have that capacity.

LINDA: **You mentioned** *E.T.*, **the movie. How do you know about movies?**

ARIEL: The spiritual evolution that you are going through is our primary concern. It is our task, our love, our mission and our joy to find even the smallest opening in the armor of your fear and, in ways that can be received through that small opening, shine the brilliance of this love inside for those who can grasp it.

We know of this experience that you call *E.T.*, for prior to its creation, and not in any form as direct as you are experiencing through Stevan now, it was guided to be created. The simplicity of its message showing the genuineness of the childlike innocence of this being from outside your realm of present understanding, with its simple truth of tremendous love and joy that meets the tremendous fear of the human mind, has been part of the continued effort to bring the truth into human consciousness.

Many ways are sought. Some are standard settings that you understand as theology or religion. Others include the cultivation of works of art, be they books or what you call movies or plays. The core spark that ignited the hearts of those who created the movie, *E.T.,* is part of our work.

*The core spark
that ignited the hearts
of those who created
the movie, E.T.,
is part of our work.*

The understanding of its impact, the change it has produced in the vibration of those who have observed it and the effect it has had on the spiritual evolution of your entire planet has been subtle but profound. The most significant impact has been on the generation that you would label *children*. The children who have seen *E.T.* have opened and have grown, not from their minds but from their hearts, through their simulated communion experience with beings of a world beyond that which you understand. This has allowed that generation of children, as they mature, to be spiritually more developed than those who preceded them. It has been happening over some time.

*The most significant impact
[of the movie E.T.]
has been on the generation
that you would label* children.

Likewise, the effect that we see of an earlier attempt to bring such knowledge through became something that you know as the radio play called *War of the Worlds*. This was from a generation whose spiritual evolution was less mature than in the time-frame you are hearing these words. The message and the reaction to it, which we have felt, was one of fear.

Please realize that the information, the communion message sent in all cases from this realm to yours, is of the highest form of love with the deepest compassion, attempting to bring an understanding that has not come before. However, the most we can do is imprint knowing. What happens from there is a consequence of your own spiritual growth.

*The most we can do
is imprint knowing.
What happens from there
is a consequence
of your own spiritual growth.*

The human mind can take pure love that is offered in unlimited quantity from this realm and turn it, through fear, into evil. It is the evil created by the human mind from which you feel the need to protect yourself, or destroy, in order to attain what you perceive as safety.

Although it is hard for you to understand, and we will really make no attempt to explain in any detail, we wish you to see how far you have come. The very same spark of divine truth and divine knowing that was sent earlier in your time created—through the fear in the human mind and the human evolution at the time—the terrifying vision that you call *War of the Worlds*.

And yet, in your metric of time, some time after that experience (and not by any means of celestial understanding a great length of time), that same knowing imprinted at a far more mature level of spiritual growth produced not destruction and fear but the most tender, childlike love that touched the hearts of many in the movie *E.T.* That very love is the message we are trying to convey, and we will use whatever words, ideas or images necessary to do that. Please know that the love and tenderness that brings a welling from deep within the human heart is pointing you to understand God.

LINDA: **Do you communicate with aliens?**

ARIEL: In some cases, communication is similar to the quality of communication that you experience from this realm. There are other cases where the communication is far superior and cases where it is very limited. There is a wide range of communication with these beautiful beings.

> *There is a wide range*
> *of communication*
> *with these beautiful beings.*

LINDA: **Is there or has there been research or autopsies on extraterrestrial corpses on our planet?**

ARIEL: It is human nature to want to understand anything that is not already understood. Whether it be the ancient artifacts of your history, trying to understand how God created the world in which you abide, trying to piece together what you call missing links of information, it is a quest of the human ego to want to know what the soul already knows.

Based on reports from journalists and from movies about the recovery of extraterrestrial bodies within your world, you question whether autopsies have been performed. It is true that such beings have encountered your fear and have been cruelly examined. Such beings have a legitimate view of humans very similar to the view that most humans have of them, the difference being that theirs is founded.

Such beings . . .
have been cruelly examined.

This topic exemplifies the dichotomy built into the human mind. What human beings cannot easily tolerate is that there could be a higher creation. Having lived and evolved at the top, so to speak, of your food chain, having dominance over all other life forms, there is an inherent weakness that prevents the mind even from opening to the possibility of a spiritual realm that is a higher order, that has total dominion over humans. But since that can only be experienced by those with expanded awareness, it is somewhat safe. It is easy *not* to believe, or to dismiss through the logic of the mind.

But when the human mind encounters a physical form— another species of a higher order with more capacity, more refined, more developed—it becomes intolerable to perceive that a human being is not at the top of the spectrum.

It is our intent in answering the questions on this topic to delineate how two different phenomena beyond what you call normal can produce such diverse responses and can essentially polarize human consciousness. One—loving communication from this realm—brings you to the height of your divine spiritual glory as a human being. It introduces a state of love, peace, trust and faith. These revelations, these experiences, bridge the mind and heart, bringing you into a state of true understanding. The other experience—encountering a life form that is not human—polarizes to the other end of the spectrum of human awareness and instills fear and suspicion, and works to erode feelings of trust and safety.

Beyond helping you see how this topic moves the mind from one end of a range of possible realities to the other, it is not our desire to expound upon these beings. If indeed you [Linda] seek to understand more and to use your written voice to create more understanding of these beings, it would be our pleasure to guide you to those who speak fluently with them and who will give voice to your audience.

Three weeks later. . .

LINDA: When we last spoke about extraterrestrials, you said you would guide me to people who are in contact with extraterrestrial physical beings. In what has seemed like an incredible series of coincidences, I've met four people who have described having such contact. Was this guidance from your realm?

ARIEL: You are starting to understand how this world in which you live works. You have an honest, heartfelt desire to seek and find something to support you in living your dream. You have requested of this realm support in attaining that desire. We have matched you with those who are living their desire and their dream, and for whom finding you is an answer to their prayers. Although divine guidance has brought them to you, it is up to you to work at the more human level of personalities and preferences, to find those with whom you can suitably work. If these are not suitable, others will simply be provided.

LINDA: What a system. These contacts are resources for another project, and I will save them for a future time.

Cover-up

LINDA: **Is there a conspiracy of silence among government agencies regarding evidence of extraterrestrial contact?**

ARIEL: The word *conspiracy* denotes the idea that some group or organization is trying to work or conspire against another. It is not as simple as that when dealing with any experience that is beyond normal limits while living within the human realm. There is a natural tendency to keep such experience secret, to keep it from the view and analysis of others. Remaining silent is not only true for this topic—the awareness of extraterrestrial life—but extends to many, many other experiences that you might consider paranormal, beyond your normal range.

Even great spiritual seers and seekers who encounter marvelous transcendent states of awareness and meet, through one of their senses, an angel or guide, in effect conspire to keep this secret. Many wonderful human beings, ranging from ordinary to saintly, have encountered beings of the angelic realm. Their instinct, because they wish to avoid the ridicule, fear and suspicion that disclosure would create, is to simply keep quiet about what they have experienced.

When the experience touches many, however, such as when many people encounter the same divine revelation or experience the same extraterrestrial phenomenon, it is difficult to keep secret that which has been seen by so many. On the one hand, there is curiosity about what has been experienced, but simultaneously there can be great fear.

Your consciousness has been biased through the artistic creation you know as *War of the Worlds*. You have been biased to think that extraterrestrial life is oriented toward attack and domination and is, therefore, something to fear. Hence, the response for most people to the possibility that an extraterrestrial being, an alien, could be present is fear.

Organizations like governments, religious groups or any other group that survives based on popularity must guard against fear to survive. It is not, in your terms, politically correct to approve, endorse or even admit that such sightings or phenomena have occurred. It would jeopardize the safety and harmony of the organization.

Yet look in your own history at the other side of that equation where, in a town you call Medjugorje, children who could be believed sighted a presence simultaneously.[2]

We bring Medjugorje to your awareness because it provides an example of normal consciousness being exceeded and paranormal phenomena occurring, but embodying and strengthening a human belief system that instills love, faith and trust. That belief system feeds upon itself and extends to build more trust, more faith. It produces the most reassuring and reinforcing experience of love—literally a bridge between the nature and essence of this realm and yours. It is used as a monument to the spiritual discipline, or religion, if you will, that embodies that belief, to prove and strengthen, bringing tremendous spiritual growth to those people involved.

---

2. Starting in 1981, the Blessed Virgin Mary began appearing to a handful of children in the small village named Medjugorje in what is now Bosnia-Herzegovina (the former Yugoslavia). She appeared as an apparition to the children every day for many years in such a way that the children could see, touch, hear and speak to her, even though others present could not. She gave messages to the children, and her presence elevated the children to heights of spiritual ecstasy. The phenomenon of apparitions of the Blessed Virgin Mary has occurred all over the world (Lourdes, France, 1858; Fatima, Portugal, 1917; Spain, 1961; Egypt, 1968; Conyers, Georgia, USA, 1995).

Sources:

    Kiviat, R. (Producer) 1996. "Miracles and Visions: Fact or Fiction," Kiviat Productions. (Film)

    DeBell, K. 1987. "Reflections on Medjugorje." Unpublished manuscript.

---

*The purpose of . . . government
is to maintain peace and tranquillity,
so such information
that would create fear
is suppressed.*

In the other case, because there is no frame of reference other than human-created fear, distrust or defense against attack, the energy of an extraterrestrial being reaching out in a state of peace to share knowledge is instantaneously misperceived. Fear reigns. Terror results. And the purpose of an organization like the one you call government is to maintain peace and tranquillity, so such information that would create fear is suppressed.

※

LINDA: **I can understand the government's motivation. However, people want to know what is going on in their world.**

ARIEL: What you will find is very much like what spiritual seekers have found. When a prophet has a revelation in the presence of a massive gathering of disbelievers, it can produce a fatal result. When a seeker of extraterrestrial life encounters an alien life form in the presence of masses of people who are nonbelievers, it, too, can produce near fatal results.

With those seeking the angelic realm as you call it, more and more have found what they are looking for. More and more come gently and lovingly into communion but remain in secrecy and do not try to share. They simply grow and evolve from the gift they have received. That, too, is happening. Many people on your planet have experienced communion, direct meetings with what you call aliens, extraterrestrials. They know by direct experience what these beings are about. They know the message they convey, and they do not share that information. When sufficient exposure, understanding and comfort with that phenomenon have taken place, as with the spiritual realm, there will be more public acceptance and more ease and safety in talking openly and sharing knowledge about these topics.

Many people on your planet
have experienced . . .
direct meetings
with . . . extraterrestrials.

You are seeing that what would have been risky even ten years ago is now more openly accepted—talking about encounters with angels, talking about spirit guides and guardians, talking about rescues and life-saving experiences. All these experiences have happened throughout your lifetime, but they are now being openly described and discussed, and this will lead to more and more sharing of knowledge and more and more understanding. So, too, in time, will your questions and your probing about extraterrestrial life forms be more openly discussed.

※

Our Selves

Karma and Past Lives

LINDA: **I'm interested in the concept of *karma*, such as a man who burned books in one lifetime, built libraries in another lifetime.[1] Please comment.**

ARIEL: The topic of *karma* is one that we could expound upon at great length. There are many thoughts we wish to share with you about this phenomenon. One of the challenges, and yet one of the opportunities of an incarnation, is to face, address, tackle and triumph over those experiences which were frailties or were stumbled over in previous experiences and existences.

A soul's mission in a life's journey is to address or face what was met with failure, backed away from or not accomplished. And through a process you don't even realize is happening in this lifetime, you find yourself back again in the same energetic setting. The characters and the situation may differ slightly in form, but the essence of the spiritual healing and the spiritual challenge in the new setting is identical.

Your example of one who burned books and then built libraries would be characteristic of what we are speaking about. Or one who *kept* books from being shared could equally well be one who is driven by some inner desire, an inner delight, to spend another lifetime writing and promoting the freedom of publication.

Often that inner burning, the inner heart's desire that causes one to direct her energy toward the expression of that inner truth, comes from a replay of past karmic experience. And while the individual is often unaware of the previous experiences, the spiritual nature—what you may call the *soul* of that being—does

---

1. This question was inspired by a psychic friend who believed that this was the karmic balance of Thomas Jefferson. Toward the end of his life, President Jefferson, in fact, oversaw the construction of every building of the University of Virginia.

indeed know exactly what is being done. The soul knows what lessons are being learned and what incredibly powerful growth is being obtained.

Whatever energy you place
out into the universe . . .
will return to you many times over.

There have been many in your history who have described karma as being like a boomerang—when thrown out, it returns. And although it is a delightfully simple, childlike analogy for the actual process, it suffices in terms of its truth. Whatever energy you place out into the universe—be it positive or negative, good or bad—will return to you many times over.

Those who put out energy of cheating or stealing, those who judge or criticize, punish or condemn, do so at the expense of having that energy returned to them, and they become recipients of those same forces. Those who put out good, gentleness and compassion, who are helpful, will indeed receive in return the energy of that same vibration and quality.

Often one of the things most difficult for the human mind (which is trapped within the timeframe of a specific lifetime) to see is this karma in action, since the speed at which the energy returns varies based on the evolutionary state of a particular soul.

There is no specific rule as to the rate of return of one's karmic actions. However, the more evolved a specific soul is and the higher and more divine the vibration that the soul attains, the more quickly such karmic energy returns as an opportunity for the soul to grow further spiritually. In some cases, the karmic energy may not return within a specific incarnation. It may be delayed and appear in future life experiences. In other cases, it will all occur within the same incarnation.

The purpose of karma is not one of punishment. Many have expressed such words. There is no sense of judgment, however. There is no abiding authority with which to condemn, praise or place any value or judgment whatsoever. Quite simply, each soul grows through the experience that has preceded it. Each soul has the opportunity to grow through the karmic process of placing a specific energy—be it what you judge as positive or negative—into the universe such that the soul's counterpart experiences additional and more powerful growth by having that karmic energy returned.

LINDA: **Regarding your example of an individual who kept books from being shared in one lifetime, "who is driven by some inner desire, an inner delight, to spend a lifetime writing and promoting the freedom of publication."[2] That description had an enormous ring of familiarity. Could you possibly have been talking about me?**

ARIEL: In answer to the general question first. It is often the case when there is a deep inner drive, an inner sense of purpose or delight, a heart's desire to express in some way, then that way is opposite and equal to a way experienced earlier in this life or in a prior life. Thus, the person is driven to counteract the energies that were put forth previously.

With respect to the specific question of your prior experience or existence and its relationship to suppressing material from being written, the more general energy around your earlier existence was one of limiting or restricting not only written but spoken words of wisdom and creativity, especially around matters of spirituality.

---

2. From the answer to question, p. 244.

The difficulty was based on fear—fear of the knowledge that was being gained and the expression of that knowledge in any form. Because of that fear, it was necessary to suppress or restrict those, including yourself, who had knowledge in matters of understanding or of spiritual insight that did not conform with existing beliefs, ways of thinking or structured systems at the time.

What you are driven to do in this lifetime is to help empower others to make up for the ways in which you disempowered others by your position of authority. In this lifetime, you have an inner drive and desire to help others grow, to help find ways to have others excel, to actually cultivate the gifts in other people and bring them to the world in ways that they might not have been able to do on their own.

So, in your own path, you like all others are working out a powerful effect of karma, and the very act of your publications will serve to greatly change the fear-based restrictive energy of the past. Even though there is fear within you, in terms of going forward, all of your energies are supporting the expansion of creative and spiritual ideas, even when they may be somewhat distinct or different from established belief systems.

✳

LINDA: **Regarding the other lifetime you are speaking of, what century was it?**

ARIEL: The predominant energy that is spoken of comes from the 16th century of your time.

LINDA: **Yow!**

✳

LINDA: **I would like to know more about this soul from the 16th century, the one who suppressed written and spoken information.**

ARIEL: Such information is always readily available. The point being pondered is the relevance and the importance at this point in your journey. But since you have asked on several occasions and it is a desire of your mind to know, we now will give you some of the rudimentary characteristics, but we would be happy to work with you to have yourself explore and reveal some of the details.

The setting you found yourself in was an official within the church, in a male body. It was your specific task to stop the heresy of people who were opening to wonderful, mystical revelation experiences with Jesus.

This undermined and threatened the establishment, for the church was built on the thesis that Jesus could be found only through the church. And yet his presence was revealing itself to many what you would consider peasants and common people—people close to the land, living in the woods, who knew the divinity of all life around them.

And while part of your heart knew they were speaking truth, knew they had found a gift that you yourself, despite your rank, had not found, your job was to refute or to prove it false. Your job was to stop the growing belief that Jesus could be found, and to excommunicate those who were so heretical. You were very good at your task.[3]

_____

3. The Inquisition was the name given to an ecclesiastical body charged with the task of detecting and punishing heretics and all persons guilty of any offense against the Catholic orthodoxy. The 16th century, in particular, saw the Spanish Inquisition. "Two features of the Spanish Inquisition are especially noteworthy: the prosecutions for 'speeches suspected of heresy' and the censure of books. . . . In 1558 the penalty of death and confiscation of property was decreed against any bookseller or individual who should keep in his possession condemned

❋

LINDA: **I would like to hear about examples of people from our history, what they did in one lifetime and who they were in another lifetime, like the book burner–library builder example I gave you.**

ARIEL: There is often tremendous importance placed on these labels or names that you assign to people. By the very nature of your question, there are implicit and underlying beliefs that certain of these people are more significant or of more interest than others.

What you will come to understand when you can see from the perspective that we are now observing you from, is that no such importance really does exist. The one [who built libraries] labeled Thomas Jefferson, from a soul perspective, is no more or no less important than one who is anonymous to history.

The quest for understanding an identity, as linked from one incarnation to another, is one which burns in many a human mind. And yet from a perspective of teaching and growth, it is of little consequence. Further, it could both provide an added complexity to understanding the words that we are attempting to speak and dilute the message contained herein to address the question of the consistency or interconnection of identity from one life experience to another. So while we understand and feel the desire in your heart to know, we will not address or answer such questions in these teachings.

LINDA: **Okay, fair enough.**

---

books." (*Encyclopedia Britannica*, Vol. 12, 1960, pp. 377, 383). "Members of the inquisitional court often referred to instruction manuals for assistance regarding the treatment of heretics." There were references to successful inquisitors who were very good at extracting confessions from suspected heretics through torture. (Bachrach, D. 1995. *The Inquisition*, San Diego, California: Lucent Books, Inc., p. 28.)

※

LINDA: **There are some startling parallels in the lives of two United States presidents—Abraham Lincoln and John Kennedy—including details or events related to their respective marriages, deaths, forensic investigations into their deaths and the assassins.[4] It seems like Lincoln's life and death were replayed 100 years later in the life and death of John Kennedy. Do these events have a karmic link?**

ARIEL: The question you have raised is one we would use as an opportunity to address an even broader issue of teaching. The question is most astute. The point that is most relevant is that the reason so much knowledge has been gained concerning the parallels of these two lives is the degree to which they were highly visible public figures.

Had they not had such visibility, no such investigative work would have been done to draw forth the incredible detail of the parallels of these two lives. And yet, in truth, if you were to apply such incredible investigative detail to all the lives in the population of the environment that you inhabit, and you were to compare and contrast billions of people, you would discover large numbers of such parallel lives.

For, while you may indeed believe that each life experience is absolutely unique, there are fewer patterns or types of life experiences than the number of people who experience them. As a result there are many life patterns which, although circumstances may be different, would play out as identical. Within each of these patterns, the phases of the life, the specific actions in the life, many key milestones, decisions or changes made, and opportunities as well as tragedies experienced, would all be par-

---

4. Lattimer, J. K. 1980. *Kennedy and Lincoln: Medical and Ballistic Comparisons of Their Assassinations.* New York: Harcourt Brace Jovanovich.

allel. The case that you specifically identified is but one of many, many such patterns that play out through the course of soul growth and development in the human life experience.

There are many life patterns
which . . . would play out
as identical.

✳

LINDA: I would like to pursue this further. Is there a karmic tie between people in different time periods? In general, is there a happening in one century that is identical to a happening with a being from a previous century? Is it possible that their bodies are inhabited by the same soul?

ARIEL: The possibility of a karmic tie from one lifetime to another is always present. The chance or the likelihood that one would incarnate into an identical life script at another point in time would depend truly upon the need that the specific soul has for experiencing the growth from that lifetime, from that life script.

It is more common to incarnate into a different life script, for in the process of journeying through a particular life pattern, sufficient knowledge, growth and development often will have taken place so a re-experiencing of the same script is not required. That soul will typically, in a future incarnation, experience a different script—one tailored to development and training for the specific areas of growth that the newly evolved soul needs to continue its evolution and growth. But there are certain cases in which a pattern is repeated and the lessons are experienced an additional time.

*[A] soul will typically,
in a future incarnation,
experience a different [life] script. . . .*

LINDA: Do Stevan and I [the authors] have a karmic tie?

ARIEL: Indirectly. The karmic tie or karmic similarity that you experience is that while you yourself have suppressed out of necessity and fear the spiritual expression of others, this Stevan has, in his past, suppressed within himself spiritual understanding and expression from the world around him, out of fear and the desire to maintain a state of safety.

The two of you, while never having experienced this in connection with each other in any lifetime, have been drawn together through our guidance and help to support each other in clearing, very powerfully, the karmic effects of the past. The union of your two souls, in guidance and harmony with the purpose of your two lives, is supporting each of you in contradicting the karmic energy of past experiences. Each of you is supporting the other in healing yourselves. As such, you two are what might be referred to in your terminology as *soulmates,* connecting for the purpose of growth, healing and transformation, not only for yourselves but for many other souls on the planet.

*You two are . . . soulmates,
connecting for the purpose of
growth, healing and transformation,
not only for yourselves
but for many other souls on the planet.*

LINDA: **Please clarify the meaning of soulmate.**

ARIEL: Soulmate is a label that we attach to souls that have chosen to unite for the purpose of spiritual growth and transformation in a lifetime. Soulmates take a very wide variety of flavors and forms in the human expression.

More common and more sought after by the human mind, especially the human ego, is the soulmate at one end of the spectrum, that is, the idealized concept of the pure romantic lover—one of deep passion and sensuality, one of tremendous, unconditional love and joy, one of total bliss and ecstasy within the boundaries of a relationship.

Yet there are soulmates who attain the same soul-level goal of growth and spiritual attainment who, from an ego perspective, are completely on the other end of the spectrum. The truth is that even souls who unite in acts of violence, including rape, incest or other crimes, experience the opportunity for permanent and powerful spiritual growth. The two souls, who from an ego perspective do not necessarily like each other and are not in ego-based harmony with each other, join together to set the stage for incredible spiritual transformation, growth and healing.

Between those two extremes are many, many possible variations on the theme of soulmate. Two souls in some form join together or mate with each other, not necessarily in a sexual or violent way but in any way designed for mutual growth and healing, mutual karmic evolution and karmic fulfillment of the life path of those two souls.

LINDA: **Could you give us an example of the karmic balance from one who devotes a lifetime to scientific research?**

ARIEL: The question you ask seeks a formula that explains the cause and effect of each possible life situation or setting. The action or dynamic of karma is not so simple or direct. The linear mapping of one life into another life, one karmic experience into another karmic experience, is not the way that karma, in and of itself, works. There are many tangential factors, including the multiple experiences of different lifetimes joining together in one very powerful karmic healing or karmic re-balancing.

There is also a process within karma that seeks to stabilize or achieve a stasis in which the negative, if you will, is balanced by positive, or that which is limited is balanced by that which is expressed. As this happens, experience after experience leads to more refined and higher levels of positive, joyful, harmonious expression.

The goal, or the path, if you will, in the process of karmic refinement is to fine-tune the soul to a point of openness of heart, of power, spiritual wisdom and tremendous compassion such that the level of spiritual attainment rises higher and higher. As this refinement occurs, the level of communion with higher aspects of the divine also increases, and the level of karmic energy that would come back to be healed is diminished.

---

*The goal . . . in . . .
karmic refinement
is to fine-tune the soul. . . .*

As people approach this state of refinement, a wonderful, wonderful level of spiritual existence arises. Others see them as truly powerful beings of a very high spiritual nature, living a life of harmony and providing tremendous insight and influence to many who come in contact with them. Simultaneously, they produce little if any karma that must be refined or addressed in future experiences. In a sense they make very few karmic waves as they pass through their journey in life.

❋

LINDA: Is a person's job part of a play-out of karmic energy?

ARIEL: All aspects of the life setting of the human experience are fitting stages to play out karmic energies. The environment of relationships is a powerful setting for such karmic lessons and growth to be experienced. The intimacy, love and power of a personal relationship makes it an ideal environment for a soul to fully express deep healing of karmic energies of the past.

Relationships in the environment of work settings, within business, within politics, within teaching, within every single walk of what you know as human life, provide excellent and ample opportunities to experience growth through the karmic energies that have returned to you.

Equally valid are the settings in which no such relationships exist. In such settings, the energy around not having a job, not having an interpersonal relationship, not having a feeling of belonging in society, in a religious structure or in some other order is also a powerful way this karmic energy is played back and experienced.

❋

LINDA: Some people have vivid memories of a past life while most have none at all. Why would some individuals remember and others not remember?

ARIEL: Simply put, the importance of past life varies amongst human experience, and each soul has a different need as to whether or not it's important to remember any or all of a specific previous incarnation. The memory of past life experiences is most closely tied with a need to resolve or heal the effects, complete the spiritual growth or resolve the karmic energies of a previous incarnation.

*The memory of past life experiences
is most closely tied with
a need to resolve . . .
the karmic energies
of a previous incarnation.*

Those people who remember past life experiences often do so in the context of healing something that is presently alive and active within a specific lifetime. For whenever there is a karmic manifestation that is unresolved or incomplete, it is replicated in some way as an energetic parallel or an energetic mirror within a lifetime. The specific form or implementation of that replication may vary, however, in a current incarnation from the form it took in a previous one.

Except for the support in healing, the knowledge of other lives is irrelevant information in terms of the growth of a soul or the evolution of consciousness. So pure searching for information about other lifetimes for what you might call entertainment value or curiosity serves little purpose.

Those people who have no recollection or no knowledge of past lives could, indeed, be those who have nothing to gain by such knowledge, or who did not bring into this lifetime specific activities to be worked upon, specific things to be healed. Those who do remember much of a previous lifetime are gaining valuable insight into the journey and the mission that their souls have in this particular incarnation.

✳

LINDA: **Is it helpful to us in this life's journey to remember lessons from a past life?**

ARIEL: The knowledge about one's prior experiences, especially as it relates to the karmic unfoldment in your current life experience, can be of tremendous value. But it is always sought and discovered only when the knowledge is both needed and useful in the evolution and unfoldment within a lifetime.

---

*Knowledge
about one's prior experiences . . .
is always sought and discovered
only when the knowledge
is both needed and useful in the evolution
and unfoldment within a lifetime.*

The reality is that there are those who are not ready for such information or whose present journey does not require it. It would not be helpful to them. Thus, they will not seek and they will not find.

And those, such as yourself [Linda], who are at a point at which it would be essential to know, find a way, discover what is necessary from the past as it relates to the juncture point at which they are living in the present.

It is wise to avoid spending, needlessly, the precious use of what you call your present moment of time in this life to explore, relive or journey into experiences of previous lives. It can become entertainment, which is possibly a distraction from one's life process and unfoldment.

The true connections to specific karmic juncture points (what you might call *karmic debts* or *lessons*) that are an integral part of your life's experience at this time, however, are very helpful to learn. Those people who need to know about these specific lives and lessons will be motivated to find them. It is a very self-contained phenomenon. It really needs no specific effort.

※

LINDA: **A famous astrophysicist, mathematician and author in the 20th century, Stephen Hawking, made a reference to the fact that he was born January 8, 1942, exactly 300 years after the death of Galileo, January 8, 1642.[5] Is there a connection between Professor Hawking and Galileo?**

ARIEL: There are several of what you refer to as *connections* between the form of spirit that you have seen as Stephen Hawking and the form of spirit that was embodied in Galileo. The principal thing we wish to teach you through your question is the character of consciousness that is expressed through these two individuals.

Each one has an extraordinary capacity to focus on aspects of the nature of the very universe which you inhabit. Each has explored areas that transcend and go beyond most minds of the time periods in which they have lived. Each one is very singularly focused, and as such is somewhat limited in many other aspects of his emotional or conscious development. But, their singular focus makes them particularly well suited to fathom depths and understandings of a very profound order using their very solidly rooted, logical and complex linear analysis capabilities.

Each one also portrays a piece of what we have tried to show you, which is that there are many roles, needs and functions that, when blended together in a mosaic that you call *life*, are each perfectly placed. In both cases [Hawking and Galileo], each one is the perfect embodiment of the life that was meant to be lived. Each one is the life form that was meant to be expressed. Neither one duplicated or in any way took from another being

---

5. Hawking, S. W. 1988. *A Brief History of Time*, Bantam Books, New York, p. 116.

that expression of life destined to be for another. Each one beautifully manifested the role and function that that soul was intended to manifest within the embodiment and the time of his life.

As to the inference in the question that they might indeed be the same being reincarnating, the strongest statement of connection that you could understand through this limited vocabulary we use to speak to you is that both have the same ability to reach what you might call a state of universal consciousness that exists in the energy field in which you live and that is rarely connected to by the human mind.

This field of consciousness, this field of knowledge, has been observed in many of your spiritual, religious and academic traditions throughout time. It is the field of knowledge that all great visionaries, seers, mystics, prophets, philosophers, mathematicians and physicists have connected with in order to propel knowledge, to propel evolution from an artistic or mathematical perspective. These two beings [Hawking and Galileo] have exemplified the ability to reach, connect with and bring back knowledge from that same space of consciousness. As a result, each has been perceived as being brilliant beyond description and having depth of understanding which is exemplary compared to their contemporaries, and each will be noted in your history as pivotal points in the evolution of consciousness.

Each has been perceived as
being brilliant beyond description . . .
and each will be noted
in your history
as pivotal points
in the evolution of consciousness.

Judgment

LINDA: **Causing physical or emotional harm are behaviors most humans judge as wrong. Please share with us your perspective on this subject.**

ARIEL: In this realm, an experience is simply what is. It is simply the experience. In this realm, all that happens is simply the instantaneous moment of pure cognition and experience. In your realm, there is first the experience and then immediately following it, you place a value judgment on that experience.

You separate yourself from the experience by judging it. The experience, in and of itself, has no way to be judged, for it is purely an experience. So it is you—your mind and your ego—that discriminates, judges and labels *good* or *bad*, *holy* or *unholy*, *right* or *wrong*. Experiencing life without judgment is not something the normal mind can do because it requires the normal mind to be transcended—something from this [angelic] perspective that is experienced at all times.

---

*Experiencing life without judgment
is not something
the normal mind can do. . . .*

✳

LINDA: **Whether it's blowing smoke in someone's face, imprisoning someone for religious beliefs or ending a life, one person has no right to impose his will on another. I don't see it as just another experience when people are suffering at the hands of another. How can you not perceive such things as bad?**

ARIEL: These things are certainly experienced by the recipient, by the victim, from an ego perspective, as a bad thing. But make no mistake about this blueprint, this plan, as to how things unfold. At a soul level, these two—the victimizer and the victim—are soulmates. They are in perfect harmony and accord, operating at a soul level in perfect unison—one soul agreeing to have the experience of being a brutalizer, the other soul agreeing to have the experience of total and, possibly savage, victimization leading to either extensive trauma or death.

From the standpoint of the human experience, there is tremendous judgment and emotion. But, from a soul standpoint, it is a very rich, very vivid, soul-level experience. It is analogous to the richness, at a soul-level, of jumping into a freezing pool of water. Although it may be unpleasant to the ego, it is a wonderful, rich experience for the soul to have.

LINDA: **When a person suffers or an animal suffers, or when one is killed, yes, I make a judgment—this is a bad thing. You're telling me it's just another experience and that there is no good and bad. I don't understand this philosophy.**

ARIEL: Please do not misunderstand our message or confuse "no judgment" with "no responsibility." From the human ego perspective, judgment is both unavoidable and essential. You have, through your judgment, established a complex framework of good and bad within which to live somewhat harmoniously.

Your moral, legal and ethical systems are based on it. What we wish you to know is that from the perspective of this realm, there isn't a judgmental frame of reference. The concept of *good* and *bad* is something specifically created by the human mind.

The concept of good and bad is . . .
created by the human mind.

❋

From this realm, what happens in life is just a range of possible experiences. The soul experiences, for example, temperature as just a range from hot to cold—not one good, one bad—just a variety of rich, incredible experiences that the human body can give to the soul to experience. It is the person who has the experience who judges, evaluates, labels and makes one better or worse than the other. And it's subjective, not absolute. For example, there are many who love to live in cold climates and judge hot as horrible. Likewise, there are many who love to live in hot climates and judge cold as terrible.

You must understand that each soul is completely responsible for its actions and their consequences in life. Each action, those judged from your ego perspective as good as well as those judged from your ego perspective as bad, creates karmic energy. Each soul will, for the purpose of ongoing growth and development, experience the results or consequences of its own karmic energy. A soul who at one time has the experience of being a brutalizer, will possibly at another time have the experience of being the victim. And while at a soul level there is no judgment on the role played, there is complete and inescapable responsibility.

*While at a soul level,
there is no judgment . . .
there is complete and inescapable
responsibility.*

❋

LINDA: **As humans, then, what can we learn from your perspective of no right or wrong, good or bad, in terms of how we live our lives?**

ARIEL: Basically that your life is guided by two forces. One is the divine force that guides you and gives you wonderful freedom of rein within certain bounds. The other is your own free will, which you may exercise within certain bounds. There is no pre-ordination, nor is there total freedom of choice. Free will and divine guidance work in harmony, one with the other.

Your soul's mission as it journeys through your lifetime is to unfold within this harmony by facing growth experiences, resolving old karma, creating new karma and coming to know God. As you follow this unfoldment, you must seek to live in a way that takes the ever-increasing love that you experience from your evolving communion with God and use it to live in a way that puts forth karma based on love. Since it is unavoidable for your mind to constantly judge, you can use your power of judgment to help guide your thoughts and actions to create karma based on love as you avoid thoughts and actions that create karma based on fear. Your power of judgment, used in this way, can be supportive and constructive in the living of your life and in the evolution of your soul. Please be aware that judgment of others, especially others of different race, religion, politics, nationality, gender or preferences, creates a karmic energy based on fear.

---

*Since it is unavoidable
for your mind to . . . judge,
you can use your power of judgment
to help guide your thoughts and actions
to create karma based on love. . . .*

Self-Discovery

LINDA: How can a person find out what is her truth, what she is meant to do?

ARIEL: In the harmony of the universe in which you live, each person has a specific function, purpose or piece in the overall mosaic of life itself.

Those in what you call the lower kingdoms of consciousness (but which are actually sometimes higher, such as this animal kingdom that you seem to feel you own) possess an ability roughly labeled *instinct*. These magnificent creatures are not encumbered by your complexity of ego separation (to the extent that you higher species are encumbered). Therefore, the specific purpose of their lives is always readily available, always known and always followed. This is reflected in activities as mysterious as migrations and movements across vast geographic territories and in the incredible knowledge of how to access food. It is also reflected in their ability to grow and live in harmony with those around them, following their instinct even to their place of death and becoming part of what you call the food chain. Each moment is lived for its perfect purpose.

If you could move beyond your sense of self-importance and self-adornment with possessions, prizes, trophies, titles and the various ways in which you distinguish, separate and identify yourself, you could move inward to that place where that primal instinct is alive and well within you. If you then follow that instinct, you will be living your life's purpose.

If you could . . . follow that instinct,
you will be living your life's purpose.

The easiest way to find, feel or experience that primal instinct is in the area you call your *heart*, through the feeling that you call *love*. As we have explained before, love is the substance of this universe. It is also the feeling or phenomenon that you experience when you are in alignment with this primal instinct, when you are doing that which is your purpose, that which is your place and mission.

Love is the substance
of this universe.

Do not confuse purpose or mission with being static. For everything in your universe is in a state of constant change. So, too, is your purpose and mission, your place, your task. If individuals are highly attuned to their instinct and have sufficient strength and daring to resist the all-too-human fears, they can spend an entire life following, working with, growing from and evolving through the process of living as their instinct describes. That person will abide in a state of love, grace, harmony and joy, and live in, what has been labeled in your words, a state of holy communion with God.

The world in which you live is open to having every single being living in perfect divine accord and harmony, following implicitly each movement of instinctive patterning, moving with hearts filled to overflowing with the feeling of love and grace, facing, dealing with and finally triumphing over fears and challenges. It is part of the design of the universe.

All too often, people are out of touch with that inner instinct. They do not experience that feeling that can fill their hearts to overflowing and bring life and passion to the very core of their being. At other times, they are well aware of their inner instinct but too afraid to act. At still other times, they are overcome by self-desire and, in effect, swim upstream fighting their instinct, fighting the very current of life, and they end up exhausted.

The miracle and majesty of the creation that you know as your universe is that it will support everyone swimming with the current, and it will support everyone swimming against the current. The evolutionary destiny, however, is that all, in time, will swim with that current, will flow with it.

LINDA: **What are the consequences of not paying attention to warning signs that one is off his life path?**

ARIEL: You have a wonderful word for this phenomenon. You have labeled it *hell*.

Myriad results take place when, in essence, the ego fights the natural call of the divine, or it hears the instinct and knows the heart's desire but does not follow it. It is much akin to, in your physical world, trying to block a mighty river. You may succeed for some time, but not without much effort, and ultimately, if you are successful, then everything downstream becomes parched and withers.

If you do not follow the flow and the harmony of your life, constantly seeking to fill your heart to overflowing and bringing yourself closer to the divine, then many emotions that stem from fear will become predominant. These include feelings of jealousy, competition, guilt, shame, anger, bitterness, apathy and depression. The list is too numerous to describe, but as you hear these words, you can understand this phenomenon.

If the flow of your life is held back long enough, it becomes like blocking the river and denying what is downstream its source of nourishment. What is downstream will wither. Similarly, the human body and the human spirit will wither. Despondency, despair, even distress and disease can occur.

If the flow of your life
is held back . . .
distress and disease can occur.

✳

LINDA: How does one tell the difference between a struggle that's meant for learning and a struggle that's a sign that we are off our path?

ARIEL: There is great insight in your question for this is one of the foremost points of learning that a soul must understand in its journey through the gift of a human life. The most important insights are to be gained by looking at the extremes of this phenomenon of difficulty or struggle.

Many a person, when encountering even the slightest amount of struggle or difficulty, gives up on the task. Sometimes that struggle and difficulty may come from outside, such as from people around you not agreeing with you, not supporting you, not encouraging you or even those who are trying to prevent you from accomplishing your task. But all too often that struggle comes from within your own mind, from all the negative and limited thoughts that try to dissuade, prevent and block you from accomplishing your task on your journey.

When your ego causes you to give up at the slightest sign of difficulty or struggle, such surrender contributes nothing to soul-level growth. The presence of struggle or the presence of difficulty is a very useful and helpful vehicle with which to develop tremendous spiritual and soul-level refinement and growth in a lifetime.

It is, however, a question of degree, for at the other end of the range of your perception of struggle or difficulty is a person who will not give up—one whose ego is trying to force its will upon the very flow or dynamic of life. This is the ego that paddles upstream despite all of the warning signs, fatigue or difficulties until exhaustion and collapse occur. Such activity is not an activity that produces the type of spiritual growth we speak of.

One of your soul's objectives is to learn how to read and understand the indescribable flow of ease versus difficulty of the universe, to learn how to know whether your life is in alignment with or in opposition to that flow. It is a key spiritual skill for you to develop the ability to learn whether a difficulty is an opportunity for growth or whether it is a signal of misdirection.

It is a key spiritual skill
for you to . . . learn
whether a difficulty
is an opportunity for growth
or whether it is a signal
of misdirection.

It is something each soul must learn to discern, and it is the key to all great spiritual growth through the human life. It is not a point that has an easy formula or an easy answer. For if it did, there would be little value in the soul-growth that could occur.

❋

LINDA: **You told us that we could never know God because there's no way to step outside and look at where God does not exist.[6] Using the same reasoning, since we cannot step outside of ourselves, does that mean that we cannot completely understand ourselves?**

ARIEL: There is much truth to what you speak.

There is much about yourself that you may explore. You may plumb many depths of awareness. You may observe yourself; you may observe your mind; you may observe the operation of emotions; you may observe your sensory feelings. You may, in many ways, attempt to grasp your identity and attempt to understand who you are and what you're all about. But because it is the ego observing and trying to understand yourself, there is a higher aspect of your identity that is blocked off from accessibility.

There is a part of you that is simultaneously "you," the separate ego self and "you," the piece of the unity. The part of you associated with the unity is not visible to your ego's vision. And as long as it is being searched for by the eyes of the ego, your totality will never be seen.

Your history has seen many, in religious as well as nonreligious environments, who have seen much more of the depth and breadth of the human experience. Whether through disciplined spiritual practices such as prayer, contemplation and meditation or by divine intervention, they have left behind, for but a moment, the part of the ego that witnesses and experiences consciousness. Without the presence of that "witness," they have stepped outside of themselves (as you have put it) and have seen far more of the truth of who they are.

※

---

6. Question, p. 313, "Unseen Universe"

Inner Teachers[1]

LINDA: What are the advantages and disadvantages of learning through another person's inner teacher?

ARIEL: The question itself points out once again the human mind's judgmental operation, which we do not have. To fragment or partition or label knowledge or aspects of reality into positive or negative, good or bad, advantages or disadvantages, is purely human.

The path of growth within this marvelous learning opportunity that you call being human ultimately comes to a single point of focus. This focal point is the direct, personal, experiential knowledge of what you call God. It is not the understanding of what other people have found, or what other people have written, or even what you have read or heard from sacred text that you call scriptures. The direct task, the most important task of any soul traveling through the journey of a human experience called life, is personally, from an area that you refer to as your heart, to know God deeply through communion.

Some people will have the great fortune to encounter that communion experience directly. They will come to know God through what you have called an inner teacher or an inner guide, or even through the communion experience with celestial energies that you might call, from your human perspective, a being outside of yourself. This is indeed one of the most profound ways to refine the depths of the experience of knowing and understanding God.

Different growth steps along the way will allow a person to encounter what you have labeled in your world a higher self, a higher sense of self, inner wisdom or inner knowing. There are many different words to describe the phenomenon of experienc-

---

1. Questions on inner teachers were submitted from our introduction author, Dr. Alfred Alschuler.

ing and understanding yourself and the universe in which you live that extends beyond the definition of the separate, distinct thing you think you are.

In some cases the experience can extend even beyond the higher self to other celestial beings such as guardians, spirits, angels and deities that are perceived by the person as being separate and distinct and coming from outside the person. And again, appreciate that this inside or outside distinction is unique to the human mind, for in reality there is a continuum that you call God which does not have such distinctions. But that is something you cannot completely grasp with your mind. It is, in essence, incomprehensible to you.

Finding someone who will awaken your inner knowledge by using his inner knowledge to help and support you in your quest is often a wonderful, transitional step. And while the knowledge does not come from your own direct experience, once heard it can have deep, deep resonance within you. It can awaken and kindle the flame of inner spiritual knowledge and, although it came through another's spirituality, openness, or the communion that another being has mastered, the information itself can provide a tremendous opportunity to awaken in you deep, soul-level knowledge and growth.

Finding someone
who will awaken
your inner knowledge
by using his inner knowledge . . .
is often a wonderful, transitional step.

However, it is but a temporary stepping-stone. For the true quest on the spiritual path, and the spiritual growth within the soul's journey of a lifetime, is to find that knowledge directly. It is the main theme and thesis of each of your religions, although it is often not practiced. It is easy to get stuck, to become complacent and to be lax at doing what is often very difficult inner spiritual work.

Within the framework of the organizations that you call religions is the invitation to use religion as a support tool as you journey along their prescribed path. Religion is a path designed to give you, first, the intellectual understanding of what you seek, and second, deep inner spiritual understanding by direct knowing, by direct communion experience.

When following the path of religion, souls often become complacent with the intellectual understanding the religion offers and, thus, do not find for themselves the deep inner communion experience that they seek. They, in essence, stay complacent with the knowledge gained from the deep communion experience of others who have gone before them.

Relying on others' inner knowledge, which they gain from their higher self or from what you label as a spirit or an angel, can also become a place to be trapped, to become complacent and to rely solely on the efforts of others and not be spurred on by the knowledge gained and the resonance attained to complete the task of finding the connection and the communion for yourself. For no matter how good that knowledge gained through the skill and the compassion of anyone who conveys it to you, it always falls short of that which you can attain through inner knowing yourself.

In that same vein, there is a calculated and understood risk that these very words that we are speaking now could become, for some, a crutch upon which to rest. But we also know the words that we speak will awaken many a heart, will inspire many a soul to complete the personal growth that they have embarked upon through the journey of their lives. There is nothing done from this realm that is extra, and there is nothing done that is without full understanding of what will transpire. So we take no risk in conveying these words through you.

The words that we speak
will awaken many a heart,
will inspire many a soul. . . .

LINDA: **What is the role of discernment as we listen to and learn from our inner teachers?**

ARIEL: Discernment is uniquely and distinctly an aspect of ego. Soul does not discern, for there is nothing to discern. Soul simply and purely *knows*. Discernment is the action the ego undertakes to try to understand what the soul already knows—to determine what is the will of ego versus what is the will of God for you.

Discernment is the action
the ego undertakes
to try to understand
what the soul already knows. . . .

Discernment is a very, very powerful tool in the development of your soul. From the strength of your strongly held idea of being separate and distinct, you then attempt to discern what is God's will for you, or in other words, what is the direction of the energy that flows in your life, what way is your soul pointing you to go? And then you take action and work against the force of your own fear, as though you have set up the hurdles over which you will then jump. This action can, from an ego perspective, feel as though it has great risk, but from a soul's perspective it is absolutely rock solid, steady and sure.

The process of discernment and then taking action and living life based on that discernment is a key path to understanding and knowing God. For as discernment is perfected, the ego comes to understand that it is but a co-pilot, at best, in your life. It is direction from God that is driving your life. Your ego is but a backseat passenger.

> *It is direction from God*
> *that is driving your life.*
> *Your ego is but*
> *a backseat passenger.*

The ego must understand that its role is to bring the will of God through you. In other words, your ego's role is to use the functions of your human body and your human resources to carry out the will of God in a way that will fit perfectly and usefully into the world around you. While the ego is very important and very needed, it is not the one that is truly the driving focus of your very life.

LINDA: **In this practice of discernment, maybe some voices are not in our best interest. Maybe there's an invisible realm that doesn't have the same healthy goals you do.**

ARIEL: The discernment that we have spoken to you about is your personal discernment, the discernment of whether the voice of ego or the voice of God is being heard within your life and within your mind.

The discernment we think you are asking about in this

question is, having received guidance that you perceive is beyond your own inner sense of self, determining whether this guidance is truly of a God-like form, a form of high vibration as you might experience it, a form that is true and loving for you, which can guide and direct you in the most healthy and positive ways.

The true process of discernment leads you to know, understand, experience and live life from a communion with what you call God. A key element of that knowledge is the direct experience of this realm and of God, and is indeed what you also label absolute, pure, unconditional love.

The very fabric of the universe is love. Thus, in the practice of discernment and the quest for knowing God, one finds higher and higher levels of love—not just an understanding of love, but the direct experience of the energy that fills your heart to a radiant overflow.

---

*The very fabric of the universe
is love.*

Energies that are reflections of your own ego, projected in a way that make them appear to be from an external source, cannot contain this level of love since they often contain a great deal of fear. Energies or influences projected by other people toward you, such as the powerful energies of a parent or the powerful energies of an enemy, can appear to be coming from outside yourself. These external energies will, because of the filtering of the fear from which they were projected, feel very limited, or possibly even something you call evil. To a person skilled in discernment, these energies cannot be misunderstood as representations of any divine realm.

> *When your soul opens*
> *to our gift,*
> *not only do we imprint knowing*
> *into your mind,*
> *we also imprint love*
> *into your heart.*

If the only element of communication from this realm were the words, images and forms that we imprint upon your mind, then the source of the communication could be questioned or mistaken. However, we communicate far more than this. When your soul opens to our gift, not only do we imprint knowing into your mind, we also imprint love into your heart. And with the feeling of love that we imprint on your heart, there can be no mistake. There is no force that exists within your own ego and no force as projected from another human that can contain, as clearly and as purely, that imprint of love that comes from this realm.

> *There is no force that exists . . .*
> *that can contain,*
> *as clearly and as purely,*
> *that imprint of love*
> *that comes from this realm.*

Coming to recognize the feeling in your heart is part of the process of discernment. As your skill in discernment increases, you will seek both the feeling of joy and radiant heart-felt love that exudes from your communion, as well as the knowledge that your mind attempts to fathom and understand.

But, indeed, whether the question is phrased as to discerning what you humorously label as a good versus evil spirit, or discerning ego versus divine, it is the same question and it is the same spiritual step that you must take to make that discernment.

Unseen Universe

Time

LINDA: You frequently refer to time as if it is a manufactured human concept, as in "your concept of time" or "what you call time." Why?

ARIEL: From our perspective, time does not exist. Time is simply this instantaneous moment, the spark of pure cognition that you might call *consciousness*. It only exists in what you have termed "this moment," "the present moment," "now." Time is only an idea fabricated for convenience by the human mind and is based completely on a cyclical characteristic of nature that allows you to create this idea. It's a convenience that allows many people to agree on a certain way of behavior. All that exists in the realm from which we speak is the eternal "now."

Time is only an idea
fabricated for convenience
by the human mind. . . .

LINDA: From my perspective, it seems as if all things are happening in the context of a past, present and future. Are all these events actually occurring simultaneously?

ARIEL: It is impossible to use any model to explain what you are trying to understand. You are trying to fit your model of time, which does not exist other than as a human concept, onto our reality by saying that past, present and future all exist simultaneously and that we span all time. Again, time only exists because your consciousness needs it to exist, to function. The best way to see it is: the present moment is all that exists. The present moment, if followed moment by moment by moment, leads to many experiences.

The human mind perceives a present moment that has occurred and has moved away from the present, and this idea is called your *past*. There is a universally agreed-upon concept amongst people that the past exists. There are even people called historians who track it. There are archeological ways to date, with very precise measurements, that thing called the past. The past truly is just a reference point being viewed in the present moment. The present moment, however, is all that exists. The future does not exist either, other than as you use the present moment to think about a present moment that has not yet occurred.

Heaven and Hell

LINDA: **Humans and many organized religions have two concepts known as heaven and hell. Do you have a comment on these concepts?**

ARIEL: We have alluded to and used these concepts and these terms in answers to some of your previous questions. Indeed what you perceive as heaven and what you perceive as hell are states of human experience. They are associated with the joy and complexity, and sometimes the difficulty, of being human. Heaven and hell occur in life; they occur in the experience from birth until death; they are manifestations of the state of consciousness that you live within during a lifetime.

Heaven and hell occur in life. . . .

You may experience within your life a state of very close communion with what you call *spirit*, *the divine*, *unity* or *God*. In this state of being, your life is filled with an outflowing of love and a receiving of love. This is a state of being in which there is total forgiveness and total harmony. This is not a state of being in which there is piety that produces forgiveness. This is not a "holier-than-thou" state of elevation, but a state of being in which the person is in such close resonance with the divine that there is an experience of unity within humanity—that is, an experience of unity within the consciousness of a soul attached to a physical body. This experience of unity is one that brings such a state of overwhelming grace and divinity into the human form that judgment doesn't exist.

It is not that all is forgiven. Rather, this is a state in which there is nothing to forgive, for there is nothing which is judged or labeled as wrong. It is a state of tremendous holiness that radiates from within and is the ultimate embodiment of the kingdom of heaven your prophets have spoken of.

Hell, on the other hand, is well known to many human beings. Hell is a state of separation, a state of disconnection from the divine. Hell is a state in which the normal, natural consequence of separation, something you call *fear*, is the predominant life force. Hell created by the life force of fear is self-perpetuating; it is self-fulfilling; it expands; and it builds upon itself.

The states of heaven and hell, as they exist, do not cease upon the moment of physical, metabolic death but are part of the transformational journey that we have described to you in previous answers.[1] It is often this phenomenon that has been understood and seen through religious teachings that describe a postmetabolic death experience of heaven, hell and purgatory.

But the broadest definition of the experience is missed. For

---

1. Questions, pp. 163–168, "Life Passages."

while the experience of heaven and hell does move past metabolic death and into the phases approaching the unity, the dominant experience of heaven and hell occurs within the span of a lifetime. Once the journey from the human vibration to that of the highest vibration of unity is complete, this realm from which we speak to you is simply a state that you would best describe as love—nothing more, nothing less.

---

*This realm from which we speak
to you is . . . love—
nothing more, nothing less.*

※

LINDA: **Are there parts of the unity beyond the human experience that oppose your efforts to promote love?** [A long pause occurred.] **Do you understand the question?**

ARIEL: We think you have asked the eternal question, namely, if the energy with which we are offering these words to enlighten may be called *good*, is there an opposite energy called *evil* which would destroy?

From the basis of the unity of all experience in the universe, there is but the life force that has many vibrations and manifestations, of which everything is a part. We wish to have you understand that creation and destruction are two separate processes.

Creation and destruction are forces within the life plan of this universe. Things are created and things are destroyed, all in perfect accord with the divine unfolding of the universe. The human mind with its incessant need for judgment places labels such as *good* on creation and *bad* on destruction. And yet if you observe your world, you will see an ever-flowing cycle of creation followed by destruction followed by creation in a continuing cycle. The overall effect of this cycle is one of tremendous expansion and tremendous growth.

As to the question of good versus evil, there is but one force, one vibration in this universe, and it is the vibration and the force of God. In the human realm, when this vibration is brought openly and freely without distortion or limit into a heart that is ready for it, it produces the most incredible love and what you would call *good*.

There is but one force . . .
and it is . . . God.

Many of your religious traditions have the most wonderful moral and ethical teachings. Within the Judeo-Christian system there are the 10 Commandments, and in the Buddhist system there are the 16 Precepts. Both are comprehensive descriptions of the actions of one you would label as *good*. What you do not often observe is that those lists describe the natural behavior of one who is in alignment with, and in communion with, the divine. Often, these lists are used as guidelines for those *not* in communion with the divine to bring them into behavioral alignment. And while they serve a very useful purpose in this capacity, they are, in and of themselves, a perfect description of the normal, natural and effortless behavior of one who is in that state of communion and connection with God.

On the other end of the spectrum created by your human need to categorize and partition is an experience of a force that you label as *evil*. Evil is quite simply the love of God passed through the distorting filter of fear within the human consciousness. When pure love from God is brought through a human consciousness filled with fear, that love is distorted into the energy that you call evil. The action of one motivated by love distorted by fear into evil often violates the guidelines of your 10 Commandments or 16 Precepts.

Evil is . . . the love of God
passed through the . . . filter of fear
within the human consciousness.

The energy itself is not evil, only the resulting consequence of the distortion from human fear is what you might call the force of evil. The essence that must be avoided is the indescribable power and force of fear for it has the ability to block your communion experience with the divine.

Fear is a very personal training ground
that each soul must traverse.

Fear is an incredible spiritual hurdle for those following the path to God. It is part of the divine plan, for nothing is extra and nothing has been left out. Fear is a very personal training ground that each soul must traverse. Sometimes fear seems like a gauntlet or obstacle course that must be navigated. There is truthfully no way around fear. Drugs and chemicals that attempt to numb fear serve only to temporarily suspend the spiritual training in your life and your soul's journey. Fear must be faced head-on and moved through. As this occurs, it will seem that the force of evil has been conquered and the force of good is triumphant.

Drugs and chemicals . . .
temporarily suspend
the spiritual training in your life. . . .

Please be clear that while, from your perception, this change is very real and necessary as an element of spiritual training, it is but a shift in your perception. For the force was always the force of God and the force of love.

Divine Plan

LINDA: **You spoke of a divine plan. Where does this divine plan come from?**

ARIEL: Everything that you experience in life is happening in a divine order. Look beyond this idea of who you think you are and look at the world around you. Look at how the cycles and the seasons move; how the entire world of animals and plants flows in perfect harmony with that divine order. Look at the relationships that exist in the minutest part of nature.

Everything is part of a giant mosaic, a kaleidoscope of life—constantly changing and forming, but all with perfect intent and purpose. And when those who are open and attuned to that ebb and flow of the creative force can be moved by it, they are most effective in supporting the entire process according to the unfolding plan of life.

It is not a plan in the sense of predestination, for you have free will. But if you align your will with that of this creative force, you will find yourself pleased beyond your wildest dreams. And in the process of doing that, you please the divine, the Creator, the thing that you label as *God*.

*If you align your will
with that of this creative force,
you will find yourself pleased
beyond your wildest dreams.*

LINDA: **Is this divine plan created before we are born?**

ARIEL: The plan has existed through the eternity that you label as time. There has never been a time before which the plan was not unfolding. And there will never be a time after which the plan is not unfolding. For the very essence and nature of life itself is growth, change and unfoldment, moving you to ever higher levels of awareness and love.

Your incarnation in this physical body at this particular time is a perfect piece of this indescribable movement called life. The only question is to what extent an individual's will can impede this creative flow. If every person on the planet you inhabit were to suddenly shift into total support and alignment with the creative flow available to them, the evolution of your species would be mystical. But it is the nature of the human experience to have some who are in that alignment and others who are absolutely swimming against the current of this alignment.

*If every person on the planet . . .
were to suddenly shift
into total support and alignment
with the creative flow . . .
the evolution of your species
would be mystical.*

The process is designed in a most elaborate complexity that the human mind cannot fathom. Through this process, not only is life itself accomplishing its plan but the individual experience of each soul—whether it swims for a lifetime against the current and finally dies of exhaustion, or it is carried with the current light-years from where it started—gets exactly what it needs in its growth. There is an individual unfoldment, training and growth and a global, universal evolution that are in perfect symbiotic relation with each other.

LINDA: **Is there an intelligence behind this divine planning, this harmony that is created, this overall master plan? How does it happen? Who does it?**

ARIEL: From the very basis of your questions, asked again from the standpoint of the separate, human consciousness, we see that again there is a desire to place this realm and the basis of the universe into a construct that fits within the segmented structure and compartmentalized viewpoint of the human mind. It cannot be done in this fashion. Once again, using words that cannot possibly describe what we wish to describe, we will attempt a description.

There is no separate being, as your question has attempted to assert, that supervises, orchestrates or directs the master plan for the myriad of souls inhabiting human form. There is, however, the one pervasive intelligence and force that is everything we speak of, including those of us who speak from this realm. By its very nature, this force is self-directing in its various forms in all manners and at all times.

There is no separate being . . .
that . . . directs the master plan. . . .

Everything that exists in the universe is formed from the consciousness that formed it. Everything is directed by the consciousness that directs it. Everything is interlinked in a way of harmony and mastery such that all things work as part of a higher-level whole, which is difficult for a component part such as the human consciousness to comprehend.

You see pieces of the mosaic. For example, you are amazed at how the things you label *ecosystems* work. Yet ecosystems are small elements of this entirety that we speak of. You are amazed at how they function, how they are self-maintaining, self-balancing and self-correcting. Even though they are made up of millions of individual components, they seem to work in harmony with each other and in balance such that they have a mind of their own. Yet the ecosystem itself has no supreme being, no mind and no structure other than that which is the essence of all its subcomponents. And its subcomponents have no mind or directive thought other than that they exist as part of the whole.

Each piece of the universe can be viewed as such an ecosystem or such a self-contained structure. And yet each ecosystem fits in harmony with the next, making a larger, grander-scale understanding, until you reach a point that the human mind cannot fathom.

But that does not stop the reality from continuing to express itself. Things that your human consciousness has comprehended, has yet to comprehend and will never comprehend are all part of a larger ecosystem which has consciousness, is self-regulating, self-generating, self-directing and is what you have labeled *God*.

*Things that your human consciousness
has comprehended, has yet to comprehend
and will never comprehend
are all part of a larger ecosystem
which has consciousness, is self-regulating,
self-generating, self-directing
and is what you have labeled God.*

❋

LINDA: Is everybody chosen for something in their lives?

ARIEL: Everybody is chosen for a specific purpose or to accomplish specific things, or at least is given the opportunity to try. The real spiritual challenge is whether or not she can accomplish it. There have been, throughout your history, many who have been chosen and who have entered into a state of communion with the divine, bringing through divine gifts in a way that was perfect for them. It is the basis of many masterpieces of art, literature and creativity. It is also the basis of heroic activities and other great accomplishments.

*Bringing through divine gifts . . .
is the basis of many masterpieces . . .
and . . . heroic activities.*

The ways that a person's purpose or divine mission can be expressed are too numerous for us to state. But each divine purpose shares the same quality—a sense of joy and closeness to what you call God. In the process of working to accomplish her life's purpose, each person attains a soul-level sense of purpose beyond any personal gain. To the soul, it feels like a holy mission. Each person who has tried to accomplish her mission has a sense of incredibly deep inner satisfaction for having worked toward and possibly finished the task.

The environment you live in, the population, the world, is being orchestrated in total harmony with the accomplishment of a worldwide, planetary or galactic purpose. But as incomprehensible as it might sound, at the same time each individual of the billions on your planet is pursuing her own purpose, her own personal soul-charter. And yet the whole creation is in perfect harmony—nothing out of balance and nothing broken. And within each person, there is total flexibility of free will to choose the actions and activities of her life, to choose a particular path or to choose none at all—to succeed or to fail in living her life's purpose.

There is total flexibility of free will. . . .

※

LINDA: I hear your words but I have a tough time reconciling the pain of those who suffer from disease, starvation, brutal deaths with the idea of a divine plan.

ARIEL: It's only from your perspective of being human that you would ask such a question. We could ask of you: Why do some people live in hot tropical climates and others live in bitter freezing cold ones? How can you explain why somebody would be so foolish as to do one versus the other? The reason is that there is an ego-based preference for one climate over another. It is what the person wishes to experience. The truth is that from the perspective of the soul, death, even catastrophic death, suffering or torture, can be a rich soul-level experience.

From the perspective of the soul,
death . . . suffering or torture,
can be a rich soul-level experience.

To the soul, experiences that the ego would judge as negative can be wonderful soul-level experiences. The experience of death in a terrible car crash is as rich and profound to one soul as the experience of writing highly successful poetry that is published around the world is to another soul. Death is just an experience, a stepping-stone. Suffering is just an experience. It is only from the ego's perspective that these are judged as bad. We can see that you [Linda] have a lot of empathy for those who suffer, for those who have losses.

❋

Soul

LINDA: Could you explain the concept of the soul?

ARIEL: This has happened before and will happen again. You wish to understand concepts in which there is no way, within the framework of your words or ideas, for us to adequately and accurately answer. And having said that, we will attempt to answer your question.

The soul is a concept of the human mind. The human mind has, at its very core, the need to establish and maintain some degree of separate identity, different and distinct from everything else around it. Even highly spiritual people who have attained the knowledge that there is a distinct unity that pervades all life still need to know that while they are all one, they are, at the same time, all separate. The soul is that part of the eternal unity that the human mind requires to be separate and distinct from other souls. So even beyond the framework of the life that you now inhabit, there is some idea that this thing, this soul, will maintain your separate identity throughout time and space.

This spiritual essence that exists
beyond the death of the physical body,
has existed and will exist throughout time.

And while that idea is true, it is also somewhat untrue. The truth is that this idea you call *soul*, this spiritual essence that exists beyond the death of the physical body, has existed and will exist throughout time. You cannot go back to a time before which this essence did not exist, nor can you go to a time after which this essence will not exist. For this essence is none other than the force of this universe, this life, this aspect which you label as *God*—this pervasive, unity of life that is in all things.

As we have explained to you earlier when we have tried to answer your unanswerable questions, the reality from our perspective is not of any separate self. We do adapt and present ourselves in different images to accommodate your need to see things as separate and distinct and to see aspects of the realm of spirit as segmented so as to be easily understood by a mind that wishes to partition and segment. But no such segmentation exists.

We do adapt and present ourselves
in different images. . . .
But no such segmentation exists.

While it is difficult for you to understand, from your frame of reference, the *lack* of separation that exists in this realm, it is equally difficult to understand from this realm the insistence on separation that you have in your realm. For the separation that you perceive is an illusion. You really are not separate and distinct from any other human being except through the physical boundaries of the body you are inhabiting. But beyond that, you really are all one—one common life force that exists as love that pervades all living matter.

Have these words helped you understand more about the soul?

LINDA: **The concept of soul is still a bit confusing. It is, on the one hand, a piece of some larger whole, some unity. But you talk of a soul that enters and occupies *a* human body, which fosters the idea of separateness. So, I see the elements in my universe as components of a giant, interdependent force. Is this a correct interpretation?**

ARIEL: You have caught on well. The dilemma is that there are two truths which are simultaneously correct yet completely contradictory. It is what the human mind has such difficulty grasping or fathoming.

The soul is an individuality, a nature, an essence. Consider it to be a piece of something larger. And while it has a separate nature, a separate characteristic, it is still part of the larger thing. It is simultaneously in unity with the whole and separate and distinct with its own nature and character.

We have tried in answers to other questions to use the metaphor of sunlight.[2] When sunlight is passed through a prism, it creates a display of the colors of light which appear to the human eye to be separate and distinct, yet each one is still part of sunlight itself. Another way we might express it is by using the simple metaphor of a puzzle composed of infinitely

2. Question, p. 121, "Angelic Life"

many pieces. Each piece is separate, each piece has its own form, its own distinct nature, yet in this puzzle no piece can ever be separate from the puzzle. Yet each piece is separate and each piece is part of the puzzle.

LINDA: **When he was in college at Oxford, Stephen Hawking said that "nothing is worth making an effort for." Then he was diagnosed with a crippling disease that would cause him to lose the use of his physical body, and the following is a quote from Professor Hawking:**

> Before my condition had been diagnosed, I had been very bored with life. There had not seemed to be anything worth doing. But shortly after I came out of [sic] hospital, I dreamt that I was going to be executed. I suddenly realized that there were a lot of worthwhile things that I could do if I were reprieved.[3]

LINDA: **His mother also attributed his scientific focus to his physical challenges. Do you have a comment?**

ARIEL: While we will not comment on the life journey of a specific soul, your question underscores a very important teaching that we will comment on. All souls need to bring forth their treasure into a lifetime, no matter what form that treasure may take.

Often there is a personality that encumbers, resists or even attempts to thwart the soul's direction. Whenever a personality wages war or tries to battle with its associated soul, the personality will lose. Much struggle and effort may take place and much of your time may transpire, but the soul always works to manifest its destiny in a lifetime.

---

3. Freedman, G. (Producer) 1991. *A Brief History of Time,* an Anglia Television/ Gordon Freedman Production. (Film)

> *Whenever a personality wages war*
> *or tries to battle with its associated soul,*
> *the personality will lose.*

As a casualty of such a war, so to speak, you might experience the effect of tremendous physical adversity through disease. There are few things that the ego finds harder to ignore than disease. While you may dislike a disease that forms, you cannot ignore it. And while you might judge it as harsh, critical or even cruel that a life could be threatened by a debilitating disease, the higher level that we might ask you to view that life by is the soul's purpose or truth within the incarnation.

In the example you described, this one you call Hawking stated that the diagnosis of disease within his body caused him to change from being bored with life to seeing many worthwhile things to do. In general, disease can cause a fire to burn within the very heart of your being such that your life can be dedicated to the pursuit of what you were placed here to do. Anything that detracts from the expression of the most meaningful soul-level purpose of your life must be eliminated so the brilliance of who you are may shine through.

> *Disease can cause a fire to burn*
> *within the very heart of your being*
> *such that your life can be dedicated*
> *to the pursuit of what you were placed here to do.*

In your own way, your soul, without comparing it to any other, has a purpose that is, in the eyes of divinity, no greater or lesser than any other. Whether or not your soul's purpose is to tap into the highest realms of knowledge or be the vanguard of physics, biology, chemistry, politics, philosophy, religion or whatever form it might take, it is the perfect expression for you, and the expression of your life that is needed and wanted by God. For the realm from which we speak has no measure of comparison.

Whether or not your soul's purpose is to tap into the highest realms of knowledge . . . it is the perfect expression for you. . . .

You might ask yourself, is there any way that your own soul is being limited, constrained, thwarted or embattled by the ego that rules the physical being and the personality associated with it? And if so, what is it you must do to bring yourself into alignment with your soul's purpose? How could you find that for which your heart, the vehicle of your soul's communication with your desires, beckons? And how can you remove the obstacles, thoughts, ideas, beliefs you have that stand in the way of that expression?

How could you find that for which your heart . . . beckons?

The soul is a powerful force and is not to be taken lightly. Heart's desires, visions, dreams, wants and needs are not just casual feelings, but are indeed strong and important messages that you give to yourself. They are to be paid critical attention.

Heart's desires, visions, dreams, wants and needs are . . . important messages. . . .

As you live your soul's purpose, the things that your personality and your ego need, the things that they strive for, will be filled to a level of overflowing that you cannot comprehend. Simply align yourself with the purpose of your life and put your efforts into following it.

❋

LINDA: **When a life that suffers disability is brought into alignment with its soul's purpose, is there any possibility of getting rid of the physical disability? Is there some avenue that person could pursue that would help him physically get over some of the challenges being experienced?**

ARIEL: Your question comes from the standpoint that the physical disease and the impending ending of the life are negatives or problems to be dealt with and avoided. It is not necessarily true in the journey your soul makes from birth to death that any such experiences are wrong or negative.

The only criteria necessary for such a, what you might call, miracle to take place is that it be in the best interest of and aligned with the soul's journey at this time. If such a circumstance benefits not only the individual vibration known as your soul but is also in harmony and accord with the overall mosaic of life, then such a miracle will occur; a reversal of disease will take place.

In many cases and in many lives, you have seen disease serve as a wakeup call for action. Action is then taken and the wakeup call is no longer necessary. In other cases, this disease not only serves as the wakeup call to focus life's effort but is indeed part of the process of growth. Even though what you call death may result, the soul has still gained, grown and evolved through the experience. Again, it is not the ego that is forcing, influencing and controlling this journey you call a lifetime. The ego is but a co-pilot in the process.

❋

LINDA: You stated earlier that you will not comment on the life journey of a specific soul. What if your wisdom could help that soul see what the future brings for it or help it heal its illness?

ARIEL: It is advisable, in general, to avoid the input or counsel of those who would predict, prophesy or foretell an outcome of a specific lifetime or a worldwide trend or event. This is a very important teaching, and we wish to say more.

One who attempts to help by prophesying, advising or predicting the journey that you would be taking, in a sense, enters into the journey and action of your lifetime with you. Knowing the flow of this river of life that you swim in, that you attempt to follow and move with, is indeed a unique and personal matter. The soul grows by testing and moving, by understanding each action and by refining the ability to fine-tune and develop its mechanism for following life—for aligning the ego's needs and desires with the soul's purpose.

When those of this realm are sought to predict what will happen in your realm, the soul-growth process is circumvented and you are robbed of your potential for soul growth and evolution. As a result, little is gained in your journey.

There is also the karmic implication of being the vehicle that imprecisely steers or directs the actions of another. This is a very complex and interwoven aspect of souls. For those who predict the evolutionary steps of another's life become part of the journey, part of that lifetime.

> *Those who predict*
> *the evolutionary steps of another's life*
> *become part of the journey,*
> *part of that lifetime.*

They do attempt, from the goodness of their hearts, to help, guide and steer the evolution of someone they care for and wish to empower. They seek to help her avoid difficulties or gain the maximum pleasures and opportunities from her life's journey. However, the energetic and karmic actions that occur from such predictions for specific lives, the evolution of society, or even changes in geography, are very complex.

LINDA: **But you've been quite candid about sharing glimpses of the future about *my* life with me, so your words on this subject seem a little inconsistent.**

ARIEL: The inconsistency is only from your perspective. Let us try to clarify this matter further.

Make no mistake that when glimpses of your future were given to you, the one who spoke those words [Stevan] took on specific karmic consequences of allowing us [Ariel] to share information that would help our work together.

Throughout the history of the evolution of what you would call humankind, such information from this realm, through the voice of one we may communicate directly with, has been used on the smallest of scales and the most grand of scales to alter or sway the direction of the unfoldment of the destiny of your race.

---

*Throughout . . . history . . . information
from this realm . . . has been used . . . to alter . . .
the destiny of your race.*

The simple example you have used of our sharing knowledge, guiding your personal work—while it may not be viewed as altering the operation or the destiny of your planet, it has at its core just as profound an impact. We offered you wisdom and advice through this voice [Stevan] to attempt to keep you [Linda] on track, to keep you from being distracted or moving in directions that were unproductive, given there is little excess of your time. It felt appropriate to involve karmically this Stevan in your activities and risk the impact of changing your life's activity and direction, and hence the very degree of success of our work together, by sharing what you might call proprietary information. However, the framework in which this work has been done directly involves only your two souls, such that the overall karmic burden taken on is minor.

※

The Unity

LINDA: Shirley MacLaine, author of *Dancing in the Light* and many other books, describes her meeting with a spiritual being that introduced itself as her "higher unlimited self," which she called "H.S."[4] Is there a difference between Shirley MacLaine's experience with H.S. and my experience with you?

ARIEL: Your question has been well thought out and reaches to the point of the most difficult of spiritual insights for the human

---

4. MacLaine, S. 1986. *Dancing in the Light*. New York: Bantam Books, 335.

mind to attain. The essence of the truth is that both of your observations are correct. Such encounters or openings, if you will, to what the human mind perceives as higher realms of consciousness are experiences of entities or energies separate and distinct from yourself and, at the same time, are encounters with a higher part of yourself. Having said that, it is necessary to explain the meaning of our words, for it is difficult for the human mind to comprehend that both realities are simultaneously true.

There is but one reality that pervades all life, and that reality is that all life is one life and all expressions of life are part of the same life vibration. There have been many ways of expressing that through your religions or philosophies. It has been stated that all things are one, all things are part of that same one, and that one pervades all things.

All life is one life. . . .

It has also been stated that all things in this universe that you are experiencing are God. They are all created by God. They are all manifestations of God. They are all part of God. These are all statements of the same truth—that everything you experience, including yourself, is part of the same pervasive energy field, the same life vibration.

So, extending from this understanding, when you reach beyond the normal frame of reference toward, in your words, an angelic encounter, you are simply meeting a part of who and what you are. Understanding it as a higher dimension of yourself, from that perspective, is quite accurate. But from that same perspective, that same underlying truth, it would have to be seen that meeting another person is also meeting a part of yourself; meeting an animal or a plant is also meeting a part of yourself. As reality is experienced from this pervasive unity, all entities—whether they be celestial or divine in nature or physically separate such as another person, plant, animal or any living form—are all, in truth, an extension or an aspect of you.

It is sometimes easy for human consciousness to comprehend the lofty understanding of a higher self, a higher nature or higher vibration as a wonderful part of who you are. But the very same principle that makes that true also makes your spouse, your sibling, your friend or your enemy a part of who you are.

And yet we said that there are two underlying realities that simultaneously co-exist. In truth they do not co-exist apart from the human consciousness. For apart from human consciousness, there is but a single, pervasive reality. It is the basis of the universe. Human consciousness, however, is unable to view itself as anything other than separate and distinct from all things outside of itself.

So powerful is the human mind's ability to hold onto this concept, this fabrication of separateness, that it even allows you to view certain aspects of yourself within your physical body as not part of you. It should seem simple to understand that feelings, disease or pain, within your physical body, are all part of you. And yet, the human mind can make these phenomena of pain or illness seem like things that are not part of who you are. They are not part of your idea, your definition or your illusion of who you are. So they appear as foreign invaders of the sanctuary of your identity.

This concept . . . of separateness . . .
even allows you to view certain aspects of yourself
within your physical body
as not part of you.

So, to a consciousness that can create separation even within the boundaries of its own physical body, it is easy to see that the mind could view higher aspects, higher dimensions, especially encounters with angelic beings or celestial vibrations, as separate and distinct, or even as foreign or alien entities. And yet it is only the mind of human consciousness that creates this framework.

So, indeed, such encounters viewed as a higher self are quite correct when experienced through a mind that can see the unity of the universe. But the same experience could be viewed as an encounter with another entity or being when viewed from the separation-based model of human consciousness.

LINDA: **You say we are one. But the Linda part of this "one" living in a mountaintop town house is a lot more comfortable than a homeless man, I'll call Ralph, living downtown in a cardboard shack. Please explain this concept that we are one.**

ARIEL: If it would help you understand, both of your interpretations are correct. There are two separate and distinct ways that *you* can perceive the reality of the universe in which *you* live. There is only one way that *we* can perceive the reality of the universe in which we *all* live.

The reality in which we and you can experience things in common is that within the reality of your town house and the reality of Ralph's cardboard shack, you and Ralph are both manifestations of the identical truth, the identical unity. You are both vibrating, living entities created in the likeness of the Creator.

You both have the ability to experience love, to experience the divinity, to experience God directly. While you are both identical—the same pervasive force—you are, at the same time, both manifestations that are separate and distinct. And that separateness is created by your ego.

The paradox, the almost unsolvable spiritual paradox, is to live both as separate and as unity at the same time. For they are different sides of the same coin and cannot be viewed simultaneously. At any given moment in time, you will either be in an experience of total unity, not only with the true nature of who you are but with the true nature of Ralph inhabiting that cardboard shelter and simultaneously the true nature of God—or you will be in an experience of the separation of you as an individual entity, separate and distinct from Ralph as an individual entity and at the same time separate and distinct from God.

The almost unsolvable spiritual paradox,
is to live both as separate and as unity
at the same time.

＊

LINDA: So perhaps the point is that we should help others because they are really our selves and such actions would help us grow spiritually. Is that the connection?

ARIEL: Yes, it comes close to understanding what we are trying to express. And if helping others is done from a true understanding, a true soul-to-soul communication, the gesture or help that is given to another, is seen almost as a gesture of self helping self, giving to oneself by giving to that other. And, yes, that help would be pure.

But all too often, such help is given not from this perspective but from the perspective of guilt, of trying to atone or satisfy a feeling of being uneasy with the quantity of your possessions, wishing to appease or mollify or reduce that level of discomfort within you. When such gestures are made from that perspective, it is not what we speak of. Rather, it is a separate being giving out of fear or guilt to another separate being. It is not so much the action but the truth, energy, or consciousness that underlies the action of giving that would make the difference.

LINDA: **You said there would be a point when we would trade places, and some part of me would be in your realm and you would be in our realm.[5] I have a concern. I'm very happy being a human. Pizza, sex, chocolate cake are among the many human pleasures not available in your realm. Would I miss these human pleasures?**

ARIEL: The question or statement you have made has many parts to it. We will address them in order.

Many of your ways of analyzing your human experience are done from a sensory feedback standpoint. The human sensory system utilizes taste, touch, sound, smell and sight to develop thoughts. You develop a structure in which there are many activities or experiences that provide a great deal of what you call pleasure. The things that you have mentioned are very pleasing, very pleasure-filled, to you. The opposite of that is also true. There are many things in the human experience filled with displeasure, such as those that are painful, annoying or aggravating.

No such pleasurable or displeasurable sensory phenomena exist within the realm from which we speak. The one common link that exists between this realm and your realm is the phenomenon you call love. Love is the pervading force of this universe that you inhabit. Love is the underlying energy in the realm from which we communicate. Within this realm all is full, all is complete.

---

5. Question, p. 151, "Angelic Life"

Love is the pervading force
of this universe that you inhabit.
Love is the underlying energy
in the realm from which we communicate.

It is only within the state of human consciousness that you have a desire that needs to be satisfied by the object of its longing—sex, food, entertainment, material possessions. What is difficult for the human mind to comprehend is that when there is no object of desire, there is no need for such sensations to satisfy that desire.

The state in which we exist, and the state that we speak to you from, is devoid of any desire. Therefore, such things are not only unnecessary, they are not even sought after. There is no thought whatsoever of them. We are so interconnected with all that is, and so filled with the state of love, that there is no room for desire. Humans, too, have the capacity to attain this state of being.

We are so interconnected with all that is,
and so filled with the state of love,
that there is no room for desire.
Humans, too, have the capacity to attain
this state of being.

The second component of your question was whether there was desire, or wanting, to be in a realm other than the one presently inhabited. That is, would a celestial entity prefer to be in a physical form, and conversely, would a human prefer a non-physical form?

We see in many, many cases souls who incarnate into the human experience and yet, while in truth it was their own soul-level choice, their own doing, their own plan, they have a deeply seated feeling of not wishing to be in the human experience. There are many souls who live life in great distress and great difficulty, constantly yearning and longing to return to the unity from which we speak.

Such souls are extremely troubled and often manifest in their lives much disharmony and discomfort—the underlying issue being their deep, deep longing to re-commune and reconnect with this pervasive state of love. And yet, within a soul's life and journey, that deep longing is the catalyst that drives that soul to achieve high states of spiritual growth or development.

It is only those who either have not started their journey in fulfillment of karmic healing and spiritual growth in a lifetime, or those who are underway but too eager to complete their journey, who have desires or thoughts of wanting to be in the angelic realm rather than in a human body. It is also those who feel overwhelmed with their pain and distress, or feel it is futile, beyond any hope or possibility, who turn to thoughts of rejoining this realm through the process of death. These are the souls who long to leave the human experience.

On the other hand, there are those souls who have attained some degree of growth and who are working rapidly through their process of karmic healing and spiritual development who see the richness, the wonder, the joy and the honor of being human.

To those in the early stage of growth or those who are stuck in their despair, being human seems to be a curse, a trap, an endless labyrinth of pain that is hopeless in its very nature. But those who have moved beyond the early stage of spiritual growth find that humanness does not end the connection with the source of this universe, nor does it end the communion with the unconditional love that pervades all things. They find that humanness is an opportunity of very rich and rare proportion, an absolutely indescribable treasure that a soul has the opportunity to experience.

There is no setting for karmic healing or spiritual attainment that is richer than the experience you call *being human*. We hope that we can emphasize strongly enough the treasure of the soul's experience at this moment of being in your human body and in your life, and that it can be appreciated to the magnitude that it deserves.

_____

There is no setting
for karmic healing or spiritual attainment
that is richer than the experience
you call being human.

_____

For, despite your ego-based evaluation of your life experience as good or bad, you have the richness of opportunity to evolve, to grow, to develop in ways that most of the time you are totally un-aware of. And yet, despite your lack of conscious awareness of this fact, you are evolving rapidly and beautifully along a path, a course, that at your soul level, you yourself have created.

From the human vantage point, life might seem to be purely arbitrary, random and chaotic, with billions of people living in isolation from each other and in self-absorption, seeking plea-sures, treasures, money, prizes and trophies. What you do not see is what we see from this realm, which is how each piece is in perfect harmony, interlinked with every other piece. You cannot make one move in life, make one choice, offer one viewpoint, get angry or be happy in a way that does not ripple through and affect the entire structure of your universe.

_____

You cannot make one move in life . . .
that does not ripple through and affect
the entire structure of your universe.

_____

Some actions have impacts of tremendous magnitude and proportion. You have seen even in your own, what you call history of time, how the action of a single person or a couple of people working together can send a shock wave, positive or negative, across the entire planetary system. And yet, at other times, the ripple seems only to pass to one person.

What you do not see is that after that ripple passes to one person, that person may pass it to the next and the next and the next. And while it may take some time, that effect can ripple through and impact the entire planetary structure. Your life is of no small consequence. It is part of a masterpiece—a masterpiece of unfathomable proportion, of immense divine consequence.

Your life is of no small consequence.

❋

LINDA: **Most humans have difficulty in that we do not feel a connection to others (other than the special person in our lives), we live in separate places, experience different things. It's very easy for us to understand that we are separate, and we don't have many occasions to feel like we are part of a unity. When I see an animal, I feel a stronger connection to it, especially my own animals, than I do to fellow humans. Please comment.**

ARIEL: It is often the case that people receive more love from animals than they do from other people. The goal would be to find the same degree of love and attention, the same degree of affection and the same degree of truth expressed with fellow human beings as you do with plants, animals or pets. The difference is that when it comes to the plants, animals or pets, you have no need to protect yourself from them, thus you are open to receiving their love.

While a dog could be, in one situation, the most loving and wonderful of companions, filling your heart and bringing you to a state of love and unity, it could also bring you, by barking and baring teeth, into fear and separation in which no such sense of love and unity is perceived.

Unfortunately it is quite common for most of humankind to experience other people as the snarling dog ready to bite—people ready to take, ready to steal. And while a dog has but its teeth to bite, people have words that can hurt, fists that can punish, ways to cheat and steal, legal systems that can sue and cripple, even political or spiritual ideologies that can judge and condemn. The array of tools that humans have to create fear or to hurt other humans is vast and powerful.

The array of tools that humans have . . .
to hurt other humans
is vast and powerful.

It is, therefore, less common to find the same degree of safety in the presence of a human as in the presence of a plant, animal or pet. It is also why most humans have a very limited number of other humans with whom they may be in that same state of peace, love or grace.

Look to the great and empowered spiritual leaders throughout your history. For they have, through their personal connection to God, allowed themselves to overcome that sense of instinctive fear of other humans. And by staying in that state of wonderful, deep connection to the truth, to the alignment with spirit, to their truth of who they are and to the love that pervades the universe, they were able to give that same sense of openness and compassion, that same sense of love and joy, to all who sought their wisdom and their counsel, including even those who would hurt, harm or kill them.

※

LINDA: **Your words remind me of Martin Luther King, Jr., who faced great adversity. He was trying to teach his followers to react with love instead of violence. Please comment.**

ARIEL: You will see in this one you speak of, as well as others who flow through your history, a common theme. It underscores a very powerful and inescapable spiritual truth that love, the force of this universe, also has a component or a characteristic of it that is destruction. The two are components of one unity.

Love . . . has a component to it . . .
that is destruction.

There have been many, many ways that you have, within the limitations of your language, tried to express those dualities, those paradoxical opposites that together form one truth. It has been called *love* as opposed to *fear*; *creation* as opposed to *destruction*; *unity* as opposed to *separateness*.

One of the difficulties that humankind, throughout its evolution, has found and will find until it attains a much higher level of spiritual openness is the following truth: whenever people are presented with a source of tremendous love, it will either bring them into a process of sympathetic and compatible resonance in which their hearts open to the truth, open to the love and blossom forth like spring flowers on a beautiful sunny day; or for people who are not ready to grow, it will evoke fear, violence or any of the various human expressions of a deep, underlying energy of destruction. You have seen a repeated pattern throughout your history where the powerful presence of love was brought to an end by an expression of this opposite force.

You have seen . . . throughout your history
where the powerful presence of love
was brought to an end
by an expression of this opposite force.

These great leaders that you speak of have been so connected to the pervading universal truth in life amongst people that the love, the connection to the source of spirit or to what you can refer to as God, moves so clearly through them. Their sight, not only visual but inner sight, is so clear, so distinct that it cannot be ignored. Anyone coming into their presence, anyone listening to their words, anyone seeing them cannot mistake the truth of their words, of their wisdom, of their knowledge and of the source they have found.

※

The Search for God

LINDA: **This is a quote from Professor Stephen Hawking's book *A Brief History of Time*:**[6]

---

6. Hawking, S. W. *A Brief History of Time*, New York: Bantam Books, 1988, 115–116.

[I]n 1981 my interest in questions about the origin and fate of the universe was reawakened when I attended a conference on cosmology organized by the Jesuits in the Vatican. The Catholic Church had made a bad mistake with Galileo when it tried to lay down the law on a question of science, declaring that the sun went round the earth.[7] Now, centuries later, it had decided to invite a number of experts to advise it on cosmology. At the end of the conference the participants were granted an audience with the pope. He told us that it was all right to study the evolution of the universe after the big bang, but we should not inquire into the big bang itself because that was the moment of Creation and therefore the work of God.

LINDA: **Do you have a comment on the pope's admonition to Professor Hawking about not pursuing this line of work because it has to do with God?**

ARIEL: Your observation underscores a dilemma in being human. The human mind is not capable of grasping God or what you label as God. No matter how brilliant, no matter how spiritual, the human mind cannot grasp, cannot describe, cannot comprehend God.

> *The human mind*
> *cannot . . . comprehend God.*

---

7. In 1632, due to the publication of Galileo's famous work that put forth the "heretical" concept of the sun as the immovable center of the universe, Galileo was called before the Roman inquisition. In an attempt to silence his flagrant contradictions of the doctrine held by the church, Galileo was sentenced to spend his remaining years in strict seclusion.

It is inherent within the very nature of being human, primarily based on fear, to try to comprehend, to try to understand and to try to know God. It is the one thing that drives all people of all races, of all times, of all levels of prosperity and of all states of health. By its very nature, however, the mind as it inhabits a human body through this aspect called *ego* creates tremendous fear. The ego is doomed to a constant process of creating fear and then trying to resolve the fear, distance from the fear or squelch the fear.

The one thing that even a very strongly directed ego-consciousness knows is that the source, the thing that can stop the fear, is this thing called God. So, driven by a desire to be at peace, to be without fear and to be safe, humankind has constantly sought this thing that you label as God. There are many paths to try to describe the indescribable and many models attempting to model that which cannot be modeled. Any system devised to describe or model God is, at best, an approximation of a truth—at best, in one of your expressions, the tip of the iceberg—but is not the totality.

Humankind has constantly sought
this thing that you label as God.

There are two paths that are the most profound paths to attempt to explain this mystery. Neither path will succeed; neither path *can* succeed.

One path is that of spirituality or religion, which becomes a highly refined, philosophical process of building layer upon layer of understanding, attempting to help those who seek to know God. But all religion—no matter what system it is presented in, or what name you give it, no matter what philosophy, structure, politics or doctrines it follows—is but a vehicle to attempt to allow you to know God directly.

Unfortunately, some people become lost in the system or the religion and, as a result, *it* becomes God to them. You should always remember that the system is simply a vehicle intended to support you in understanding that which cannot be understood. It is designed to propel you into a direct experience of God, which is beyond understanding, through a process we have called *knowing*.

Some people become lost in the . . . religion
and, as a result,
it becomes God to them.

The other path is of science. It is also designed to help you understand that which cannot be understood. This model scientifically approaches an understanding of the beginning of creation of the universe. If you were to step back and put down all bias, all judgment, you would see that both are attempting to explain, in different language and from different viewpoints, the identical thing.

Both are correct, although both are different. The problem is that both are trying from within God to describe God. The only way to describe something—the only way to model it—is to step outside of it where you can observe it, where you can see it in every facet of its complexity. You cannot model the operation of a human cell unless you can step outside and look at one, test one, sample one. From inside a cell, you could never understand its complexity. The dilemma the human mind faces is that there is nowhere it can go such that it can step outside of God and look back. Such a place does not exist for the human mind.

---

*The dilemma the human mind faces
is that there is nowhere it can go
such that it can step outside of God and look back.*

In questions such as this theoretical approach of the big bang, the obvious extensions are: Who created it? Who created the matter from which the big bang followed? Was there ever a time before which that matter did not exist? Will there ever be a time after which that matter does not exist? Only those who know God, who have met God through direct experience, can begin to fathom the answers to such questions. Religion and science are developing very precise, accurate and wonderful models, which, due to politics, seem to compete with each other.

---

*Religion and science . . . due to politics,
seem to compete with each other.*

There is no competition, no right or wrong other than what the human mind fabricates. The goal is to know God. The goal is to find and meet God.

We thank you for your question.

✳

Biblical Life

Jesus Christ

LINDA: Who was Jesus Christ from your point of view?

ARIEL: The being, the person you know by the name of Jesus Christ in your history, was the embodiment of the potential that you are all, as a race, evolving toward. He was the living presence, the simultaneous experience of total and complete unity and yet fully in the experience of being human.

He was . . . the simultaneous experience
of total and complete unity
and yet fully in the experience of being human.

This being was the embodiment of a most precious spiritual ideal that humans are moving toward and striving for, even if they do not understand. This spiritual ideal is simply described by your word *forgiveness*, and yet, even in saying these words, we fear that you do not understand what we have said. For many do not understand even what this most precious of souls, you know as Jesus, had said.

One of the needs in the process of spiritual growth and evolution is to inspire, motivate and teach without taking away the opportunity to learn and to grow. If you reflect not only on the life, experience and wisdom of this particular being named Jesus but also on other beings who have brought important knowledge by the very lives they lived, these beings have characteristically not been directly responsible for the knowledge they taught. They, in many cases, did not leave behind any documentation. Although the most precious master Jesus was capable of writing, he did not leave behind a written form of his teaching. And, while there were others near Jesus who were capable of writing down every word he said when he said it, this, too, was not done. This was no mistake. For Jesus, living the embodiment of this simultaneous reality of man and unity, was to be seen, to be felt, to be experienced, and his force can still be felt in the hearts and in the minds of humans to this very moment in your time.

---

*His force can still be felt
in the hearts and in the minds of humans
to this very moment in your time.*

The human opportunity, the human delight, is to take the vagueness or the purposely ambiguous and sometimes contradictory descriptions of events, circumstances and details of the life of this most precious master, and to focus on what he conveyed. What he said and what he lived was a life of forgiveness. He lived a life practicing forgiveness, not from a mindset of superior attainment from which he would take pity on you and forgive you, but from a state of such love through unity with God that the need to separate, judge and condemn was absent.

---

*What he said and what he lived
was a life of forgiveness.*

Jesus lived in a state of being, filled with love, where there is no judgment, which, for humans, exists only during a communion experience with God. In the state of communion, you can experience the forgiveness that this most precious master demonstrated, not only through his words but through his life and even through his process of death. This is, indeed, the true teaching that was demonstrated and that has been handed down in the form that you call religion. But, in its pure sense, forgiveness that results from the state of love through unity with God was the entire teaching. It shows you, most certainly, where you are headed in your evolution.

There is, however, much complexity in the process of spiritual growth, and it is the trick of the ego to misconstrue spiritual knowledge for spiritual growth. Thus, the mind will readily focus on the externals, the circumstances or the details, and miss the point of Jesus' teaching that is right in front of it.

❋

LINDA: **The first twenty-five years of Christ's life are not recorded in our history. Could you tell us something about his early years?**

ARIEL: Your question itself underscores our previous answer in many respects. There is no mistake that the details of the life of this most precious being were not recorded or handed down. You might think it strange that, even when those around him understood his greatness, it was not until many years of your time passed by that things were recorded. As such, the details that have been described are contradictory and vague.

Do you not see that the lack of exact recording occurred because it is not the details that you are being guided to look at? The details are an encumbrance and only give the mind, the ego, an opportunity to miss the spiritual point of the actual incarnation of this most precious jewel. It would go against the goal and the process for us to enlighten you on the details of these unrecorded years, for it is not the details of the life that are important—it is the message. It is the embodiment of the total state of love, the total state that a human can experience when he or she is simultaneously and paradoxically human and in communion with God, that is, simultaneously in a state of total forgiveness and a state of total humanity.

It is not the details of the life
that are important—it is the message.

❋

LINDA: **Has the soul of Christ re-entered a body since his most famous incarnation on Earth?**

ARIEL: No, not in the sense of the normal concept of a soul attaching to a physical vessel for the duration of what you call a lifetime. Please understand, again with our apologies, the difficulty in trying to convey the pure truth of the state of, if you will, the soul of this most extraordinary being.

In the model that we have created for you, his soul is purposely abiding between the state of close connection with his loved ones and the total immersion into the state of complete unity with God. As a result, this most extraordinary soul can, in essence, touch the lives of his loved ones. To this soul, to this being that you associate with the name Jesus, the term *loved ones* applies to all of humanity. For there is no one—no human being of any religious discipline, economic background, political alliance or any way that you label, categorize or differentiate yourselves—with whom Jesus has not infinitely and deeply connected.

There is no one . . . with whom Jesus
has not infinitely and deeply connected.

He has the ability—especially in times of tremendous fear or despair in the heart of a human being—to enter in and join you in deep, deep, beyond-description communion. When he shares, even for a moment, a connection to the very physical body in which you live, he leaves behind a sense of utter peace and tranquillity, utter resolution and dissolution of any fear. This soul serves as a universal bridge to the divine, allowing for momentary communion experiences. And our use of the term *momentary*, in your terminology of time, can be from but seconds to years of time.

To be graced with an experience of being touched by the very heart of this soul, and through that touching being infused with a level of your own personal communion to the divine, brings you to a state of forgiveness, a state in which there is basically no judgment, hence nothing to forgive. Therefore, forgiveness exists by its own nature.

---

*When [Jesus] shares . . . a connection
to the very physical body in which you live,
he leaves behind
a sense of utter peace and tranquillity,
utter resolution and dissolution of any fear.*

You have used many terms to describe this beautiful, beautiful state of grace available to you. The term *Holy Spirit* has its own connotations and meanings, which in some cases are identical to what we have just described and in other cases are different.

The point we wish you to understand is the following. There is correctness in saying that this presence of Jesus, this living Christ, in your language, or the presence of the Holy Spirit can remove your fears and bestow forgiveness upon you. The forgiveness and the removal of fears come not from a magic wand waved over you to pardon you or absolve you. The forgiveness we speak of is the result of the communion experience that we have just described. It is the result of a touching of your heart to the heart of Christ through a communion in which the love of

God is so infused through this vessel, the living Christ, that it brings about a state of total release from fear and a state of total forgiveness within you.

※

Adam and Eve

LINDA: What is the purpose of the story of Adam and Eve?

ARIEL: Adam and Eve is quite simply an attempt to tell you the absolute, unknowable, unfathomable truth, but at the same time present a mystery which creates confusion, which creates difficulty of understanding. It is the most exquisite and infinitely complex description. It can be easily misunderstood by being viewed in its most simple presentation of a childlike story. But within it is the answer to every mystery you wish to know. It is not, however, on the surface of the story. As you have often seen, this knowing that we try to convey is done through metaphor, through image, and by raising questions that have no answers but which bait your mind to seek understanding and to cultivate its own direct knowing.

---

*Within it is the answer
to every mystery you wish to know.*

Most simply put, the story of Adam and Eve is the most accurate and beautiful description of the creation of this universe, and the creation of everything within it, that has been presented. And, at the same time, it is incorrect to interpret it literally.

We would do you great disservice by explaining in great detail the correct interpretations. We leave that task to your own mind and your own heart. But we ask that anyone hearing these words, if you are stuck in a simplistic interpretation of each of the elements as a literally true story, we ask you to look deeper, for in the story of Adam and Eve you will find a most beautiful expression of many things that we have used much of your time and many of your words to try to explain.

❋

LINDA: Why would humans be told not to eat from the Tree of Knowledge? What does the Tree of Knowledge represent?

ARIEL: Most simply put, eating from the Tree of Knowledge means, at its most profound level, taking fear into you, bringing in the substance that you might call *ego* or a separate idea of self, from which fear springs. Once fear has been brought into the consciousness, once it has become manifest in the mind, the communion with God is broken and you are, as you see it, cast out of paradise.

> *Eating from the Tree of Knowledge means . . .*
> *taking fear into you. . . .*

Before knowledge, there was peace, love and joy. There was, as is so brilliantly and graphically portrayed, this garden, a paradise. However, this most indescribably perfect, brilliant and infinitely complex creation you understand as humankind, was given the opportunity to evolve through direct communion with God or to experience the fear that eating from the Tree of Knowledge creates. *Knowledge* in this piece we are explaining to you means knowing yourself as separate, having a sense of self-importance. Such knowledge sets up a different path for the evolution of human growth and human development. And yet the goal is to return, even after eating from the Tree of Knowledge, to the union that was present prior to the disobedience.

Knowledge . . . means
knowing yourself as separate. . . .

Having eaten from the Tree of Knowledge, the journey by souls through the human experience took a different path—the excursion into the environment of fear created by the knowledge of one's own identity as separate. That was, however, simply a route taken in developing the evolutionary potential for spiritual growth. And as we have tried in so many ways and in so many words to show you, the goal is to return home, to return back to that garden. Hopefully words from us at this time will reach those who will understand the message we are trying to convey.

The goal is to return home,
to return back to that garden.

LINDA: **What is the significance of Adam and Eve being cast out of the Garden of Eden?**

ARIEL: Having taken knowledge and knowing one's separation, knowing one's illusion of self, there is incompatibility with being in the garden, in the unity, in deep communion with God.

The term *cast out* needs to be understood. It may be helpful to understand that the emphasis should be placed on the incompatibility of being in the garden and at the same time in a state of self-knowing or knowledge. In a sense, the knowledge itself caused the casting out, for when the mind is no longer in a state of peace and unity with the pervasive force of this universe, that is, in a state of deep communion with God, it is fragmented and separate. It is no longer abiding within what this story describes as the Garden of Eden.

The knowledge itself
caused the casting out. . . .

And yet, in a sense, it might be viewed as a punishment, a casting out, a banishment. It is indeed no such penalty. It is simply a natural consequence of the evolutionary path, the spiritual course of development, of growing back into union with the divine, returning to the Garden of Eden while still having had the experience of knowledge.

Humankind has chosen, with the support and love of what you call God, to move along this evolutionary path. You're headed in the direction of the return. Having eaten from the Tree of Knowledge, you will come to understand and be nourished by the Tree of Life. You will become aware that knowledge has separated you into parts, and the part that we call *soul* is eternal.

You're headed in the direction
of the return.

❋

LINDA: **What does the Tree of Life represent?**

ARIEL: The Tree of Life represents the source of God's love. When one eats of the Tree of Life he is infused with the essence of this divine love and given the gift of life—not just life in the human form, but life of the soul. This life is eternal. Having taken in the treasure of the Tree of Life, the soul is infused with the eternal life of God.

This life, given to the world, can manifest in the form of a human life as well as in the form of what you call angelic life. The life itself is the constant, only the form of the expression of life is changing. The Tree of Life is God's loving gift to his precious children. It is the source of all life surrounding you, as well as life that you have not yet discovered. It is the source of life in what you call the *realm of angels* and life in what you call *other realms*.

All that exists is fed from this very Tree of Life. It is the source that nurtures life in all its forms. The fact that you are alive hearing these words means that you have in essence eaten from this magnificent tree and are blessed with a life force through a soul that is eternal. Please honor this most precious gift and honor with gratitude the most loving source of this gift. Please also honor the manifestation of this life, this soul, in your present form. Your very life is a most precious expression of the Tree of Life. Please avoid judging, comparing, criticizing or destroying this, the most precious gift that God can give you. Put aside your thoughts of separateness and their resulting judgments. Join your heart with the very Creator of this Tree of Life and honor the miracle that you are.

_____

Honor the miracle that you are.

_____

※

Cain and Abel

LINDA: **In the story of Cain and Abel, Cain killed his brother Abel because God preferred Abel's offering. Can you comment on this story?**

ARIEL: Once knowledge has been brought into the human soul, once the Garden of Eden has been left, there are two ways of looking at all things—through the mind of ego and through the heart of soul. As a result, this question of offerings as a method of conveying one's love of God *to* God can take two forms.

Once knowledge has been brought
into the human soul . . .
there are two ways of looking at all things—
through the mind of ego
and through the heart of soul.

It can take the form of an expression of love from the heart. This form comes first and foremost from the deep, deep personal union that one attains by transcending the effects that the knowledge of separate self has provided and moving into a state of uniting your human heart with the heart of the divine. This offering is the highest offering that humans can give to God, for in that moment of deep and eternal union, they are sacrificing their idea of separation; they are sacrificing their sense of personality or separate ego-self that has been brought from the Tree of Knowledge.

Other offerings include ideas, important acts that one performs—prayers that one routinely recites, physical offerings that one makes, gestures, prostrations, expressions of many forms that are intended to convey love to the divine, love to

God. These cannot and do not compare to the expressions of love from the heart. The essence is to see that these activities that honor, respect, love and praise God come through ego. While in form they may look beautiful and reverent, they do not achieve the praise of God or the blessings of God that offerings made from the heart achieve. This story is trying to show you these two possibilities.

Ideas . . . prayers that one routinely recites,
physical offerings . . . gestures, prostrations. . . .
cannot and do not compare
to the expressions of love from the heart.

Exodus

LINDA: In the story of Exodus, God divided the Red Sea to allow the Israelites to escape the Egyptian army. How would you describe the parting of the Red Sea?

ARIEL: As is often the case in trying to comprehend that which is incomprehensible, those who attempt the most holy task of reviewing scripture to understand the spiritual truth that it conveys often are caught up or sidetracked by the simpler aspects of the scriptures that the mind can hope to fathom. As a result, not only in the question you have raised but in many, many questions that human minds have raised throughout your centuries, there is a great deal of questioning, controversy and seeking of explanation for miracles or phenomena that seemed to be unexplainable.

The dilemma is that while the mind then seeks to explain how such a supernatural phenomenon might have occurred or how different events took place, it utilizes everything from seeking understanding of specific astrological alignments or meteorological events to searching for the vessel that you understand was Noah's—and you miss, in many cases, the spiritual teaching being conveyed within the scriptures you call the Bible.

Please do not delay your spiritual quest or growth trying to understand these, what we would almost call, insignificant details of the truth. Look into the message that is conveyed by these most treasured words in these stories. Please look beyond the surface aspects, the details, the chronologies and look into the mysteries, for in them, where the eye of knowledge cannot see but where the heart of compassion can read, clearly lies, time after time, stories that say in their own way the exact same words we are saying now.

Please do not delay your spiritual quest . . .
trying to understand
these . . . insignificant details. . . .
Look into the message. . . .

It is a most frustrating aspect of your human journey to have all the wisdom and the knowledge in front of you, but based on your level of spiritual understanding, to be blind to it. And yet, while the mind is blind, the soul is not. Take stories such as Exodus, which are meant to be read again and again and again, reading not from the mind but from the heart. Each time this happens, the soul is nurtured, the message is understood and, in time, if you are fortunate, the part of you that has gained what you call knowledge will indeed also understand what the soul already knows.

*Where the eye of knowledge cannot see . . .
the heart of compassion can read. . . .
while the mind is blind, the soul is not.*

Return to Eden

LINDA: You spoke of the journey that begins in a state of innocence and communion with the divine—a place known as Eden. You spoke of the journey away from Eden, and then the journey back as we move toward spiritual unfoldment.[1] It's a wonderful metaphor, but the concept is abstract. Can you explain it in more concrete terms?

ARIEL: At the moment you are born, you begin a journey, a journey returning homeward to Eden. Ultimately, in the very process of your human incarnation, you will—at the end of your physical life—be called home. But that is not the homecoming we speak of. What we speak of now is the journey in which your soul, living harmoniously in your human form, follows a spiritual path explicitly and perfectly orchestrated for you. It is a homecoming in which, while remaining fully alive, healthy and happy within your experience of being human, you in a sense return to Eden. This homecoming that we speak of is living in the state of harmony and sanctity of the purpose and flow of your own life.

Homecoming . . . is living in the state of harmony . . . of the purpose and flow of your own life.

Within the infinity of love in which you abide, there is a place and purpose for every act, every living thing, every one of God's loving creations. There is a harmony and a flow that occurs within life. It moves like an invisible river. It has a force—the life force. It has a path along which it flows. It has currents; it has backwater eddies; it has obstacles. All is in perfect accord.

---

1. Question, p. 151, "Angelic Life" and question, p. 327, "Biblical Life"

The opportunity exists for each and every person to learn to sense the flow of that life force and use her heart as a compass to guide her journey. You can learn how to flow with the current, letting it move your life along the very path the divine has laid out for you. When you do find that flow, and release yourself into its current, you will discover how beautiful and easy life can be. You will discover how supported you are, how interconnected all living things are. You will feel the presence of angels of this realm surrounding you, guiding you, loving you and helping you. You will be guided to help others and to serve the divine.

The opportunity exists for . . .
every person to learn to sense
the flow of that life force. . . .

You will also find times in which the current moves very quickly—times in which you seem to be swept through life faster than is familiar to you or faster than you are comfortable with. These are times of great growth and positive change and transformation. These are also times that test the strength of an inner state of spiritual solidity called *faith*. For, even as you experience the flow of life and connect to the presence of God's will for you, the part of you that is ego will be along on the journey with you. This ego part of you will constantly find opportunities to challenge your faith with your fears.

The times you will feel most comfortable in your journey are times when your ego is most satisfied and at peace. These are times when the flow is moderate and the ego is reassured by the very activity of your life that indeed God is present and guiding you. However, these are times when it is not true faith at work. Rather, it is a pseudo-faith based on the demonstration of the power of the divine in your life. This pseudo-faith will not withstand difficulties. It will not withstand challenges or accept opportunities for your development of spiritual strength, and therefore is not the faith we speak of.

This ego part of you
will constantly find opportunities
to challenge your faith with your fears.

The faith that we speak of resides in your heart, within the very center of your being. It is faith that does not require external verification or validation for it to be strong and solid. It is a faith independent of the outside world—a faith in yourself. But more importantly, it is a faith in the power of God working through you. This is the faith upon which the very foundation of your life rests.

The faith that we speak of
resides in your heart. . . .

It is not a faith based on understanding or what you have heard from others or what you have read. These are good starting points for the journey, but what we speak of comes from "knowing," a faith based on direct experience, the mystical union or communion with the divine. For indeed, challenge to your faith can only come from within you. While there may be external events that cause your ego to produce fear, those events in and of themselves do not challenge your faith.

When one has developed true faith, one will be in harmony

with the current of life and feel the presence, loving guidance, compassion and care that God has for each and every being. And from this basis, things of the world—things that might to a judgmental separate ego be perceived as setbacks, losses, difficulties or challenges—are indeed none other than experiences in the flow of your life, that the divine has lovingly guided you into to build your strength, redirect your journey, teach you something you will need to know, cause you to meet someone who is important for you to meet or to build an aspect of character that is necessary for what will come. Most importantly, in the moment of its occurrence, it is the opportunity to refine and hone and strengthen this aspect of inner-self that we have called *faith*.

When faith is at its pinnacle, life is lived without any conscious awareness of faith. This is because you become the embodiment of faith, you maintain your state of communion or connectedness to the divine and live in constant union with the force, love and harmony of God. Faith becomes a way of existence, an expression of your true nature and a claiming of your birthright. Faith is simply the living, loving expression of who you are.

> *Faith is simply the living, loving*
> *expression of who you are.*

As you journey on the spiritual path of your life, we ask you to view every occurrence that upsets your inner experience of faith as an opportunity to deepen your state of prayer. In prayer, you should beseech the divine to guide you and show you ways to build your faith. It is a time to reflect on the revelation of the words of the divine through scriptures and to bring those scriptures into your heart. It is a time to go within, quieting the mind and opening the heart through meditation. And it is a time to work to heal the wounds of the ego part of yourself that has been so traumatized by the events of your life.

_____

The process of building faith is . . .
the process of journeying home. . . .

_____

The process of building faith is indeed the process of journeying home, for as you bring yourself into alignment with this river of life and build an inner foundation of faith that becomes a natural expression of your being, you will discover something that has always been true. You will find that you have not only brought yourself into alignment with the river of your life, but that you have *been* the river of life all along. As this occurs, in that moment, you return to Eden.

❋

LINDA: **We each travel a different path on this journey toward karmic healing and spiritual unfoldment. As a result, others will likely have questions I haven't asked—questions that would help them move through their lives more efficiently. Would you consider answering questions from our readers?**

ARIEL: Yes. We find that the best way to convey knowledge is to be given the opportunity to speak to a mind that is thirsty. The thirstiest of people are those who ask questions, for they are the ones truly seeking answers.

The format you have created for the work that we have been doing with you is designed to elicit that most wonderful human response of questioning. The fastest path to spiritual growth is to raise questions where there are no questions, and then to provide the process where the spiritual journeyer may find her own answers.

The fastest path to spiritual growth is
to raise questions . . .
and then to provide the process
where the spiritual journeyer
may find her own answers.

Questions from people other than yourself would create an ideal environment for us to continue our expression of truth and knowledge and to reach as many hearts as we can. But make no mistake, it is *we* who decide what we will answer and how we will answer. Again, our goal is always to use what has been asked as the platform to give the knowledge that we wish to convey. We will, in many cases, either not answer a question or not answer it in a way that the questioner has sought, for many questions that will come to you and through you will be of a nature incompatible with our goals and objectives, and hence will not be dealt with.

Questions from people other than yourself
would create an ideal environment
for us to continue our expression
of truth and knowledge
and to reach as many hearts as we can.

LINDA: Will you give the readers guidelines as to what questions you would choose to answer?

ARIEL: We ask quite simply for questions that will propel not only the questioner but all who share in the knowledge obtained from the answer. The questions that are most important to the questioner are the ones we wish to deal with, those that are the very basis of life's quandary. Those that are of the most pressing importance to a person's journey will be the ones that will convey the most impact to the spiritual evolution of mankind.

Those that are driven by ego, those that ask about self and personal attainment, those that question things that have less global bearing provide less of a forum within which we can work. Those burning questions that come from the soul are ones we seek, for those are the ones through which we can most effectively do our work.

Those burning questions that come from the soul
are ones we seek,
for those are the ones through which
we can most effectively do our work.

❋

LINDA: Is there an ideal time for this book to reach the public?

ARIEL: The wisdom that is contained in the book is most valuable at a time when people are most interested in and open to receiving it. Curiosities have been piqued and much has been done to satisfy the initial curiosities, but the depth of what is contained in these words goes beyond mere curiosity and will satisfy and nourish deep spiritual needs.

You are in a time of tremendous planetary change and spiritual unfoldment, and our words are designed to quench people's spiritual thirst. The earlier in your time that you may produce the work and offer it to people, the better. Because what will come after will take much energy. You will be surprised how much work and how much continued activity this simple task of publishing this one book will create for you. The sooner this particular phase of our work together is completed, the sooner later phases may commence. If you could optimize your work— to trade off ultimate perfection for timeliness—timeliness would be the more beneficial of the two choices.

---

*You are in a time of
tremendous planetary change
and spiritual unfoldment. . . .*

✳

LINDA: **Is there information you would like me to share with my fellow humans?**

ARIEL: There is so much to say that it is difficult to answer such an invitation.

We wish first for you to understand the gratitude that we have for allowing these words not only to be heard by your ears [Linda], but to be shared through your [Linda's and Stevan's] efforts in writing for others to read. We have sought many times and in many ways to find people with whom we could share our wisdom, our guidance and our teaching, and who would have so thorough a way of expressing these words as you do.

There has never been a time
like the time that you presently exist in,
in which so much opportunity is available. . . .

We wish very much to let people see and understand what is happening at this point in what you refer to as time. In the journey of the consciousness of humankind, there is an awakening, an opening of the capacity that has always been there but has been somewhat limited to those few who had a very strong and powerful spiritual connection. What we wish you to see is that there has never been a time like the time you presently exist in, in which so much opportunity is available to allow the heart to open, to allow the consciousness to grow and expand. This had been reserved for those few seekers who, through their efforts, could find this individual space of attainment.

You have seen changes in which
there are now loving environments
where there once was hostility.
But you have also seen changes
in which there is now hostility
where there once was peace.

The vibration of energy, the power of love, the force of the universe that exists on your planet has never been as powerful or as strong as it is at this moment in time. You have seen many of the reactions that this force of love has created. You have seen changes in which there are now loving environments where there once was hostility. But you have also seen changes in

which there is now hostility where there once was peace. Both
are an effect of this powerful force that is leading you through a
process, allowing those who are open to join and to grow—to
join with each other and to grow in the heart's energy, love and
power that is available to them. This is a time to call forth, to face
the fears, to face the internal challenges and dare to be what you
were designed and created to be.

---

*This is a time to . . . dare to be
what you were designed and created to be.*

It must be apparent to you by now that the path to your highest
prosperity is to follow your heart. Prosperity is measured in love,
wealth, health, well-being, joy, harmony and enthusiasm. All of
those categories have the greatest opportunity to become abun-
dant when you simply follow your heart and live your dream.

---

*The path to your highest prosperity
is to follow your heart. . . . and live your dream.*

There is a truth, which has been conveyed in many of your writings, that you were designed and created by the Creator in the
Creator's likeness, that you are created in the likeness of God.
And this is very true. You are created in the likeness of love. God
is the energy of love. God is the energy that, through the power
of this force called *love*, brings creation to the universe. You are
that same force; you are that same power. You are the love that
brings creation into the universe, and now is a time of great
awakening and opening to that power.

> *You are the love that brings creation*
> *into the universe, and now is a time of*
> *great awakening and opening*
> *to that power.*

We wish this to be a message for people that the time has come to arise out of fear and darkness, out of the times and feelings of separateness, to embrace the truth, to embrace the power that you are and that is within you. This is our message.

STEVAN: There's a beautiful image coming through of what Ariel is trying so hard to explain to us.

ARIEL: If you've ever watched a droplet of water on a windshield of a car or on a windowpane, it may be small when it starts the journey, being pulled by gravity. And, as it moves, it often bumps into the next droplet, joins with it and the two droplets, now bigger, keep moving. It hits the next, which joins in. By the time it hits the bottom, it's either an incredibly large droplet or almost a little stream of water. Gravity was what motivated its journey.

These droplets are analogous to love. The words that we offer are these droplets of the pure essence of love that is the building block in the structure of the universe in which you live. Gravity in this metaphor is the thirst of the souls that live in your world. Their yearning to have that thirst quenched literally pulls this truth toward them. You, yourself, are one of those droplets, yearning in your own way but also serving. So as we pass the gift of love to you, as you draw it in, it joins with you; you pass it to the next and it joins with them. And what ends up happening is that from the tiniest droplet as a starting point, we will serve to quench the thirst of the world.

From the tiniest droplet . . .
we will serve to quench
the thirst of the world.

The world is still very angry, very fearful, very bitter. There are few people whose thirst has been quenched and there are many people, the number always increasing, who we must reach. There are others like yourself, with their own ways and their own words, who deliver the droplets of love that we share.

Even if you contribute every ounce of your life force to serve us in this work, you cannot quench all of the thirst that is present, so we enlist many like yourself. You do not compete with them, and please do not compare yourself to them. For unlike trying to quench the thirst of a thirsty person with water, the love that we offer must come in different forms. It must come in different ways because the nurturing and the nourishment has to be tuned to the capacity of the recipient. Therefore, in some cases we speak in beautiful poetry; in other cases, in lofty theology; in other cases, childlike stories; and in other cases, as truth voiced as distinctly and concisely as we can. Not every mind is ready to receive all forms of our truth, so we offer it in a variety of forms and in a variety of ways, hoping one form will reach a heart and that heart will be filled.

The love that we offer must come in different . . .
ways because the nurturing and the nourishment
has to be tuned to the capacity of the recipient.

The heart that reads your book, and is filled, becomes the droplet that then touches the next by sharing the book as a gift or talking about its messages. That person alone may inspire ten others to receive their own nourishment. And they become droplets. And, until the entire world is nourished and all of the thirst for spiritual nourishment satisfied, that pull, very much like gravity, will pull the knowledge and the love through people, until all are filled.

❋

LINDA: **We're coming toward the end of this collaboration. Do you have any final words?**

ARIEL: Let us be very clear. You, yourselves [Stevan and Linda], may be coming to an end of some needed human partitioning or phasing of your collaboration with us. We are not coming to an end of our collaboration with you. While we will not be able to have you understand this, we are in a sense just at the beginning.

We are not coming to an end of our collaboration. . . .

We would be pleased to continue working with you in answering more of your questions, or questions that arise from the answers we have given here. There is much, much more that we wish to convey through you, if you wish to work with us.

We would be pleased to continue working with you. . . .

Our work begins in this realm with passion that you cannot even imagine. It is why on many an occasion when you would express your gratitude to us for giving our words to you, it was so paradoxical because you cannot understand the passion we have for this work, or the delight we would have if you would spend twenty-four hours a day working with us. We have an ocean of knowledge, information, poetry, images and wisdom to convey to help the dilemma of your culture and people on your planet. It is our reason for existence—to give this information. So when we find people like you who will support our effort, not as a burden but as a passion in their own lives, we are truly, truly joyful.

Read the accounts time and time again in scriptures of all forms and in all religions. There is a way in which nourishment from the very Tree of Life itself is fed into the hearts, souls and minds of humans. You will see repeated over and over, if you look with an eye that knows what to look for, the way in which this process works. There is always a conveying of information that produces a great uplifting for those who are ready to take in the love and the wisdom that is conveyed.

There are those, however, who will take these words, take the love and the wisdom that is conveyed, and as it is brought into the scope of their consciousness, their egos will react with fear. There can be a reaction, both what you will label as positive and negative, to this information now being infused into your consciousness. But if you will look at historical accounts, this is always experienced: information is infused, a reaction occurs and information is then infused again.

We will work periodically to infuse knowledge, wisdom, truth. We then allow the growth to occur, and when it is time, we convey again, allowing more growth to occur. As long as our work, our words, our knowledge and our wisdom can be effectively conveyed through your [Stevan and Linda's] human skills and can reach and change the vibration, the spiritual level, to move it closer to the divine, closer to union with God, we will infuse through you, time and time again, more of this knowledge and more of these words. If using your gifts ceases to be effective in attaining the purpose that we began with, then we will draw this work to a conclusion.

❋

LINDA: **During these past two years that we've been talking, you have been a major factor in changing my life in a direction that has brought me personal joy, professional satisfaction and health. I want to thank you for helping me grow into the role of publisher and author. And on behalf of Stevan and myself and the people of Earth, thank you for your wisdom, your knowledge and your message.**

ARIEL: We acknowledge your words and once again convey that we deeply understand your gratitude; we deeply understand your sincerity. The energy of your words of gratitude and the truth that underlies them were already understood by us prior to your uttering them.

We thank you for embarking on this task. We thank you for daring to complete this first of your phases. We thank you in advance for the tremendous growth that each of you will experience from what ensues from this first step. We thank you for daring to grow through all aspects, both those that you might label as wondrous and those that you might label as difficult.

But please know that in the journey there is tremendous love, tremendous gratitude and tremendous safety for all who travel toward the unity with God and who, even after having eaten from the Tree of Knowledge, return to Eden.

❋

Index

A

Aaron, 47
abduction, alien, 228–29, 230
Abel, 330
abortion, 175–76, 208
Abraham, 3, 152
Acts, 71
Adam and Eve, 325–26,
        327–28
AIDS, 187–90
alcoholism. See drugs
Ali, Mohammed, 29
alien. See Extraterrestrial Life

alignment, 221, 265, 268, 284,
        286–288, 297–99, 311, 340
Allah, 124
Alschuler, Alfred S., 2, 97, 270,
        356, 357
alternative, 88–91, 98–99,
        180–83
Amos, 18
angel, 95, 106–107
Angelic Life, 116–54
anger, 146–47, 266
animal, 144, 145, 160–61,
        195, 201–205, 228–29,
        264, 310–11

apocalypse, 39, 60, 198–99
apparatus, 126
Ariel, 2, 69, 84–88, 91, 98, 102
Association of Beneficents, 14, 57
Assagioli, Robert, 26
astronaut, 224
astronomy, 19
astrophysicist, 258
attachment, 138, 164, 166, 176, 178, 203–205
aura, 89
Aurobindo, S., 34, 43, 47, 50, 74, 75
Auroville, 43, 50
authorization, 18, 30–31, 57, 65–66, 73
autopsy, alien, 235
awakening, 65, 180, 188, 272, 344–45
awareness, 127, 130, 133, 153, 166, 206, 217, 236, 269

B

baby. *See* children
Bach, Richard, 7
Baha'u'llah, 43, 47, 49–50, 75
Bahai, 43, 75

Bailey, Alice, 4, 10, 32, 35–36, 38, 72, 74, 75
Bartholomew, 4
Beatles, The, 56–57, 76
Beethoven, 40
Berchtesgaden, 51
Berlioz, 40
Bermuda Triangle, 199–201
Besant, Annie, 25–26, 73
Bible, 104, 147–50, 332. *See also* scripture
Biblical Life, 320–33
big bang, 314, 317
birth, 126, 175–78
Blackfoot, 23–24, 73
Blake, Robert, 34–35, 74
Blavatsky, Madam, 26
Boehme, Jacob, 33, 74
Bosnia-Herzegovina, 239
Bradbury, Ray, 10, 32–33, 72, 74, 76
Brahms, Johannes, 13, 37–38, 40, 74
Brockmann, R. J., 73
Brown, Rosemary, 40–41, 71, 75
Buddha, 47, 59
Bunyan, John, 27–28, 73
Byron, 13

C

Cain, 330
cancer, 187, 193
career, 159–62
Carey, Ken, 80
Carmelite, 5–6
cataclysm. See apocalypse
Catherine, St., 14, 34, 43, 47, 48, 49, 54, 74, 75, 76
Catholic, 3, 49, 248, 313–14
Cayce, H. L., 75
cell, 184–85, 316
Center Of Being, Inc., 79
century, 127, 251
chakra, 39
challenge, 55, 162, 175, 190–91, 211, 244, 290, 295, 298, 337–39, 345
channel, 80–82, 85, 86, 94, 95–97, 98, 120, 123–24, 212, 213, 215
Charcot, J. B., 73
Charillus, 22
children, 176–77, 186, 233, 239
Chopin, 40
Chopra, Deepak, 220
Christ, Jesus, 8, 27–28, 47, 48, 59, 65, 66, 79, 80, 152, 153, 248, 320–25
Christian, 152, 154, 158, 284
cognition, 117, 127, 135, 206, 260, 280

collaboration, 348
Columbus, Christopher, 26–27
communication, 15, 20, 38, 82, 98, 99, 106–107, 109, 117, 118, 130–33, 134–36, 139–40, 147–48, 152–53, 176, 202–203, 212, 225–226, 227, 235, 236, 276, 297, 305
communion, 78–79, 149–50, 151–54, 205, 263, 265, 275, 282, 321, 326, 338, 339
conception, 176–77
consciousness, 47, 62–65, 72, 75, 76, 94–95, 108–109, 116, 119, 127, 135, 141, 143, 144, 152, 153, 164, 167, 168, 214–16, 225, 236, 258–59, 280, 288–89
conspiracy of silence, 3, 238
contact (spiritual), 43, 46–47, 219
contact (extraterrestrial), 228–37
Conyers, GA, 239
Cooper, Col. Gordon, 224
creation, 57, 216–219, 220, 283, 290, 314–17, 325, 345
Creator, 195, 216, 286, 345
Creme, Benjamin, 4
criminal, 208, 210

criticism, 109–12
Crow Indians, 23–24
cults, 58–61, 76
Cummins, Geraldine, 32, 73
Curran, Pearl, 41–42
Curtayne, A., 74, 75, 76

D

Daimon, 65
Danskin, W., 4, 71
death, 14–15, 22, 23, 41, 49,
    72, 163–72, 175, 185–86,
    213, 291–92, 298
death penalty, 208–10, 248
Debussy, 40
deLoach, Etel, 89
delusion, 2
depression, 215, 266
desire, 92, 103, 106–109, 111,
    244, 246–47, 265, 266,
    297, 307, 315
destiny, 110, 156, 160, 266,
    295
destruction, 196–97, 283–84,
    312
devil, 53, 54–55
Dickens, Charles, 55
Dinnage, R., 73
dinosaur, 207

disability, 298
disaster, 187–88, 198
discernment, 16, 52, 200,
    273–77
disease, 88–89, 180–84,
    186–88, 266, 291, 296,
    298, 303
divine, 14, 150, 152, 161–62,
    170, 174–75, 190, 218,
    254, 277, 282, 284, 303,
    324, 328, 329, 330,
    336–40, 350
  communion, 205, 290
  direction, 201–202
  guidance, 80, 153, 263,
    287–88
  information, messages, 98,
    135, 137, 215–19
  inspiration, 63
  intervention, 269
  plan, 86, 149, 283, 285–89,
    291
  presence, 129, 217
  realm, 128–29, 178,
    275–76
  spark, 157–58, 234
  speech, 6, 8–9
  will, 110–11, 150, 263
divorce, 157–59
doomsayer, 198
doomsday, 60
dream state, 132
droplet, 346–48

drugs, 285
Dunn, Kathi, 184

E

E.T., 232–34
Earth, 194–98, 217, 224–25, 226–27, 231, 314
Earth, Life on, 179–222
ecosystem, 225, 289
ecstatic, 2, 8, 17, 25, 44–46, 70
Eden, 154, 327–29, 330, 336–40, 350
Return to Eden, 335–50
Edin, 85, 92–93, 154
education, 40, 41–42, 65–69, 76
ego, 108, 119, 131–33, 135, 137, 138, 141, 146, 157–58, 160–62, 163–64, 167, 174–75, 180, 185, 188, 191–94, 200, 205, 209–10, 214–16, 219–21, 225, 229, 235, 260–62, 266, 267–68, 269, 273–77, 291–92, 296–99, 304, 315, 322, 326, 330–31, 337–40, 342
Emmanuel, 4, 12, 18, 72

emotion, 10, 144–45, 161, 180–81, 213, 261, 266, 269
encounter, angelic, 224–32, 235, 238–40. *See also* Extraterrestrial Life
encounter, alien, 97, 127–29, 130–31, 134–36, 151, 227, 238, 240, 302–304
energy, 57, 63, 75, 79, 82–85, 89–90, 92, 102, 112, 120–21, 126, 129, 142, 144, 152, 156, 157–58, 164, 176, 181, 190–92, 195, 202, 206, 213, 220, 231, 244–47, 252, 253–55, 259, 262, 263, 273, 275, 283–285, 302, 305, 306, 312, 343, 344–45, 350
creative, 136
healing, 84
karmic, 176, 190–92, 244–47, 252, 253–55, 262, 263
personal, 63, 156, 157–58
system, 83, 90
therapy, 79, 85
enlightenment, 53, 199, 322
enrollment, 43, 52
environment, 145, 194–201, 255, 290, 327
epidemic, 187–88

Euthyphron, 22
Eve. *See* Adam and Eve
evil, 16, 50–53, 59–60, 234, 275–77, 283–85
evolution
  human, 75, 104–108, 124, 150, 226–27, 229, 234, 259, 287–88, 300, 327, 328
  of inner voices, 62
  karmic, 253
  spiritual, 64, 106–108, 121, 149, 152–54, 170, 187, 208, 231, 232–34, 263, 320–22, 342
excommunication, 248
Exodus, 73, 331–33
extrasensory, 135
Extraterrestrial Life, 224–41
Ezekiel, 3

F

faith, 31, 337–40
Fatima, 239
fear, 45, 147, 152, 153, 157, 169, 172–75, 180, 192, 198–200, 219–20, 225–27, 229, 238–40, 247, 266, 275, 282, 284–85, 305, 311, 312, 314–15, 326–27
feelings, 83, 137, 141, 144–47, 162, 169, 171, 180, 266, 276, 297
fetus, 175–76, 178
Fodor, N., 76
Foreman, George, 28–29
Fox, George, 43, 49, 75
Frakes, Jonathan, 224
Frazier, Joe, 29
free will, 66, 110–11, 153, 263, 286, 291
Freud, S., 8, 68, 71
Friml, Rudolf, 11
future, 152–53, 161, 209, 245, 251, 280–81, 299, 300

G

Gabriel, 14, 44–46
Gaia, 196
Galileo, 258–59, 313–14
Gallup Poll, 70, 95
Gandhi, Mahatma, 29–30, 73
gay, 190
geography, 198, 199–201, 300
Gershwin, George, 37
Ghose, A., 74
ghost, 127. *See also* spirit

God, 4, 6, 10–12, 14, 19,
        25–31, 34, 38, 44–50, 53,
        57, 59, 65, 69, 70, 80, 84,
        120, 124, 126, 129, 143,
        145, 148–50, 158–59,
        169–70, 174, 186, 187,
        194–95, 200, 205, 206,
        211, 216–17, 218–22,
        232, 234, 235, 263, 265,
        269–71, 273–75, 282,
        284–86, 289, 290, 293,
        296, 302, 304–305, 311,
        313–17, 321–25, 326–31,
        336–39, 345, 350
Gold, Herbert, 55, 72, 74, 76
good, 261–62, 283–85
government, 211, 224, 238–40
Great White Brotherhood,
        12–13, 58–59, 76
Greeley, Andrew, 70, 71
Grieg, E., 40
guidance, 16, 90, 136,
        153–54, 194, 263, 275,
        339
guide. See spirit
guilt, 169, 266, 305
Guyon, G. M., 7, 33–34,
        36–37, 71, 74

H

Hadamard, J., 76
hallucination, 7, 70
Halpern, Steve, 37, 74
handicap, 31, 191
happiness, 144
Hardy, Sir Alister, 70, 71
harm, 260, 311
Harmon, W., 72
Hawking, Stephen, 258–59,
        295–96, 313–14
Hayden Planetarium, 224
heal, healing, 49, 74, 83, 84,
        89, 175, 180–84, 228,
        255–56, 299
health, 180–90
heaven, 3, 27–28, 55, 281–83
hell, 27–28, 55, 172, 266,
        281–83
heresy, 248
heterosexual, 190, 191–92
hierarchy, 14, 119–20, 128
higher self, 10–11, 83, 135,
        270–72, 301–304
history, 2–5, 49, 72, 74, 76,
        104, 108, 122–24, 142,
        147, 151, 309, 322
Hitler, Adolf, 50–51, 75
HIV. See AIDS
hoax, 60, 108
holiday, 216–17
Hollywood, 97

Holy Spirit, 59, 64, 153, 324

homecoming, 336

homosexual, 189–93

Horton, W., 73

hostility, 231, 344–45

Howard, Harlan, 11

Hughes, D.J., 94, 215

human, 118, 126, 138, 145–47, 186–87, 192, 197, 200, 211, 218, 230, 231, 236, 263, 265, 270, 274, 281–83, 292–93, 310–11, 314–15, 326–27

human energy system, 83, 85

I

illness. *See* disease

image, 105, 120, 126, 134, 136–137, 140–142, 171, 293, 325, 346

imprint, 184, 233–34, 276

incarnation, 244–45, 249, 251, 255–56, 287, 323

information
  alien-related, 224, 240
  divine, 98–99, 103, 105–107, 132–34, 135, 139, 143, 271, 300–301, 349

psychic vs. channeled, 212–13

sensory, 116–17, 192

spiritual, 90, 94, 112, 248

superior, 18, 19, 68

See also communication, message

inner dictation, 7–8, 32–33, 35–37, 57

inner teachers, 6, 34, 64–69, 76, 270, 273–74

inner voices, 2–22, 25–28, 30–35, 36–37, 39–40, 43–55, 57–59, 61–68, 70–71, 80–81, 94

innocence, 154, 232, 336

inquisition, 3, 248–49, 314

insight, 68, 98, 99, 132, 134–36, 214

inspiration, 18, 25, 29–30, 63, 68, 137

instinct, 160–61, 202, 203, 238, 264–66

Integrated Energy Therapy®, 83, 85, 90, 102

intuition, 131–32

Isaiah, 30

J

James, Henry, 15
Jaynes, G., 73
Jaynes, J., 76
Jefferson, Thomas, 13, 244, 249
Jeremiah, 3
Jesus. *See* Christ, Jesus
Joan of Arc, 8, 31, 62, 71, 73, 76
job, 254–55. *See also* career
John, 4
John, St., 7, 14
Johns Hopkins University, 89
Jonathan Livingston Seagull, 7, 88
journey, 71, 72, 74
    human, 145, 150, 154, 200–202, 332, 344
    life's, 163, 176–77, 244, 251, 256, 257, 299–300
    soul's, 159, 164, 173, 184, 191, 263, 267, 285, 298, 308, 327, 336–40
Judeo/Judaic, 152, 154, 284
judge, judgment, 123, 177, 188, 192–93, 209, 210–12, 246, 260–63, 282, 283, 316, 324
Jung, Carl, 10
justice, 208, 210–12

K

Kabbalah, 4
karma, karmic, 111, 113, 172–73, 176, 190–93, 209, 212, 244–59, 262, 263, 299–301, 308
Keeper of the Stones, 81
Kennedy, John F., 250
King, Martin Luther, 26, 73, 312
Kirlian photography, 89
Kirsch, Jonathan L., 95–96, 97
Klimo, J., 94
Knight, J. Z., 4
knowing, 116–17, 135, 139–40, 141, 203, 233–34, 272, 273, 325, 327–28, 338–39
Koran, 50
Krishna, Gopi, 38–39, 75
Krishnamurti, 26
Kundalini Yoga, 39, 75

L

Langer, W. C., 75
language, 38–39, 42, 139
Lattimer, J. K., 250
law, 95–97, 208–12

Leadbeater, Charles, 26
leader, 148
Life, 95
life form, 201, 236, 240, 329
Lincoln, Abraham, 250
Linton, Charles, 36, 74
Liszt, Franz, 13, 40–41
Litvag, I., 75
love, 145–46, 164, 166,
    168–69, 170–71, 186,
    234, 263, 265, 275, 276,
    282, 306, 312–13,
    321–22, 330–31, 344–45,
    346–48
  bond of, 117
  God's, 28, 148–50, 284–85,
    322, 324–25, 328, 329
  homosexual, 189
  meaning of, 67
  message of, 125
  of pets, 202, 310
  romantic, 253
Lowell, 72
Luther, Martin, 26, 73

M

MacLaine, Shirley, 11, 72, 97,
    301
Maclean, Dorothy, 10, 72

maggidem, 3–4
Mariccio, Victoria, 23–24
Mark, 8, 71
marriage, 156, 158–59
Mary, Virgin, 239
Master, 4, 32
Matthew, 8, 71
McAneny, L., 95
McCartney, Paul, 56–57
McCready, William, 70, 71
Medjugorje, 239
Mentor, 4, 14, 65
message, 37, 52, 82, 83,
    124–25, 297, 322, 332
  Ariel's, 69, 85–86, 87–88,
    171, 234, 346
  channeled, 80–83
  communion, 233
  teaching, 84
  value of, 58
metaphor, 121–22, 168, 193,
    194, 200, 346
miracle, 31, 42, 46–47, 66, 76,
    89, 193, 217, 298
miscarriage, 177
Mishlove, J., 72
mission, 18, 30–31, 43, 49,
    50, 104, 199, 217, 244,
    263, 265, 290
Mohammed, 3, 43–46, 47, 49
Monteverdi, 40
Montgomery, Ruth, 4
Moore, Mary-Margaret, 4

mortality, 184
Moses, 3, 30, 46–47, 148, 152
Moss, Thelma, 89
Mozart, 40, 56
Multiple Personality Disorder,
    94, 215
music, 37–38, 40–41, 142
mutilation, 229
Myer, F. W. H., 72
mystical, 48, 70, 79, 152,
    214–15, 287, 338

N

Nathanson, Linda Sue, 2, 4,
    30, 69, 85–86, 88–94,
    102, 355, 357
National Opinion Research
    Center, 70
National Public Radio, 72, 73,
    74, 76
Nazi, 15, 51
near-death experience, 171–72
New York Times Magazine, 70,
    73
Newsweek, 95
Nietzsche, 10
Noah, 148
Noetic Sciences Bulletin, 95
Nostradamus, 198

O

Oates, Stephen, 32, 73
Olafsohn, Olaf, 20
Oliver, E.D., 95
Oliver, Frederick, 7, 36, 71,
    74, 96
one. *See* unity

P

paradigm, 67–68
paranormal, 94, 95, 149, 224,
    238–39
Parapsychology Foundation,
    94–97
parent, 176–77
past life, 244, 255–58
Patience Worth. *See* Worth,
    Patience
peace, 137, 315, 324, 326, 328
Pelikan, J., 73
pet. *See* animal
Peter, 7
Peter III, 20
Philo, 63
phobia, 68
Phylos the Tibetan, 7, 36, 96
plague, 187
plan, divine. *See* divine plan

planet, 71, 74, 96, 152–54, 188, 190, 194–95, 199, 201, 224, 225, 227, 228, 231, 235, 240, 287, 290, 310, 344, 349
plant, 201, 206, 302, 310, 311
pleasure, 193, 201, 306
Plutarch, 22
Podmore, F., 72, 74, 76
Pope, 314
Pope Gregory XV, 6
pray, prayer, 174, 175, 217, 219–22, 330, 339
prediction, 60, 198, 300
pregnancy, 177
Princeton Religion Research Center, 70
prism, 122, 124, 294
profession, 159
prophecy, 153, 198–99, 299
prophet, 3, 18, 148, 240
Prophet, Elizabeth Clare, 58–60
Providence, 51
psychic, 22–23, 64, 212–13
psychopathology, 71
psychosis, 2, 62, 214–15
Puccini, G., 11
purgatory. See hell

R

Rachmaninoff, 40
racist, 12
radio, 41, 72, 73, 74, 76, 118, 123, 139
Ramtha, 4, 14
reincarnation, 186
religion, 63, 64, 70, 76, 124, 156, 158, 212, 218, 221, 232, 239, 272, 281, 302, 315, 317, 322, 349
Religious Experience Research Unit, 70
research, 70–71, 88–89, 93, 98, 215, 235, 253
responsibility, 10, 54, 57, 67, 261–62
return
  to Eden. See Eden
  to God, 47–48, 54
  of karmic energy, 245–46
  to unity, 307–308, 327
revelation, 57, 59, 60, 75, 133, 137, 236, 238, 240, 248, 339
Rheingold, H., 72, 94
right
  (correct), 112, 160
  (prerogative), 67, 224, 261
  (vs. wrong), 109, 209, 211–12, 260, 263, 317
righteousness, 28

ripple, 309–10
Roberts, Jane, 80
Rodegast, Pat, 4, 12, 18, 72
Rossner, Judith, 33, 72, 74, 76

S

safety, 137, 204, 225, 229, 234, 236, 252, 311, 350
  in numbers, 192
Saul, 8
Schiller, C. H. S., 42
schizophrenia, 215
Schubert, 13, 40
Schucman, Helen, 4, 6–7, 9, 36, 66–67
Schumann, 13, 40
Schweitzer, 40
science, 18–19, 66, 93, 94, 230, 313–14, 316–17
scripture, 19, 59, 66, 150, 270, 331–32, 339, 349
Sczarmach, P. E., 71
Second Coming, 153
segmentation, 293
self, 54–55, 120, 213, 216–17, 221, 269, 305, 342
  -abandonment, 53, 54
  -criticism, 32
  -deception, 38, 61
  -discovery, 264–69
  -expression, 85, 154
  -healing, 181–83
  -identity, 206
  -knowing, 327–28
  -transcendence, 47–50, 54, 57, 68
  higher, 10, 11, 83, 201, 270–72, 301–304
  polyphonic, 63
  sense of, 204, 275
  separate, 174, 293, 326–27, 329, 330
  superficial, 63
senses, five, 89, 99, 116–17
sensory, 130, 153, 170, 306
separate, separation, 293, 303, 310, 327
  at death, 164, 166
  ego, 138, 264, 304, 330
sex, 306
Shaw, George Bernard, 62, 76
sickness. See disease
Sidgwick, Henry, 70
Sign, The, 21–22
sin, 27–28
Sinai, 47
Sinetar, M., 161
Skutch, R., 71, 72, 74
society, 57, 109, 161, 189, 208, 209, 255, 300
Socrates, 21–22, 72

soul, 98, 119, 126, 128–29, 157–60, 177, 178, 183–87, 193–94, 200, 208–10, 211, 244–46, 252–54, 261, 262, 273, 290, 291, 295–99, 307–309, 327, 328, 329, 330, 332, 342
and healing, 181–82, 183–85
and past life, 255–56
at birth, 175–78
at death, 163–71
concept of, 292–94
growth, 134, 162, 250, 251, 267–68, 285, 287–88, 336
of Christ, 323–24
animal, 203, 205
flower, 206
homosexual, 189, 191
human, 161
unlimited, 11
soulmate, 252–53, 261
space, time and, 25, 38, 48, 64, 192, 292
spaceship, 230
Spangler, David, 4
Spear, John Murray, 57–58
Spielberg, Steven, 231
spirit, spirit guide, 11, 14, 16–17, 31, 53, 64, 66, 70, 71, 72, 74, 76, 82–84, 99, 107, 109, 110, 111, 121, 127–34, 148–49, 152–54, 160, 162, 177, 180, 181, 183, 188, 191, 205, 208–12, 214, 216, 217, 231–34, 236, 238, 244, 252–54, 255, 258, 266, 267–69, 271–72, 277, 282, 285, 290, 292–93, 301, 304, 305, 308, 313, 320, 324, 327, 328, 336–38, 339, 340–44, 348–50
group, 17, 57
evil, 64, 277
Holy. See Holy Spirit
human, 107, 266
realm of, 205, 214–15, 236, 293
spiritual, spiritualism, spirituality, 31, 66, 71, 72, 74, 76, 99, 109, 111, 129, 134, 154, 162, 180, 208, 211, 217, 244, 246–47, 269, 285, 301, 311, 314–15
challenge, 244, 290
commentary, 50
community, 48
connection, 183, 184, 344
counseling, 79
dimension, 160
discipline, 239
ecstasy, 53, 79, 239
entity, 95–97
essence, 188, 205, 209, 293

evolution, 121, 149, 152,
    231–33, 342
existence, 254
experience, 70
expression, 252
glory, 236
groups, 14
growth, 50, 79, 111, 128,
    150, 160, 177, 187, 188,
    233–34, 239, 245,
    252–53, 255, 267–68,
    271–72, 305, 308, 322,
    327, 328, 332, 336–41
healing, 49, 83, 84, 89,
    180–84, 244, 252–56, 340
ideal, 320
journey, 148, 191, 210,
    340–41
need, 342, 348
openness, 312
paradox, 304
people, 3–4, 71–72, 292
tradition, 151, 216, 259
union, 184
vibration, 153, 231, 350
St. Joan. See Joan of Arc
St. Thomas. See Thomas, St.
Steiner, Rudolf, 26
Stevenson, Robert Louis, 10, 72
Stewart, David, 24
Strauss, Richard, 10–11
struggle, 26, 30, 55, 134, 137,
    174, 191, 210, 267, 295

subconscious, 141
suffer, suffering, 134, 161,
    172, 186, 193, 213, 261,
    291–92, 298
suicide, 45–46, 172–75, 186,
    213
sunlight, 122, 294
supernatural, 332
Swedenborg, Emanuel, 13,
    18–21, 36
Sweet Truth, 34, 54

T

Tao, 124
telephone, 118
television, 58, 95, 118, 123, 139
Ten Commandments, 30,
    148–49
Teresa, St., 5, 8–9, 25, 31, 32,
    34, 35, 71–74, 152
Thayer, Stevan J., 2, 4, 13,
    78–88, 90, 353–54, 357
Theosophy, 26
Thetford, Bill, 9
Thomas, St., 8
thought, 5, 7, 10, 32, 56, 81,
    82, 131–32, 136–37, 139,
    141, 144, 170, 220, 263,
    267, 289, 297, 306, 329

Tibetan, the, 4, 10, 35, 38. *See also* Phylos the Tibetan

Timarchus, 21–22

time, 104–105, 110, 120, 127, 151, 165, 195, 226–27, 241, 251, 280–81, 287, 342–43

Time, 95

Torah, 4

tragedy, 193–94

transcend, transcendence, 38–42, 47–50, 58, 65–69, 200, 238, 258, 260, 330. *See also* self-transcendence

transgression, 27

transplant, organ, 184–85

Tree of Knowledge, 149, 326–27, 328, 330, 350

Tree of Life, 329, 349

trial, 210–12

Tribbe, 72, 74

tuberculosis, 58

Tyson, Dr. Neil DeGrasse, 224

unity, 116, 128–29, 130, 138, 143–44, 167, 168, 178, 180–81, 205, 225, 269, 282–83, 292, 294, 302–305, 310, 312, 320–22, 323, 328, 350

universe, 167, 180–81, 194, 220, 224, 225, 264–66, 268, 275, 283–84, 288–89, 293, 294, 302–303, 304, 306, 309, 313–17, 325, 344–45

V

Van Dusen, W., 72, 75

Vatican, 313

vibration, 37, 119, 120, 122–23, 128–29, 139–40, 142–43, 163–65, 167, 168, 169, 233, 245, 283–84, 344, 345

Victor, 13, 16

Virgin Mary. *See* Mary, Virgin

vision, 11, 21, 46, 142, 214, 239

visionary, 90, 93, 214

Voice, 3–4, 5–6, 18, 19, 26–27, 29–30, 36, 70–71, 81, 274

U

UFO, 224

unconscious, 62, 68, 94, 141

Underhill, Evelyn, 63, 71, 76

unholy, 260

W

War of the Worlds, 233–34, 238
Warner, M., 71, 73
wave, 126
Weinberg, Dale, 138
Wesley, John, 20–21
whole. *See* unity
Wolff, L., 76
Worrall, Olga, 89
Worth, Patience, 13, 41–42
wrong, 104, 109, 209, 211,
    212, 260, 263, 282, 317

Y

Young, Meredith, 4, 80
Yugoslavia, 239

Z

Zen, 79, 81

From the Authors

We'd like to give a special thanks to Alfred S. Alschuler for his insightful Introduction. Alfred S. Alschuler, Ph.D. in Clinical Psychology from Harvard, is Professor of Education at Appalachian State University. He has published 20 books and over 130 articles on human development and potential.

We would also like to thank our readers for the kind words of gratitude they have shared with us for bringing Ariel's powerful, life-changing messages to them through *Interview with an Angel*. We continue to receive new information from Angel Ariel and share her ever-expanding vision through television, radio, seminars and the Internet. If you would like to experience more of Ariel's wisdom and obtain our appearance and teaching schedules, please visit our Web sites.

Blessings

Stevan J. Thayer

Stevan J. Thayer
www.centerofbeing.com

Linda Sue Nathanson

Linda Sue Nathanson, Ph.D.
www.edinbooks.com